The Power of the Prosecutor

The Power of the Prosecutor

Gatekeepers of the Criminal Justice System

Joan E. Jacoby and Edward C. Ratledge

An Imprint of ABC-CLIO, LLC

Santa Barbara, California • Denver, Colorado

Library of Congress Cataloging-in-Publication Data

Jacoby, Joan E., author.
  The power of the prosecutor : gatekeepers of the criminal justice system / Joan E.
Jacoby, Edward C. Ratledge.
    pages cm
  ISBN 978-1-4408-4218-4 (hardback) – ISBN 978-1-4408-4219-1 (ebook)
  1. Prosecution–United States.   I. Ratledge, Edward C., author.   II. Title.
  KF9640.J29 2016
  345.73'01262—dc23   2015029438

ISBN: 978-1-4408-4218-4
EISBN: 978-1-4408-4219-1

20 19 18 17 16   1 2 3 4 5

This book is also available on the World Wide Web as an eBook.
Visit www.abc-clio.com for details.

Praeger
An Imprint of ABC-CLIO, LLC

ABC-CLIO, LLC
130 Cremona Drive, P.O. Box 1911
Santa Barbara, California 93116-1911

This book is printed on acid-free paper ∞
Manufactured in the United States of America

To the memory of
Dr. Edwin Zedlewski (1941–2013)
With gratitude for his ceaseless commitment
to improving criminal justice through research and
his willingness to try something
different that might fail but usually did not.

Contents

Preface

The Power of the Prosecutor presents a realistic discussion of the unique powers held by American prosecutors in more than 3,000 communities to make decisions about whether to accept or reject cases, what charges to file, and whether their dispositions are acceptable. What may seem irrational or even discriminatory to many is made understandable by this comprehensive description and analysis of a process that relies on discretion to introduce flexibility into a relatively restricted set of choices, and its importance in providing checks and balances to our system of criminal justice.

Hidden between law enforcement agencies and the courts, the prosecutors' discretionary powers and their roles in bringing about just dispositions are laid open, relationships with the other members of the criminal justice system are described, and the factors that play a substantial role in their effectiveness are discussed in detail. Five well-known cases are analyzed from this decision-making perspective.

The authors together have more than 60 years of experience working with local prosecutors and criminal justice systems throughout the United States and their counterparts internationally. Primarily funded and supported by Department of Justice grants, they have conducted a wide range of research, evaluations, management studies, organizational analyses, and cost studies in these areas. They have traced the development and changes in prosecution since the early days of LEAA until its most recent ventures into community prosecution, and the benefits of computer technology in the form of artificial intelligence and expert systems. As a result, this book presents a broad perspective of prosecutors grounded in local environments and differing in policies and priorities about what constitutes their role as gatekeeper of the criminal justice system.

Our view of prosecution is that of social scientists; we are not lawyers. But we have had the opportunity to work with professional prosecutors in the hundreds across this country for more than four decades. They have been very generous with their knowledge and hopefully we have helped them with our expertise. We hope you enjoy this comprehensive portrayal of the power of the prosecutor to bring about justice, equity, and improvement of our system of criminal justice.

We have benefited, too, from those who have assisted us in one way or another in the preparation of this book. They are, alphabetically, Rebecca Bedford, Daniel Brown, Amirah Ellis-Gilliam, Roberta Gibson, John Laznik, David Racca, and Tibor Toth. All are members of the Center for Applied Demography & Survey Research, University of Delaware.

In addition, we wish to acknowledge the support and assistance of the staffs and resources of the University of Delaware's School of Public Policy and Administration, ABC-CLIO, and in particular Jessica Gribble, acquisitions editor for Praeger.

Regardless of the assistance we have received, we alone are responsible for the content of this book.

JEJ
ECR

Introduction

Prosecutors' discretionary powers long have been a matter for discussion, both for and against. Some even suggest that the actions of prosecutors are either illegitimate or simply wrong. Most of these exchanges, while interesting, reflect a lack of understanding about prosecutors and the power assigned to them by statutes. The objective of this book is to shed light on the prosecution function and the essential need for discretion to insert flexibility into prosecutions based on relatively rigid systems of law. This book describes the policies and strategies prosecutors use to exercise discretion despite forces to the contrary, and to produce dispositions that are both reasonable and appropriate for the individuals and communities served.

Discretion requires making decisions from among a limited set of choices. The decisions made by prosecutors reflect both the policies and priorities in place. The goals of other agencies, especially law enforcement, the community, and trends in social justice may also influence these decisions. It is this situation that muddies the outputs of local criminal justice systems and makes differences among jurisdictions almost impossible to interpret. Why did prosecutor A accept this case, while prosecutor B rejected it? Why did defendant C get a jail sentence, while defendant D was placed on probation for the same charge? Is plea bargaining good or bad? Is it even fair?

Prosecutors have the power to make these decisions, starting with choosing which cases to accept for prosecution and which to reject or divert from the system. This is the prosecutor's most powerful choice. However, it also depends on the quality of the police investigation that preceded a case's arrival in the prosecutor's office. Poorly managed or trained police departments are not likely to produce high-quality police reports and evidence to support arrests. Similarly, inexperienced assistant prosecutors reviewing the police reports and evidence are not likely to spot evidentiary weaknesses or legal insufficiencies that call for either more investigation or outright refusal to file the case. The wrong charges may be filed without supervision or training. The decisions made at the gate affect the courts' workloads, the caseloads of public defenders, and other agencies in the system like probation, jails, and corrections.

All cases accepted have to be disposed. Much like an accounting system, there are various ways for this to occur. Some cases will be dismissed and all charges dropped, others will end in a jury trial, but the vast majority of cases will be disposed by a plea of guilty. Plea negotiation is the most prevalent means of disposition in all courts. However, it varies substantially based on the prosecutors' priorities for prosecuting cases and the policies of prosecutors, defense counsel, and judges with respect to sentencing. What are those policies and priorities and how do they affect the way a case is disposed? Why are they different across the country? Add to this the tolerance of the community for various crimes and it is not surprising that one jurisdiction may have completely different dispositional patterns from another.

In the second part of the book our attention changes to the matter of understanding why some cases do not result in expected outcomes. This is a broader inquiry into the scope and power of prosecution because it focuses not just on the prosecutors' decisions but the effects that other criminal justice agencies can have on adjudications. The question asked is to what extent the prosecutor's decisions could have produced a more satisfactory case outcome and why those decisions were not made.

Five notorious cases examine this issue. They include newly elected Cyrus Vance Jr.'s decision to prosecute Dominique Strauss-Kahn (DSK), managing director of the International Monetary Fund (IMF), for the sexual assault of a hotel maid in New York based on premature investigation of the facts of the case and its ultimate dismissal. Another prosecutor with years of prosecution experience was appointed to the job of district attorney in Durham, North Carolina, just as the Duke lacrosse team rape case began. The case grew in a crucible of massive media interest, a university town that disowned the athletes without adequate information, and a university administration and faculty that behaved poorly. The situation required a seasoned chief prosecutor to keep the situation under control. Unfortunately, Mike Nifong was a newly elected prosecutor and was unable to handle the case, to his own detriment. Through a series of unprofessional and ethical missteps he was finally disbarred and the defendants cleared by the attorney general.

Even more complicated is the tale of deteriorating police-prosecutor relations and a longtime prosecutor in the JonBenet Ramsey murder, which was never actually a "case" and is still unsolved. In contrast, the murder of little Caylee Anthony in Florida yielded unexpected results when Casey Anthony, her mother, was acquitted by a jury trial on charges that might have been "a bridge too far." Finally, the O. J. Simpson trial represents the epitome of things that can and did go wrong and examines the role of the prosecutor in this television spectacular.

When one examines case outcomes as they are affected by the decisions prosecutors make, it is easier to understand why there are such vast differences, and why simple numbers like convictions don't explain very much about the quality of justice in the United States. However, examinations like these shed light on the factors that affect or influence prosecutors. Opportunities for changes in direction and scope of criminal prosecution and adjudication are always present and probably should be undertaken by more prosecutors. While traditional prosecutions are carried out daily with reasonable and appropriate dispositions, new forms of participatory leadership have brought significant changes and improvements to the entire system, extending the outreach of prosecutors into activities and roles not imagined 20 years ago.

Innovations like community prosecution, drug courts, and the potential of computer technology, especially in the areas of big data analysis, artificial intelligence, and expert systems, are addressed. Despite all these advances, however, the core of prosecution remains relatively simple—namely, the establishment of policies and priorities uniformly applied throughout the office. Within these confines is the need for good management and administration so that the practices and procedures ensure equity and justice.

CHAPTER ONE

What Is Discretion and Why Do We Care?

Discretion is the power to make decisions. In the criminal justice world, discretion is woven throughout the actions of those who seek to bring about justice. Its character is the combined results of the decisions made by police, prosecutors, judges, probation officers, and defense counsel. Like a fingerprint, discretion produces uniquely different patterns of dispositions that give the criminal justice system complexity and variety.

The opposite of discretion is the absence of choice. In that world, each path leads to only one destination. Without choice, our criminal justice system would be flat, very predictable, and in the end, unfair. Each offense would receive the same treatment; each offender would be given the same sentence. All rapes would be treated in the same way; all rapists would receive the same punishment. Without discretion, the punishment would not fit the crime, nor would it reflect the offenders or their victims.

Discretion allows the decision makers in the criminal justice system to select preferred destinations and the best route to get there. Serial rapists move along a path destined for imprisonment, while date-rape offenders could possibly move toward probation. Laws provide the specifications for criminal offenses for criminal justice agencies, but the exercise of discretion determines how the laws are implemented or enforced, which leads to a multidimensional map with differences across local criminal justice systems in the nation.

Of all the players, the prosecutor is the most important and powerful in the exercise of discretion. The prosecutor alone has the legal authority to pursue prosecutions and to file charges that will be prosecuted. Those decisions set each case on a path to a disposition that the prosecutor and indirectly the community served feel is appropriate.[1] The prosecutor's power stems from a set of five decisions that are unreviewable and cannot be changed without his or her approval.[2] Those decisions are:

- The decision to accept cases for prosecution
- The decision to decline to prosecute
- The decision to divert offenders to alternative programs or activities
- The decision to select charges
- The decision to dismiss charges or cases[3]

This core set of discretionary decisions is different from many other decisions made in the criminal justice system. No one can overturn them. There is no appeal. As a result, that core set makes the prosecutor the most powerful participant in the criminal justice system, and they make prosecution the most variable and complex function of all those performed in the adjudication process.

Prosecutorial discretion affects not only the disposition of cases but also defines the nature of the adjudication process. Since the prosecutor is usually an elected official responsible to the local community, the use of discretion often reflects the desires of that community as well. Prosecutors can establish charging policies that control which cases are processed by the courts, choose plea bargaining policies that affect the way defense counsel and the courts reach dispositions, and make sentence recommendations or perform other activities that influence the sanctions imposed. In the end, the prosecutor's decision will be influenced by determining if a prosecution is in "the public's interest." States, counties, and cities may and do have different views on that question and the prosecutor will be influenced by those feelings. Ultimately the quality of community life may be improved or degraded by the guidelines prosecutors establish about which crimes will be tolerated and which will not.

If light is to be shed on the prosecutor's discretionary powers, those core decisions must be examined closely, especially the factors that influence the decisions to accept, reject, divert, charge, and dismiss cases. By doing so, the forces that drive prosecutions and distinguish one local criminal justice system from another can be observed.

There is substantial agreement among prosecutors about the factors they consider in making decisions. In fact, research has also shown that differences in prosecutorial decisions can be explained almost entirely by these factors and not by some other unknown forces.[4] They include whether prosecution is in the public interest, the costs of prosecution, the evidentiary strength of the case, the seriousness of the offense, the nature of the offender, and the actions of the participants in the crime. Each factor is considered in making decisions, but they are given different weights depending on the prosecutor's policies, priorities, and expectations.

Take the case of a hit and run accident in which the victim was hospitalized with serious injuries. The offender was found and arrested. A search of criminal history files found no prior offenses. The accused was gainfully employed and was remorseful about the event. In addition, the offender admitted the offense but explained being too scared to stop. Prosecutor A viewed the offense as horrific and took actions that would show the community that this behavior would not be tolerated in this case or others. He placed the highest charges on the case and proceeded with prosecution, seeking some jail time as a punishment. Prosecutor B, on the other hand, looked at the defendant's clean record and was wary of ruining the future of the young man based on one mistake. She recommended a diversion program that included extensive community service in rehabilitation facilities, a suspended license, a driver's training program, and a course in ethics at the local community college.

Same crime, different decisions and outcomes! Prosecutor A gave priority to the seriousness of the offense; Prosecutor B, to the circumstances of the offender. The same factors were considered, those concerning the offense and the offender, but the importance assigned to each radically changed the tenor and outcome of the prosecution.

To fully explore the dimensions of discretion and its impact on criminal justice, the influence that the community and the other players in the criminal justice system have on prosecution and its ability to obtain appropriate dispositions for the prosecutor needs to be understood.

Unreviewable Discretionary Decisions

The courts have consistently upheld the prosecutor's right to decline prosecution. Although it may appear from complaints appearing in newspapers and on television that prosecutors abuse this power, this is generally not true. The majority of cases referred for prosecution are accepted.[5] Typically prosecutors review (or "screen") more serious cases involving felonies and some misdemeanors for evidentiary weaknesses. The rate at which these cases are declined generally reflects the quality of reports submitted by law enforcement agencies in the jurisdiction and the prosecutor's standards for charging.

Decisions to use diversion as an alternative to prosecution are mainly directed at offenders charged with less serious offenses, although many jurisdictions make an exception for drug cases if treatment or rehabilitation seems like a reasonable alternative to formal prosecution. Usually, diversion requires the defendant to participate in a program or activity and meet other conditions such as making restitution. If the defendant successfully completes diversion, the charges against him or her are dropped. In some cases charges may not have been filed at all so there is no need to dismiss them upon completion of the diversion. If the defendant fails to complete the program, prosecution is initiated.

The prosecutor has unreviewable power to dismiss cases or charges. This authority is the foundation for plea negotiations as well as the means for ensuring equity in prosecution. Many a case has "gone south" after it has been charged. Defendants flee the jurisdiction, witnesses refuse to cooperate, and crucial evidence can be lost. Dismissals provide the means to remedy the situation or promote reasonable and appropriate dispositions that tailor the punishment to fit the crime.

Dismissals are court-sanctioned activities that dispose of cases in one of two ways. An outright dismissal of charges clears the offender of all charges filed. A dismissal with leave dismisses the charges but reserves the prosecutor's right to reinstate the charges at a later date. A common use of this type of disposition occurs when the defendant has failed to appear at a court hearing and a warrant for arrest cannot be served because the defendant cannot be located. A dismissal with leave closes the case for the record but allows the prosecutor to reinstate the case if the defendant is ever located or arrested. In some instances, if the defendant is serving time on another charge, it allows the prosecutor to reinstate the new charges after the defendant is released from prison.

Dismissals occur only after cases have been filed in the court. They differ in this respect from declinations or rejections, which are made before cases have been filed. In the absence of statutes to the contrary, historically only the prosecutor has the power to dismiss a case without judicial approval as long as the reasons are stated in writing.[6]

This discretion is especially important because it allows the prosecutor to negotiate with defense counsel about dispositions. In a typical scenario the prosecutor offers to dismiss some or all charges for a consideration, usually a plea. As will be seen later, the power to dismiss plays its most important role in the adjudication process rather than at intake and charging.

Dismissals typically occur at the charging stage only when cases are filed in the court prior to prosecutorial review. Under these circumstances, the prosecutor cannot decline a case for prosecution but rather must formally notify the court that he or she is dismissing the case for some specified reasons. Decisions to dismiss are based on the same variety of factors that play in the decision to decline. The difference is that cases filed in court before being authorized by the prosecutor have to be dismissed if the prosecutor does not want to prosecute them.

Deciding which cases to accept for prosecution is the heart of the prosecutor's discretion. Decisions will vary from office to office because they are influenced by the nature of crime in the jurisdiction, the prosecutors' policies and priorities, community expectations, the media, the quality of investigation by law enforcement, the seriousness of the offense, the evidentiary strength of the case, the nature of the offender, and a variety of other influences. Of all prosecutorial decisions, this is the most important because it is at this point that "the wheels of justice" are set in motion. Because the decision involves the consideration of so many factors, and because prosecutors can give different weight to the importance of the factors, one prosecutor's office may look entirely different from another's.

Going hand in hand with the decision to accept cases for prosecution is the decision about what charges to file. Charging decisions reflect the prosecutor's assessment of the seriousness of the case, which translates into an expected outcome. These decisions may also indirectly reflect the prosecutor's anticipated strategies about how dispositions will be obtained, by negotiated plea or by trial. Prosecutorial policy that sets priorities for prosecution and their expected outcomes is a major contributor to the variations seen between prosecutor's offices.

Only the prosecutor has the authority to charge violations of statutes or ordinances. Cases may be charged as felonies, misdemeanors, or violations. The distinguishing feature among them is the range of sanctions associated with each. Motor vehicle or ordinance violations have the least serious sanctions consisting of fines, points, court costs, and perhaps restitution or driver's education. In some jurisdictions, prosecutors may not even have jurisdiction over misdemeanors or violations. It depends on the structure of the court system—whether unified or not—and whether traffic violations are handled administratively or in municipal courts. Misdemeanors cover a wide variety of offenses and their sanctions range from fines to jail, typically sentences of a year or less.[7] Felony charges are the most serious because they carry with them the potential for lengthy incarceration and in some cases, even death.

Discretionary Decisions Subject to Review

The core set of decisions defining the prosecutor's discretionary power are unreviewable. Those unreviewable decisions can be distinguished from a second set of decisions that also support the prosecutor's ability to further exercise discretion during the adjudication process with the objective of expanding the ability to achieve reasonable and appropriate outcomes. However, these decisions are less certain since, to varying degrees, they require the agreement of others in the system, especially the court and defense counsel and to a lesser extent law enforcement agencies.

The prosecutor has the discretion to institute practices and procedures that improve the efficiency of the adjudication process and increase the likelihood of obtaining acceptable outcomes. The primary decisions focus on:

- Participation in plea negotiations
- Providing informal discovery
- Making sentence recommendations
- Postconviction activities including presentence investigations, parole, or probation hearings

The decision to undertake any of these is totally under the prosecutor's control, but their impact may be weakened because they are subject to agreement by other agencies or the courts.

For example, a prosecutor may present a plea offer and be willing to negotiate with defense counsel about conditions for a guilty plea, but there is no assurance that this will happen if the defense counsel refuses to cooperate. To expedite dispositions, prosecutors may choose to open their files to defense counsel and provide them with early discovery as it becomes available. Discovery is a procedure whereby the prosecutor shows the defense what evidence is in hand about the defendant's offense. There is no assurance, however, that defense counsel will take advantage of this information to hasten dispositions.

Similarly, even though some prosecutors help probation departments conduct their presentence investigations by supplying them with information from their files, there is no guarantee that probation's recommendations will favor the prosecution or even be accepted by the judge. Judges may also reject plea agreements and ignore sentence recommendations. In these circumstances, the prosecutor's decisions may be overturned or modified by forces beyond his or her control.

Nonetheless, decisions to use these practices are discretionary for prosecutors. If they choose not to use them, there is no authority that can require them to do so. Many judges seek the prosecutor's sentence recommendation and others refuse to involve themselves in negotiations between defense counsel and the prosecutor. In later chapters, we will see that the value of these procedures is such that their implementation is viewed favorably because their effects are positive for the entire adjudication process.

Factors Affecting Decisions

There are factors that routinely affect the core set of discretionary decisions. This section examines five of the primary factors that prosecutors consider:

- In the public interest
- Evidentiary strength
- Seriousness of the offense
- Nature of the offender
- System capacity, resources, and costs

Depending on the decision being made, these factors assume different levels of importance. Sometimes one factor may act as the primary justification for a decision. In other cases, the same factor is almost irrelevant in selecting a course of action. In the following sections, each of these decisions is examined with respect to how the factors change relative to the core set of prosecutorial decisions.

The ABA standards[8] recognize that some cases should not be prosecuted because they "are not in the public interest." The public interest can be defined in a number of ways. In addition to being a consideration for declinations and dismissals, the public interest may also play a role in accepting cases and charging them at the highest levels.

Cases may be declined for humanitarian reasons, such as when the prosecution of the wife of a codefendant will deprive a family with young children of their mother and force them into foster homes. In this instance, charges may be dropped or reduced against the wife if the husband pleads guilty.

Public interest reflects what a community thinks is important, its values and norms. As a result it can support the nonenforcement of laws or proactive enforcement. Probably the best example of nonenforcement occurred when prohibition was the law of the land. Violations of the sale and consumption of alcohol were winked at and largely ignored until, finally, prohibition was repealed. In other instances, community values and norms play a large role in the selective enforcement of the law. One community's attitudes toward adultery, pornography, or consensual sex between same-sex adults may call for the immediate prosecution of these offenses. In another community, these activities are tolerated, arrests are not expected, and prosecutions are rare.

Sometimes cases may not be prosecuted if prosecution would result in a loss of public support or respect for public institutions of government.

It may be in the public interest not to go forward, for example, with cases involving misconduct by police officers. Catching an off-duty police officer in a drug bust, or in a sting operation conducted against prostitution, are misconduct issues for which there are internal law enforcement agency remedies. Public prosecution would achieve no additional purpose in punishing the officer but it could erode respect for the agency.

Under these circumstances, although "in the public interest" is an amorphous term, it is an important factor because it allows the prosecutor to decline cases when prosecution would only cause more serious harm or damage to other public interests than the punishment of an individual.

On the other side of the coin, however, public interest may justify a higher priority for prosecution than otherwise might prevail. Practically guaranteed to be accepted for prosecution are cases involving offenders who have violated the public trust or community values. Such crimes may include embezzlement of public or church funds, illegal activities for personal gain or wealth, and sexual molestation of children and youth, to name a few. In upholding the norms and values of society, both the justice system and the prosecutor let public interest be a defining factor in giving priority to these offenses. It should always be remembered that this country is a union of 50 states and that the criminal law is a matter for each state. The laws and the punishments vary between states because that is what the citizens of each state desire.

The most important basis for declining cases is that they lack evidentiary strength. This term describes the strength of physical evidence, testimonial evidence, or constitutional protections. If the evidentiary problems cannot be overcome, then prosecution is simply a waste of time and resources. It is better to decline cases under these circumstances.

Despite intensive screening at intake, some cases are accepted for prosecution and later fall apart. When this happens, and the evidentiary weaknesses are substantial, then it is in the prosecutor's interest to either become more liberal in the plea offer or dismiss the case. The evidentiary strength of the case is the foundation upon which all prosecutions rest, and the most influential consideration for decisions about how to proceed.

Problems with physical evidence usually arise if the chain of custody is broken. If the movement of physical evidence cannot be accounted for as it changes hands, then it cannot be conclusively linked to the defendant. The fact that defense counsel claimed that O. J.'s bloody glove was planted by the police is one example where the claim could not be rebutted conclusively.

Sometimes these weaknesses can be overcome by the presentation of other evidence; sometimes they cannot. Crime scenes may be contaminated, especially if police have accidentally destroyed evidence or disturbed its location. Trampling through the grounds of a crime scene is not good police procedure, especially if it destroys footprints or tire tracks. Many prosecutors will send experienced assistant prosecutors immediately to serious crime scenes just to preserve evidence.

Some cases are lost because evidence is missing from the police property storage room where it should have been, or is damaged or lost in crime labs. If the chain of custody is broken for a sample submitted for DNA testing, the results can be challenged. If this is all the evidence in a case and it is flawed, there are few options left for prosecutors other than rejection or later dismissal.

Testimonial evidence also has to be considered. Here the issues focus on the cooperation of the victim and witnesses, their credibility and competence, and whether the testimony can be corroborated. Victims of crimes and witnesses to crimes are often fearful of reprisals. This is very obvious when gangs are involved. As a result, victims and witnesses may be reluctant to testify; some may even disappear. Without their testimony, the state may find it impossible to prosecute.

Prosecutors can subpoena victims to appear in court, but they can't force them to testify. Prosecutors can also prosecute cases even if the victim refuses to press charges. All crimes are considered to be against the state, not the victim. Most often, however, if the victim or witnesses are reluctant, the case will be declined or dismissed. The situations where this occurs are many and varied. In domestic violence cases, often the victim has a change of heart and refuses to testify or does not see the incident as a "crime" but rather a family matter. In cases involving citizen complaints, the parties may end up settling their disputes their own way out of court. In other instances, the victim may also be "guilty" and, therefore, reluctant to testify. A good example is a "John" caught in a prostitution raid. They are not likely to be star witnesses for the prosecution.

In a case involving a drunk-driving negligent homicide, the witness's testimony was crucial for the prosecution. The only problem was the police "forgot" to tell the prosecutor that the eyewitness was a drug addict whose brain had been burned out by speed. In another case, the witness was a cellmate of the defendant, who had been detained pretrial, and who was looking for a reduced sentence in return for cooperation with the police. The problem of whether the witness is credible is a major issue. As one prosecutor said, the perfect witness is a middle-aged nun with 20/20 vision and excellent hearing.

Another difficult consideration is whether the witness's testimony can be corroborated. To use an old adage, two sets of eyes are better than one.

If the testimony cannot be corroborated by others or by other physical evidence, then the situation falls into a "she says, he says" argument with neither side able to prove the case, and the defense is able to introduce reasonable doubt. Research on prosecutorial decision making also indicates that the strength of the case improves if there is more than one police officer who can testify to the incident.[9]

Although they are last to be mentioned, not the least in importance are the constitutional issues that must be considered in weighing the evidentiary strength of the case. It may be impossible to survive problems created because Miranda warnings as to an arrested defendant's rights were not given, improper searches were made, inappropriate lineups held, and wiretap procedures violated. Sometimes the problems arising from violations of these constitutional protections are insurmountable, and the case has to be rejected.[10]

There are numerous examples of how cases have been dismissed because of constitutional issues. Many of them are known to the public only when highly publicized cases have been overturned on appeal.

There are minimum legal and constitutional standards that must be met. However, once those standards are met, then the decision about what cases are accepted depends on the charging policy of the prosecutor and the anticipated dispositions.

Standards for evidentiary strength are set by policy. In some offices, any case that is legally sufficient, meaning that there is reason to suspect the defendant did what is charged, is accepted for prosecution even if the evidence is marginal. In other offices prosecutors accept cases only when they judge that they have enough evidence to win at trial. In the middle are cases whose evidence appears to be sufficient and that are most likely to be disposed of by a negotiated plea.

If prosecutors are seeking the highest sanction in a criminal case, such as imprisonment for the longest time allowed by law, then the evidentiary requirements have to be at the highest level to support this goal. In contrast, if another prosecutor with the same case is seeking at least some prison time, then the evidence does not have to meet the same high standards as in the first instance. In the long run, what the prosecutor considers as reasonable and appropriate punishment defines, in large part, the evidentiary requirements of the case.

The seriousness of the offense defines the value or priority that the community and the prosecutor give to crimes. Some cases are accepted regardless of evidentiary issues or any other factors. Most notable are cases involving crimes so heinous or notorious that they must be prosecuted. These cases have wide name recognition because they reach such high levels of media attention: the O. J. Simpson case; the Manson case in California; the case of necrophiliac Jeffrey Dahmer; the Muhammad-Malvo sniper case in the Washington, D.C., metropolitan area; John Hinckley's assassination attempt on President Reagan; and the list goes on. There is no way that these cases ever would have been declined once an arrest was made. Most end up as high-profile jury trials covered on Court TV.

If cases fall under the rubric of special advocacy groups, they too may be likely candidates for prosecution. Probably most familiar is the advocacy group called Mothers against Drunk Driving (MADD), which pushes for the prosecution and punishment of drunk drivers. There are a myriad of advocacy groups. They advocate—or oppose—gun control, birth control, environmental pollution, child abuse, and a host of other social issues. Depending on how vocal they are, they may put pressure on the prosecutor's decision to accept cases. Strangely enough, sometimes prosecutors find themselves in a situation where competing interest groups nullify their influence on the decision. In the long run, special advocacy groups may place the prosecutor in the uncomfortable position of having to balance special interests against the greater interests of public prosecution.

For example, if environmental groups are pressing hard for criminal sanctions against a major polluter of the drinking water in a community, the prosecutor may not have enough staff and investigative resources to handle this case in addition to the others in the office. However, because the pollution has the potential for inflicting more damage if left unchecked, the prosecutor may decline to prosecute but look to other agencies and the courts, either civil or federal, for environmental protection relief.

Public interest and media attention may define the seriousness of the offense, but in the everyday working world, the bulk of the cases in the criminal justice system rarely receive special attention. The seriousness of the offense is colored largely by the amount of personal injury or property loss or damage.

Top priority is given to cases involving violent crimes like murder, rape, robbery, and aggravated assault. The seriousness of the injuries or the number and sometimes the age of the victims increase priority. Thus, prosecuting a serial rapist case would be given a higher priority than prosecuting a single rape case, and cases involving very young or very old victims would rank high on the priority for prosecution scale. The seriousness of the offense typically requires prosecutors to commit extra resources to such cases, which are most likely to go to trial and warrant prison sentences.

Prosecutors may impose their own priorities on the seriousness of the offense depending on community fear and the prosecutor's own perceptions of what is serious. They can include crimes involving guns, drug crimes, gang-related crimes, drunk driving, and teenage alcohol consumption, among others.

The amount of property loss or damage also defines the priority of a case for prosecution. These cases involve property loss or damage from burglary, larceny, motor vehicle theft, fraud, and bad checks. The larger the amount of damage or loss, the higher the priority for prosecution. For example, a case involving the embezzlement of hundreds of thousands of dollars will receive more prosecutorial attention than one of pilfering from the cash register.

The vast majority of property crime cases receive little media attention, in part because they are so common and the loss or damage is minimal. Auto theft and shoplifting are endemic; most burglaries occur during the daytime when few victims are about, and theft is often corrected by restitution.

Some cases are so trivial that criminal prosecution is considered too harsh a response. They are the candidates for alternative programs like diversion or community service, which require the defendant to admit responsibility and make reparation. Their priority for prosecution is so low that they "waste prosecution time." Typical examples include disputes between neighbors over trespassing or damage to their property, claims about dishonest business practices, or even passing bad checks. The one exception is that a suspected major offender, a so-called career criminal, may be prosecuted for a minor offense if that is all that can be proven.

Prosecutors have the authority to make rules about which cases will not be prosecuted. For example, drug offenses would not be prosecuted if less than one ounce of marijuana is involved; cases involving solicitation, gambling, or larceny for less than $50 would not be prosecuted. In addition to having the discretion to state what will not be prosecuted, prosecutors can also define the use of other remedies such as filing cases in small claims court, or using mediation or dispute resolution programs. Some cases at this level of seriousness often settle themselves after a cooling-off period.

The vast majority of cases, however, do not fall into these categories. They comprise drug offenses and property crimes like burglary, larceny, shoplifting, and simple assaults. If the seriousness factor is not high for prosecution, they receive routine processing with a goal of early disposition. For these "ordinary" cases, prosecution relies more on the evidentiary strength of the case than the seriousness of the offense.

The seriousness of the defendant's criminal history adds to the priority of the case for prosecution and is considered in all prosecution decisions. First offenders typically receive more leniency in charging and prosecution decisions, be they whether to prosecute the case, recommend diversion, or make a lenient plea offer. If the prosecutor believes that there is little chance that the defendant will recidivate, and the damage from prosecution outweighs the punishment for the immediate crime, then it may well be in the best interests of the offender to drop the case. However, as we noted earlier, the views of one prosecutor may not be shared by others. It is the prosecutor's prerogative.

Obviously the career criminal or the violent offender is not viewed in the same way. When defendants have well-defined criminal career ladders, their cases will not be dropped no matter how insignificant. As one prosecutor put it about career criminals, he would prosecute them for "spitting on the sidewalk" because doing so would provide an opportunity to argue for pretrial detention, which would keep the offender safely locked up, and to add enhancements to the charge or sentence.

Defendants who have violated the public trust also receive priority attention. A recent example of this is the Enron prosecutions for crimes that effectively wiped out the life savings of many Enron employees. Similar priority, although with less spectacular coverage, would be given to a bank manager or stock fund manager who embezzled millions of dollars that rightfully belonged to a large number of people. These examples spotlight the relative importance given by prosecutors if they are compared to a shoplifter who stole a $20 scarf.

In general, the seriousness of the offender's criminal history takes on added significance in considering diversion, the benefits of treatment and rehabilitation programs, and the appropriate sanction. With few exceptions, criminal history plays a large role in prosecution decisions.

An exception to the general rules regarding the offender's criminal history is confidential informants (CI) and the special handling that they receive from knowledgeable prosecutors. CIs provide the police or prosecutor with testimony or evidence in return for immunity, reduced charges, or improved conditions if they are presently imprisoned.

In Illinois, some of the prosecutors who participated in multijurisdictional drug task forces (MJDTF) drew up contracts with informants that specified their duties, the amount of drugs that were to be seized, or a minimum number of busts that had to result in a specified time period. The contract spelled out what the prosecutor would do if the conditions were met, and what would happen if they were not met. The contract was signed by the CI, the prosecutor, and the law enforcement agency. The prosecutor retained the contract.

The seriousness of the offense, the nature of the defendant, and the evidentiary strength of the case are the three major factors that affect the discretionary decisions to accept cases, reject them, place charges, and seek expected levels of punishment.

In general, cases are most likely to be accepted if they involve serious offenses for which strong evidence exists to prove that offenders who have extensive criminal records committed them. If they have also caught the media's attention, they will receive even more intense scrutiny. They are also more likely to be disposed at the highest levels and with the most severe sanctions.

There are not enough resources to enforce every violation of the law in any jurisdiction. There are not enough police, prosecutors, defense counsel, judges, probation officers, social service agencies, or even jail or prison capacity to allow this. As a result, choices have to be made about which laws are enforced and which arrests are given less than priority attention, if at all. So, serious crimes, especially those involving violence, take precedence over resources, while public order crimes like drinking or urinating in public, or barroom fights are often tolerated.

Selective prosecution is a way of life in every jurisdiction. It is especially visible if the courts are heavily backlogged and the prosecutor's office is understaffed. A lack of resources or court capacity leaves prosecutors with few options. They can decide not to prosecute certain types of cases, transfer them to other prosecution agencies, or divert them to alternative services or programs.

When the office does not have the capacity to prosecute every case, workload can be reduced by not prosecuting certain types of cases. A common example is bad check cases. Some offices will issue letters to persons passing bad checks notifying them that this is an offense and will be prosecuted unless the offender makes restitution. Other offices take an additional step and actually collect the money for the companies that have been victimized. Other examples involve cases where the injury is minor or the dollar amount of the theft is less than some specified amount.

Transferring work to other prosecution agencies or government agencies provides instant relief to the caseload. In cases where there is concurrent jurisdiction—that is, where offenses can be handled in municipal or city courts—a viable solution is to transfer them to those courts. Similar situations may also occur when there is federal jurisdiction over an offense in addition to the state's jurisdiction. Some of the most creative responses to a lack of capacity look for remedies other than criminal prosecution. Those may include the use of civil suits, abatements, or code violations to enforce laws.

Some cases may be transferred to alternative programs such as mediation, dispute resolution centers, and citizen complaint bureaus. All these options reduce the number of cases accepted for prosecution.

Diversion is a commonly accepted alternative to prosecution. However, it is important not to think that insufficient resources are the only reason for diversion. Diversion provides some defendants with an opportunity to take responsibility for their offenses and make amends without receiving a criminal record.

If a large number of cases could be diverted, it might substantially reduce workload. The decision to use or recommend diversion is entirely up to the prosecutor. Some operate their own programs, establishing activities like consumer complaint centers that are manned with volunteers. Others use programs or services like mediation or community service programs that are run by agencies in the community. Other prosecutors prefer to use the court's diversion programs. The choice is theirs.

There are two forms of diversion. Pretrial diversion is entirely under the prosecutor's control since the cases are not filed in the court and never will be if the conditions imposed by the prosecutor are satisfied. Typically, these are less serious cases that, under other circumstances or in other jurisdictions, would not even be in the criminal justice system. They may involve neighborhood disputes, trespassing, vandalism, damage to property, dogs running loose, and so on. Frequently both parties are satisfied with apologies and restitution. Mediation and community service are common alternatives to prosecution.

Court-sanctioned diversion occurs after charges have been filed. Typically the court orders the defendant into a diversion program based on the prosecutor's recommendation. These court-sanctioned programs may include dispute resolution, drug and alcohol treatment programs, community service, job training, anger management programs, and restitution, among others. They reflect the services that are available in a community and the priorities of either the prosecutor or the court.

Regardless of the type of program, whether prosecutor or court-ordered, the prosecutor holds the hammer that increases the defendant's compliance. Failure to comply with the conditions will activate the criminal charges and prosecution.

The costs of prosecution also affect what is prosecuted. Sometimes prosecution is simply too costly either in terms of investigative time or other prosecutor resources. Complex cases such as white-collar crimes or high-priority cases such as death penalty cases may have to be transferred to the state attorney general's office for prosecution if that is possible. In other instances, staff are "borrowed" from another prosecutor's office. The choices are based on which cases are affordable and which are not.

Some cases incur costs that exceed the prosecutor's budget, or are not worth the expenditure. This is an issue when cases require expert

witnesses, the extradition of defendants, or travel for out-of-state witnesses. They may be declined simply because there are insufficient funds
in the budget for these expenses. The hard reality is that prosecution costs
money and resources, and some cases may have to be rejected, even if
reluctantly.

The bottom line is that capacity, resources, and costs play a powerful
role in the prosecutor's decisions about how cases will be handled. More
imaginative prosecutors will seek ways to sanction the offender. Instead of
extradition, the holding jurisdiction may be able to prosecute the defendant. If the defendant is on probation, the criminal activity may permit
revocation of probation and immediate return to prison. With prosecutorial discretion, the prosecutor has many options for dealing with caseloads.

How Prosecutorial Policy Affects Discretion

Prosecutorial policy dictates how much weight is to be given each of the
factors. Policy then becomes the explanatory factor in describing most of
the variation among offices, even those in the same state operating in the
same legal environment.

The importance of policy can be explained in relation to the prosecutor's environment with the following overview:

The local jurisdiction has a large influence on the prosecutor's work
since it differs in population and socioeconomic factors, including the
nature of its crime. It is within this setting that prosecutors are elected and
from which they develop their policies and priorities.

A conservative, hard-line approach to prosecuting offenders would
not sit well in an affluent community where the predominant crimes are
against property and where drugs are used by the sons and daughters of
wealthy households. Contrast this with a prosecutor whose community
contains substantial public and subsidized housing, where violence and
drugs are rife. It is not difficult to understand how a hard-line approach
would be more acceptable in this community than in the first.

It is the prosecutor's policies and priorities about which crimes are most
important and how offenders should be sanctioned that set the tone and
direction of the office. To implement policy requires an organization that
aligns the appropriate personnel and resources with the workload in the
office and its administrative activities to increase productivity.

The organization develops practices and procedures that are consistent
with the stated policy and priorities in the office, which then brings about
the anticipated dispositions in an efficient manner. The practices and
procedures produce outcomes and dispositions that are equitable, reflect

the policy of the prosecutor, and hopefully reduce some of the problems affecting the local jurisdiction.

Policy and the effects of policy are most easily observed in the decisions that are made and the choices selected. This relationship allows us to analyze policy using decision-making techniques. By looking at the choices selected from all the choices available, the effects of policy on the outcomes of the choices, usually dispositions, can be seen.

The most important prosecutorial policy involves charging. It is at this point that not only are the prosecutor's priorities declared regarding crime and its seriousness, but also the expectations about dispositions and how they will be achieved. Charging policy produces vastly different operations and outcomes, which affect the efficiency and productivity of the entire adjudication process.

The major factor driving charging decisions is the prosecutor's assessment of what charges are most likely to produce dispositions that the prosecutor can live with. Charging involves three elements:

- The prosecutor's policy with regard to the standards needed to bring charges
- Charging that will produce acceptable dispositions and appropriate sanctions
- Choosing a venue for prosecution that increases the chances of obtaining the expected disposition and sanction

The charging decision considers the totality of the case, the offense, offender, evidentiary strength, community values, and the potential sanctions associated with the charge. For serious misdemeanors and felonies, prosecutors usually have charging policies that are a reflection of their interpretation of the role of prosecution and its priorities. There are three basic policies that govern charging decisions:

- Legal sufficiency
- System efficiency
- Trial sufficiency[11]

Legal sufficiency is the lowest standard for accepting cases and charging. It simply states that a case will be prosecuted if it is legally sufficient; that is, the elements of the offense are present. With this policy, the requirements for evidentiary strength are minimal, based merely on the presence of the elements as defined by the statutes. Considerations about the nature of the offense and offender are not very important.

In one sense, this policy is best suited to lesser misdemeanors and violations than the more serious misdemeanors and felonies because the charges brought by police at the time of the citation or arrest are rarely changed by the prosecutor. These cases flow through an assembly-line process where they receive only a cursory review for completeness. The charge itself is not especially critical because it can be adjusted by offers from the prosecutor to plead to lesser charges. For example, the prosecutor will reduce a speeding ticket for a guilty plea, or dismiss a larceny charge if the defendant makes restitution, or dismiss a destruction of property charge if the defendant makes repairs and reimburses the owner for damages.

When legal sufficiency charging policies are applied to serious misdemeanors and felonies, different results occur. With minimal acceptance criteria, few cases are declined at intake and the old GIGO (garbage in, garbage out) principle is activated. This means that the prosecutor has to adjust more cases or dismiss them later in court. As a result, compared to more restrictive charging policies, there are more dismissals for lack of evidence, and that forces the prosecutor to rely on plea bargaining to obtain dispositions.

System efficiency policies use charging criteria that look beyond the mere elements of the crime and seek speedy dispositions. The standard for charging is whether cases can survive a probable cause hearing, which is a court hearing used where a judge decides if the defendant probably did what is being charged. If so, then the defendant is charged and processed in ways that promote early disposition. The fact that this policy relies on the use of plea bargaining to speed up dispositions inserts the issue of sanctions into the charging process. In other words, selecting a charge takes into consideration what would be the bottom line for an acceptable negotiated plea.

In one prosecutor's office, the charging assistants were instructed to write on the file jacket what they considered to be the lowest acceptable offer, and trial attorneys were instructed to be guided by this advice. This procedure means that the intake and charging attorneys have some trial experience. If inexperienced attorneys were assigned to the charging desk, the policy and standards would be meaningless.

Trial sufficiency policies are the most complex and difficult for prosecutors to implement without good management. These policies state that the charges placed should be provable at trial. They do not anticipate changes in the original charges, and they expect successful outcomes if the cases go to trial. Unlike system efficiency, which relies on plea bargaining to obtain speedy dispositions, trial sufficiency assumes every case may go to trial. In real life this does not happen because there is simply not enough trial capacity to allow for it. Rather, many cases are rejected outright at intake, a high proportion of cases are disposed by a guilty plea to the original charge, and the others are disposed by pleas to reduced charges. Few dismissals occur because of the intensive case evaluation at intake.

Because most of the system's discretion is lodged in the charging process, trial sufficiency policies reduce the need for discretion later in the trial stage. As long as the original charge cannot be changed without approval from the charging attorney or his or her supervisors, the trial attorneys are not given much discretion. Since dismissals are viewed as indicators of improper charging, they too have to be approved by the charging assistants before this action is taken.

Not many prosecutors make charging decisions with trial sufficiency standards because these policies require a level of management in the office that is difficult to implement and sustain. More frequently this charging policy is reserved for special programs that deal with violent crimes, violent offenders, or career criminals. Managing this policy at a program level is easier to do than for an entire office.

Charges and Expected Sanctions

Charges are placed with the expectation that they will be disposed successfully and that the sanctions imposed will be satisfactory to prosecution. Criminal statutes generally define violations by the sanctions that can be imposed, or the maximum allowable sanction like a fine of $10,000 or 24 months in prison, or both. Sentencing guidelines also describe the range of sanctions that can be imposed based on the type of the offender and the seriousness of the offense.

So, for example, if a prosecutor charges first-degree rape that includes premeditation and force, a sentence with a long prison term is being sought. On the other hand, if second-degree rape or even assault is charged, this lowers the sanctions that are possible even to the extent of allowing for probation. The level of the charge is directly related to the sanctions that could be imposed after a guilty plea or conviction.

If these statutes were the only ones defining crimes and their sentences that prosecutors had to consider, then linking the charge to the sanction would be a relatively straightforward process. But legislatures have also passed laws that make charging a more complicated decision because they enhance the sentences that can be imposed or even mandate specific sentences. Most visible are habitual offender statutes, enhancements, mandatory minimums, and "three strikes, you're out" legislation. Their existence allows the prosecutor to "mix" the sanctions and "match" the sanctions to what is charged. In other words, they increase the prosecutor's discretionary power at charging.

Habitual offender legislation and enhancements allow the prosecutor to increase sanctions for defendants. They usually are based on the length of the defendant's criminal record, although some apply to certain offenses, like drugs. Enhancements or habitual offender laws state under what circumstances they can be applied to increase the severity of the sanctions.

Habitual offender laws may apply to repeated arrests for drunk driving so that licenses can be revoked if suspended. They can be used to increase the likelihood that career burglars will receive some jail or prison time. These laws have been a major weapon in incarcerating repeat offenders or career criminals for offenses that rarely produced custodial sentences. For example, the most likely sanction for burglary is probably probation. But certifying the defendant as a habitual offender increases the probability of receiving a sentence with prison time. If the goal is to seek incapacitation, the enhancements to the charges certainly help.

Adding capital murder charges to a homicide is the most severe enhancement possible because it places the defendant at risk of being put to death. This charge also starts a complex and costly undertaking that eats up court time, staff time, and money. It also automatically puts into play a string of appeals after conviction and the imposition of the death penalty. Accordingly, decisions to place these charges are made only after lengthy review and discussion.

One would think that prosecutors would favor mandatory minimums, which mandate minimum sentences for the conviction of certain crimes, because they mandate incarceration for crimes that previously could have received lesser sentences. This is not necessarily the case. Mandatory minimums generally do not receive favorable reviews by most prosecutors because they limit the ability of the prosecutor to "fit the punishment to the crime."

The most common offenses subject to legislated minimums are possession of a gun during the commission of a crime, usually a felony, and selling or distributing drugs within a specified number of feet from a school. California has a "three strikes and you're out" law that requires imprisonment after conviction for a third felony.[12]

The problem created by mandated minimum sentences is that they take away the prosecutor's discretionary power to tailor sanctions to fit individual cases. In the long run they reduce the prosecutor's ability to negotiate dispositions that are more reasonable and appropriate than those mandated by the law.

A Detroit, Michigan, prosecutor described the dilemma presented in charging a case involving a very young teenager who was caught shoplifting in a major department store. When the defendant's handbag was searched, the police found a gun in the bottom. The mandatory gun law required the defendant to face one year in jail even with no prior criminal history. If a gun had not been in the picture, the shoplifting charge would probably not even invoke probation, given the defendant's age and lack of record. Most probably, for this first time offender the sentence would have been community service as a condition of diversion. The issue facing the prosecutor was to charge the case in such a way that the mandatory minimum was not invoked. Typically cases subject to mandatory minimums are charged as attempts, in this case, attempted shoplifting.

Enhancements increase the discretionary power of prosecutors because they allow them to increase the severity of sentences if added to the original charges. Mandatory minimums and three strikes legislation, however, present obstacles to prosecutors who seek a lower sanction than those mandated, although they still retain the power to lower the charge to one not requiring the mandatory minimum.

Sentencing guidelines have also strengthened the prosecutor's charging discretion because they add certainty to the sentences that are likely to be imposed. Most sentencing guidelines essentially are a grid, with one column classifying offenses into categories like drugs, property crimes, robbery, assault, and so on, and the rows classifying the criminal history of the offender according to his or her criminal record—for example, no prior record, prior record but no active sentences, prior record with active sentences. Inside each cell in the grid is a range of sentences from which the judge can select. The sentencing judge has the discretion to go outside the range based on mitigating or aggravating factors. But if the judge does so, the reasons must be specified in writing. No one single matrix exists because each state has developed and implemented guidelines consistent with their statutes.[13]

When sentencing guidelines are available, prosecutors often refer to them in the charging process to make sure that the "punishment fits the crime." If the prosecutor wants jail time as a possible sentence, he or she can check the guidelines to make sure that the charge selected includes the possibility of jail. If the prosecutor selects a lower charge that does not include jail, then that sentence is ruled out.

The charge that is placed also may affect the defendant's eligibility for other programs, especially diversion programs. There is an increasing acceptance of using diversion, mediation, dispute resolution centers, citizen complaint bureaus, alcohol and rehabilitation programs, community service, and a host of other programs to avoid prosecuting the offender through the criminal courts. Many of these programs have eligibility criteria for entrance, some of which are linked to the charge and the seriousness of the charge. Prosecutors who want to direct the offender into these programs take these entrance criteria into consideration when they place the charges.

The level of charges, felony or misdemeanor, and the actual charges are really about the type of sanction that would be acceptable to the prosecutor. So the level of the charge placed on the case cannot be untangled from the prosecutor's expectations about the likely outcome of prosecution. For the majority of cases, the decision of what to charge is based on a combination of factors, primarily resting on the seriousness of the offense, the criminal history of the defendant, the strength of the evidence, and, in the end, a preferred sanction.

The decision of what to charge is not the end of the charging process. There are other strategic decisions that prosecutors can make that affect the way cases are prosecuted, increase the chances of getting preferred outcomes, and reduce workload in the office. The most common considerations include decisions about jurisdiction, meaning which court will prosecute; timing, when charging decisions will be made; and location, where the case will be prosecuted.

Prosecutors are not restricted to trying cases in the local jurisdiction. Criminal cases arising in one jurisdiction may be prosecuted in a number of venues. Depending on statutes or agreements, they can be transferred to the office of another local prosecutor, or prosecuted by municipal prosecutors, the state's attorney general, or the federal U.S. attorney.

Although each venue has its own jurisdictional requirements, there is enough overlap between the offices that makes some transfers possible and often beneficial to prosecution. Every offense that shares concurrent jurisdiction with one or more prosecution systems is, theoretically, eligible for a change of venue. These opportunities have given the prosecutor additional strategies in achieving preferred dispositions.

In some instances it is more efficient to consolidate a number of cases into one prosecution than to conduct them separately. Persons charged with passing bad checks all over the state, or burglars who practice widely throughout a metropolitan area or even in two cities are good examples. When prosecutions are split between two or more jurisdictions, consolidation is an attractive solution because it strengthens the plea bargaining position of the prosecutor. Now an offer to dismiss charges in the other jurisdiction if the defendant pleads to charges pending in the local jurisdiction is possible. It may also have the added benefit of making the defendant eligible for sentence enhancements under habitual offender statutes or even for mandatory prison terms.

The drawback to this advantage is communication, or the lack thereof. The present state of information systems operating statewide for local criminal justice systems usually cannot provide information to one prosecutor about cases that may be pending in other jurisdictions. Unless staff phone or e-mail other offices to check whether they have cases pending against specific defendants, there is little chance that they will discover other pending cases, thereby nullifying the benefits of a transfer.

Colorado is an exception. The state has developed and implemented a system called "ACTION," which allows each of the 22 prosecutor offices to communicate with one another and with the state's central database. It is now routine procedure for the staff to check incoming cases against the central database to determine whether there are other pending cases in other offices. This is a major advancement for prosecution!

Some cases may be prosecuted either by the local prosecutor in state courts or by a municipal prosecutor in municipal courts. These concurrent jurisdiction cases typically involve ordinance violations, some misdemeanors, and in some cases, traffic and moving violations.[14] Generally, procedures are agreed upon by the two prosecutors and guidelines prepared for police and magistrates stating in which court the different types of cases will be filed. For example, all ordinance violations will be prosecuted in municipal courts and all misdemeanors involving injury or property loss or damage will be prosecuted in state courts.

Conflict is a continual issue in concurrent jurisdiction cases. Part of it stems from the fact that the sanctions in municipal courts from violations of ordinances and traffic laws are usually substantially less than sanctions available from violations of state statutes. If the local prosecutor wanted stiffer penalties for certain crimes, the case would need to be filed in the state court, not municipal court.

Another part of the conflict is due to the desire to keep the revenues resulting from fines and fees. For many municipal courts, the revenue from fines and fees goes into the general fund, providing the local government with substantial income. Thus city prosecutors may be reluctant to transfer "high fine" cases to the local prosecutor and lose the revenue from them.

This was illustrated in one state by a continuing problem with driving under the influence (DUI) cases. DUIs filed in municipal court could generate fines for as much as $500. But the local prosecutor had made the prosecution of drunk drivers a top priority for prosecution. If they were tried in his office, the sanctions imposed could be far more severe than a fine, and, in some cases, the defendant would be eligible for statutory enhancements available only in state courts. So the conflict between the two courts was ever-present, one seeking to keep the high revenues, the other seeking stiffer penalties. The problem was exacerbated by police, who were not following existing guidelines that called for DUI cases to be filed in the state courts.

Establishing mutually agreed upon guidelines for prosecuting concurrent jurisdiction cases not only reduces conflicts but also can provide creative solutions to some of the more systemic problems created by legislation and the courts.

In a jurisdiction in the Northwest, the city attorney and the district attorney had reached a mutually successful way to handle juveniles who were disruptive in school and destroyed school property. There was little the district attorney could do if the complaint was filed with his office. Procedures called for the student to be processed by the juvenile court division, which would decide, first, whether the case should be adjudicated, and then, months later, what action should be taken. The process was so slow that the student could be out of school or at least in the next grade before anything would be done. Swift, sure, and certain justice was out of the question.

The city attorney, however, was not bound by these restrictions. If the complaint was filed with the city, the city attorney could file a complaint citing municipal ordinance violations and order the parents and the student to appear in court by a specific date, usually within days of the incident. The parents could be held accountable for their child's actions; fines and restitution could be imposed. Swift, sure, and certain justice was now attainable.

In some states the attorney general has criminal as well as civil jurisdiction. If a local case has consumer protection or interstate trade implications, then based on this broader scope, it may be transferred to the attorney general or to a statewide grand jury for further investigation before charges are placed. In a few instances, the attorney general may take over a local prosecution, but these events are rare and usually reflect situations where the local prosecutor is not prepared, or there is an issue of public corruption that requires an involuntary takeover. These occasions are so exceptional that they are not a factor routinely considered by prosecutors.

Federal prosecutions by the U.S. attorney's office are another story. Because federal legislation tends to impose harsher and more severe penalties than state legislated sanctions, transfers to the U.S. attorney's office (USAO) are often desired for serious or complex cases. For example, federal law allows for the death penalty in cases like drug trafficking, while some states like Michigan do not permit the death penalty for any violations of the law. Federal law may also have mandated minimums that do not exist at the state level, thus making federal prosecutions more desirable.

The problem, of course, is whether the U.S. attorney's office will accept a change of venue and prosecute the state's case. Some federal guidelines prohibit prosecution of cases below a certain dollar limit. This particularly applies to complex drug and organized crime cases. Other reasons for rejection by the U.S. attorney's office are essentially the same as those used by local prosecutors: the courts or the office may be overworked and backlogged, the case is not in the interests of the public, and there are other cases pending that have a higher priority. The decision may be negotiable but it belongs to the U.S. attorney and cannot be changed.

Back in the 1970s, San Diego's district attorney, Ed Miller, had a number of cases that could have been prosecuted federally but were rejected by the U.S. attorney's office, citing a lack of resources. Ed Miller came up with a creative idea. Why not have his assistant district attorneys "cross-designated" as assistant U.S. attorneys (AUSA)? In this manner, those cases could be prosecuted in the federal courts. The courts and the U.S. attorney approved, and this became the first recorded use of local prosecutors designated to prosecute in federal courts. Later the concept was used in reverse, when some AUSAs were designated as state and local prosecutors to assist the prosecution of complex cases, usually drugs, in state courts.

In the end, it is primarily the prosecutor who decides where cases are to be tried. Sometimes these decisions are not always for the best. Take the O. J. Simpson case. Los Angeles's district attorney, Gil Garcetti, had the choice of trying the case in Brentwood where the murders occurred or downtown where Garcetti's central office was located. The demographic makeup of the two jurisdictions was that Brentwood was predominately white and affluent, and downtown Los Angeles predominately black, Hispanic, and poor. Defense counsel's strategy of making race the issue, not the murders, tipped the scales in favor of an acquittal. A jury in Brentwood might have forced defense counsel to use other strategies with different results. It was just a questionable choice of venue.

The Long Reach of Discretion

Thus far, the discussion has been about the elements of prosecutorial discretion as related to decisions made about individual cases. But the prosecutor's discretion affects more than just cases. It defines many features of the criminal justice system and the citizens of the local community.

In the criminal justice system, the discretionary power of the prosecutor reaches back to law enforcement and forward to courts and corrections. Whenever prosecution interacts with other agencies or the courts, it can influence policy, procedures, and practices by the power of its discretionary decisions.

Prosecutorial charging policies set the standards for what is acceptable police work and police reporting. Those policies also define the priorities of the prosecutor with regard to prosecutions. Since every case in the system is not given the same level of attention—for example, murders require more work than simple drug possessions—priorities play an important role in the interface between police and prosecutor.

In serious crimes, prosecutors may have a great deal of input, advising detectives about the evidence needed to support arrests and where additional information is needed. This type of cooperation was seen during the 2002 sniper attacks in the metropolitan Washington, D.C., area when the task force formed included not only the law enforcement agencies of the surrounding jurisdictions but the local prosecutors as well.

The prosecutor has the power to influence and even change law enforcement policy. This is apparent if the priorities placed on crime by the two agencies are not in sync. If the prosecutor's priorities spotlight specific offenses like domestic violence, shoplifting, bad checks, child abuse, or drunk driving, it influences police decisions to arrest since it is clear that these cases will get more attention than others.

When priorities are not in sync, the work of the police does not receive special attention. Police crackdowns on shoplifting, for example, are ineffective if the prosecutor only prosecutes cases that exceed some dollar value of the goods lifted. Similarly, violent offender programs run by the police department are rarely as effective if the prosecutor treats those designated like any other felony in the office. Coordinating policy, procedures, and practices between the two agencies opens the door for prosecutorial involvement and influence.

The most important effect of the prosecutor's discretionary power is that it defines the workload in the courts. The decisions to accept, reject, divert, charge, and dismiss give the prosecutor almost total control over the gate leading to the courts.[15]

To critics, this power is threatening. The critics fear that it will lead to unbridled injustices. But they forget to look at the checks and balances surrounding this power. They include the various interests of the police, defense counsel, judges, the media, special advocacy groups, and the public. The importance of checks and balances was best exemplified when, in 1986, England created the Crown Prosecution Service as an independent entity under the director of public prosecutions. Crown prosecutors replaced the old police-dominated system of solicitors who were hired by the police department to prosecute cases under police guidelines.[16] Crown prosecutors are now an independent body exercising much of the discretionary power American prosecutors enjoy.

The critical measure for testing the impact of discretion is whether this power strengthens equity in the justice system, produces reasonable and appropriate dispositions, and increases the efficiency of the adjudication process.

Some prosecutors do not exercise much control over the gate. There are still prosecutors who do not screen cases or give them only a cursory review. Usually this occurs with misdemeanor prosecutions. By taking this position, prosecutors have, in effect, transferred control over the gate to law enforcement and reduced the effectiveness of checks and balances in the process.

Most professional prosecutors define what goes through the gate consistent with their personal views of their role and responsibilities. These views vary from that of prosecuting all crimes as long as they are legally sufficient, to establishing priorities for what constitutes the most serious offenses and allocating resources and time so they can be given sufficient attention. Much like triage, some cases are simply not prosecuted or are given only minimal attention because others are more important and need extra resources.

Prosecutors define their roles in different ways, from being an extension of law enforcement, to being a manager of cases, a policymaker, or a community leader. Each definition establishes boundaries around what is accepted, how it will be prosecuted, and to what end. The prosecutor's policies toward plea negotiation, discovery, and sentence recommendations, in large part, establish the relationships between the prosecutor's office, the courts, and defense counsel.

By the prosecutor's controlling the gate to the court, the court and defense counsel are the recipients of only those cases that the prosecutor accepts. They implicitly march in response to prosecution priorities and respond, indirectly, to the resources that prosecutors direct to cases and prosecutors' policies about plea bargaining and discovery. The guidelines and standards established for making discretionary decisions reach deep into the courts, affecting how cases are disposed and what sanctions are imposed.

Not to be ignored is the impact of prosecution on corrections and other postconviction activities. The war on drugs is a good example of how the major push to prosecute drug dealers and users filled prisons and jails to capacity and expanded the prison-building industry. The recent shift by the federal government to fund more rehabilitation efforts such as drug courts, in addition to existing drug task forces, is an indicator that the old strategy has severe limitations and new ones are needed to correct the prison population problem. But not to be forgotten is the fact that it was the prosecutors who sent the cases into the courts and looked for incarceration as a preferred outcome. If prosecutors change their priorities or seek different types of sanctions, the effects on prisons, jails, and probation and alternative programs will be ordained.

In seeking reasonable and appropriate dispositions, prosecutors may find themselves involved in postconviction activities such as presentence investigations conducted by probation officers, or in opposing parole. Each time the prosecutor becomes active in these areas, the influence of the office seeps further into the criminal justice system. The achievement of the office's goals is one effect, but the more important effect is being able to have influence on the workings of other parts of the criminal justice system.

The cases that the prosecutor decides to accept and dispose of by plea negotiation, dismissal, or trial, and the working relationship with the defense bar define to a large extent what is known as "the local legal culture."[17] The prosecutor may not have complete control over all aspects of prosecution, but the effects of the prosecutor's discretionary power can be seen in the practices and procedures used in the adjudication process.

The discretionary reach of the prosecutor is felt in every aspect of the criminal justice system. Prosecution policies and priorities let prosecutors mix and match their discretionary decisions with strategies to bring about what each defines as desired dispositions. As a result, it is little wonder that local criminal justice systems vary so widely.

Many think that the influence and power of the prosecutor stops at the courthouse. But this is far from being the case. In many jurisdictions, prosecutors have become policymakers and leaders. These are prosecutors who look beyond the courts and criminal justice and see the needs of the community. The local prosecutor's influence and elected status can be used to confront community problems and push solutions. The values or policies guiding prosecution ultimately reflect community concerns about crime, even about what constitutes crime.[18]

The fact that most prosecutors are elected requires this sensitivity to community values if only as a means for political survival. But more importantly, it gives the people a say in deciding what is important for prosecution and what is not. The existence of special advocacy groups like MADD or environmental protection groups bear witness to the pressures that the public and the media can place upon prosecutors to listen to their priorities. Some of these pressures are one-sided and could create potential biases in prosecution. It is up to the prosecutor to consider all sides and maintain balance, a sometimes difficult and unpleasant task.

The prosecutor's discretionary power coupled with the office's locally elected status may produce a complex prosecutorial environment that is driven by politics and policy. Balancing the two forces involves treading a fine line between holding positions that are responsive to the community and being true to stated policies and priorities for prosecution. Politically, there is always an opponent waiting to challenge for the job.

If prosecutors reach out into the community as they have with community prosecution, they become problem solvers, using the law in creative ways to reduce problems and the elected status to persuade other agencies, offices, or programs to help. The full range of power and influence can be seen in Multnomah County, Oregon, where District Attorney Michael Schrunk implemented the most comprehensive attack on community problems with a community prosecution program.[19] When starting the program in 1990, Schrunk said that if the office's felony caseload increased, the community prosecutor would return to the courthouse to try cases. Years later, the community DA program is alive and well.

Prosecutor leadership extends also to providing a vehicle for solving problems in the community. Almost too numerous to mention are the prosecutors who have written grant applications for joint programs with the police, or those who have pulled together law enforcement agencies, school principals, officers in juvenile court probation, and their own attorneys to find ways to stop gang violence before it starts by removing troublemakers from the scene. The current funding of community prosecution programs is a good example of some of the ways that the quality of community life can be improved because of the involvement of the prosecutor.

Even without community prosecution, the quality of community life may be improved or restricted by the standards and guidelines established by prosecutors about which crimes will be tolerated and which will not. The long-term effects of discretion may be observed in communities that have reduced crime, increased public safety, and improved the quality of life. Although not all of these effects may be directly attributable to the prosecutor's discretionary decisions, indirectly, high-quality prosecution services play a large part in creating a safe and secure environment.

Discretion Is Shared by Many

It is tempting to believe that the prosecutor is the sole possessor of discretionary power. But many other actors also exercise discretion, which affects crime, public safety, laws, and the courts. They include, among others, citizens, police officers, defense counsel, judges, and probation officers. Each one's choices or decisions affect what is in the criminal justice system, how cases will be disposed, and with what results.

Discretion starts with the citizen or victim of a crime who decides whether to call the police or not. Victimization surveys like the National

Crime Victimization Survey (NCVS) indicate that some types of violations of the law like household crimes or domestic abuse are rarely reported to police. Some victims choose not to report crimes because they feel that nothing can be done. However, some crimes are regularly reported because they are covered by insurance, like auto theft. If the crime is not reported, or if witnesses are not willing to testify, the chances of arrests occurring are diminished.

Police have the authority to decide when there is probable cause to believe that a crime has been committed. They also exercise enormous discretion in deciding whether to make arrests. Typically, these decisions are influenced by the citizen's demand for an arrest, or the offender's attitude and behavior. Police discretion is most clearly seen when they are attempting to maintain order or play a peacekeeping role. If police decide to only give a warning or caution for a moving violation, for example, or if their orders to back off, cool down, or go away are followed, arrests may be avoided. In some states, magistrates have the discretion to issue warrants for the arrest of individuals based on citizen complaints.

The importance of decisions to arrest or not is crucial to the criminal justice system. When arrests are made, the next part of the criminal justice process, namely adjudication, begins. If arrests are not made, the criminal justice process never starts.

The adjudication process has three major players also having discretionary power. Judges exercise discretion in their decisions to detain or release a defendant pretrial and to set bail or to bind over defendants for trial or dismiss cases. Judges rule on motions, accept or reject negotiated pleas, determine guilt or innocence in bench trials, and sentence defendants after conviction or guilty pleas. To a certain extent, legislation or statutes have limited some of these discretionary powers. This is especially true of pretrial detention decisions, which must take into consideration the constitutional rights of the defendant; and sentencing, which has to conform to the limits set by sentencing guidelines and some of the sanctions mandated by the legislature.

Judges also bring to the courtroom a personal view of justice and the role of a judge in applying it. How judges define themselves can have a significant impact on how cases are processed. Judges are often referred to as "hanging judges," lenient judges, even absent judges. There are judges who "run a tight ship" and there are judges who are amenable to what the prosecutor and defense counsel agree upon. The procedures judges follow, the decisions judges make, and the case management abilities of judges all have an impact on the course of cases through the courts. It is this course to which prosecutors and defense counsel must respond.

Probation officers also have discretion in recommending sentences in their presentence investigation (PSI) reports. The influence of probation officers is more limited than that of most of the other participants in the adjudication process because it is tempered by two factors: the extent to which specific recommendations agree with the judge's view of appropriate sanctions and the amount of agreement between the judge and the probation officer about the factors that produce successful probations.

Probation officers also have discretion in deciding what constitutes a technical violation of probation resulting in a warning, or a violation that revokes probation. These decisions directly affect prosecution since a recommended termination reopens the prosecutor's case and puts it back into the courts for the imposition of sentence.

"Defense counsel has considerable authorized discretion in the preparation of the defense, particularly in the advice offered to defendants and in the strategy to be pursued in plea bargaining or trial proceedings."[20] In most cases involving public defenders, the discretion of defense counsel may be affected by the daily working relationships with the prosecutors and judges. Public defenders too have to conform to the procedures and processes in place in the courts. Nevertheless, the public defenders' interpretation of their role in representing clients may delay the processing of cases through repeated requests for continuances, or increase the work of the court by producing a large number of pretrial motions.

Especially important is their strategy for negotiating reductions in charges and other plea offers. It is here that the interface between the prosecutor and defense counsel becomes important. Some defense counsel take on an adversarial role with the prosecutor by keeping trial strategies private and refusing anything but limited plea negotiations. Other defense counsel assume a more administrative/managerial role, work with the prosecutor to keep cases moving, and look for speedy dispositions. However the defense counsel structures that role, prosecutors have to respond and adjust to those procedures and policies.

Nevertheless, despite the tremendous amount of discretion spread throughout the criminal justice system, it is the prosecutor who is the focal point. The inputs and outputs of the criminal justice process are largely governed by the prosecutor's decisions to decline to prosecute, accept and charge cases for prosecution, use other alternatives to prosecution, or dismiss cases. There are other discretionary decisions made by prosecutors that have substantially important effects, but these are minor in comparison to this basic set that opens the door to the judicial system and sets the course to disposition. Once inside, other discretionary decisions are possible that, while influenced by others, still allow the prosecutor to direct the course of the case through the system. These decisions focus on case management, the relationships prosecutors have with the other participants in the criminal justice system, and the nature of the prosecutor's involvement with the community.

The American prosecutor is unique among peers in other countries because of the level of discretionary power. The American prosecutor also has the freedom to make decisions and select a course of action from a set of actions. Those decisions are not reversible by others, and the action selected is based solely on that power. The discretionary power of the prosecutor, then, affects the internal workings of the office, its relationships with those agencies and the courts that do business with the office—namely, the criminal justice system—and the community the prosecutor serves. How it is used and even abused sets the foundation for a fascinating study of discretion and the prosecutor's prerogative.

CHAPTER TWO

Discretion and Policing

Toward the end of the 1960s, when Washington, D.C., along with many other cities, was the focus of Vietnam War protests, soaring crime rates had prompted President Nixon to announce that he would put a police officer on every street corner in the district. D.C.'s chief of police, Jerry Wilson, telephoned the district's director of the Office of Crime Analysis (OCA).[1] Wilson was frustrated with the department's inability to control crime and suggested that the U.S. attorney, who served as the district's local prosecutor, was failing to successfully prosecute cases the department submitted. Wilson had never met the U.S. attorney and viewed him as an opponent rather than an ally. The OCA director advised the chief to establish a relationship with the U.S. attorney. Both needed to communicate, even though the result would not always be satisfactory to them.

A few years later, the newly formed Law Enforcement Assistance Administration (LEAA) convened the first-ever national conference on police-prosecutor relations in Washington, D.C. About 200 attendees representing chiefs of police, sheriffs, and prosecutors met in the ballroom of a local hotel. Like guests at a traditional wedding, the police sat on the left side of the main aisle and the prosecutors on the right. It took a few years and lots of LEAA funding for joint police-prosecutor programs against career criminals and repeat offenders to get police and prosecutors to sit at round tables and design and develop workable, coordinated programs for their communities.

LEAA ended a long history of self-imposed isolation by police and prosecutors. The concept of cooperation and coordination between the two agencies became an accepted best practice over time. However, there was no well-defined way this interaction took place. It took time and much trial and error to discover the best way for any particular jurisdiction to coordinate. Even today some prosecutors and law enforcement leaders prefer the old way: the police investigate and the prosecutor will take it from there. However, for many if not most jurisdictions a new age of police-prosecutor interaction was born. Prosecutorial discretion at the earliest stages became noticeable and, over time, more powerful. In fact, by extending the reach of discretion deeper into law enforcement activities, both police and prosecutors reaped the benefits of joint activities, coordinated programs, and totally new forms of policing and prosecution.

In contrast to the "world before LEAA," the importance of police-prosecutor relations is now self-evident. Most agree that investigations and arrests by law enforcement agencies are the starting point for almost all the subsequent work in the criminal justice system. Police priorities direct the focus of investigations. Police training, practices, and procedures define the quality of the cases referred for prosecution. And police responsiveness to prosecutor requirements can substantially affect dispositions. Prosecutors set adjudication priorities through charging decisions. Those decisions are largely based on the product submitted by police and define the workload of the prosecutor, defense counsel, and court, which ultimately impacts the safety and security of the public.

In this chapter, the focus is on the dynamics of the police-prosecutor interface as it is shaped by discretion exercised by the prosecutor and the degree to which the prosecutor can influence police activities. Specifically, the factors that set the boundaries for police-prosecutor relations are examined. The nature of these relationships can either extend the influence of the prosecutor or constrain it. The evolution of the prosecutor's power and influence in the police-prosecutor interface is described in terms of these relationships and how various programs have helped or hindered the progression—from acting as an officer of the court to being a community leader. It is clear that prosecutors can have enormous influence on law enforcement productivity through arrests and ultimately on public safety.

Before looking at the police-prosecutor interface and how it is impacted by the prosecutor's discretion, it is important first to examine some of the factors that cause wide variation among local criminal justice environments.

Factors Affecting the Police-Prosecutor Interface

Any examination of policing in the United States will find that its authority and funding sources are basically local in nature. As a result, there is limited uniformity in policy, priorities, operations, and resources. The same is true for prosecution. By examining the overall landscape, the factors that are important in making the interface between police and prosecutor work more or less successfully can be identified.

There is no question that the quality of police reporting is the primary factor affecting prosecution. Its impact can be discerned in the variety of complaints by prosecutors who deal with police departments that do not train investigators and street cops to prepare acceptable reports of incidents and arrests:[2] "They have no clue about what it takes to make a case. Do they get any training?" "It's the Keystone cops. They can't even protect a crime scene." "If only they would give us more info, like who the witnesses are, and what will they testify to."

By the same token, prosecutors are not always blameless either. They are not universally hailed as the good guys by police. Listen to some police officers' complaints: "The prosecutors never come to the crime scene even when asked." "Every time I bring a case over, the prosecutor finds something wrong with it." "We work cases, he breaks them down." "I call for advice about a search warrant and get a baby assistant who doesn't know anything about them." "Each time I call over, I get a different assistant DA [ADA] who wants something else."

The quality of police training and the professionalism of the department directly affect the ability of officers to collect and protect evidence, give Miranda warnings, prepare and exercise search warrants, collect witness statements, protect the chain of custody, and document all these activities in a report for the prosecutor. This may be a lot to ask of local police departments if they are inadequately funded and trained. However, police departments generally measure performance using clearance rates. The clearance rate reflects that an arrest has been made for a particular offense. They are less concerned with a conviction. That is someone else's problem, namely the prosecutor.

While the quality of policing is the most important factor affecting the police-prosecutor interface, achieving almost the same level is the quality of police reports. It goes without saying that decisions made by prosecutors for accepting or rejecting cases are based primarily on the police report and its contents, supplemented by interviews with the police and witnesses. But listen to the complaints in this area.

From the prosecutors: "A major weakness in our prosecutions is lousy police reports." "I know they aren't Shakespeare, but can't these guys even write?" "I'm a trial lawyer. I don't have time to train everyone in report writing." "The departments differ so much, how can you count on getting good reports?"

From the police: "We give them as much information as we have at the time, but they want it all wrapped up in a neat package." "What they want depends on which assistant is on the warrant desk." "Sure there is some delay but blame the desk sergeant[,] not me." "Now just how is it my fault that lab reports always come in late?"[3]

Prosecutors do not have to live with the problems associated with less than adequate police training and professionalism. Prosecutors can exert some control over the quality of police reporting and successfully reduce or eliminate many of the complaints.

Although police reports typically are the first concern of prosecutors in the police-prosecutor interface, they are not the only ones. Changes in the local criminal justice system environment can occur slowly since they usually are the result of new legislation, changes in existing statutes, or changes in criminal justice system policies. If this effect on policing is ignored or given only cursory attention, prosecutors may suffer as a result. Consider habitual criminal legislation, which allows prosecutors to raise the ante against defendants with multiple convictions. It seems very clear that without access to criminal history records, this legislation would be meaningless. How else would you know the suspect was a habitual offender? If criminal histories, or "rap sheets," as they are often called, were only sporadically received from police when submitting an offense report, then the prosecutor's ability to use this new legislation would be diminished.

This is a simple example but it points to the prosecutor's responsibility to inform police of new legislation or changes in statutes that affect them, which, in turn, affects prosecution. How police are informed varies almost as much as how crimes and arrests are reported. Some prosecutors believe in the written word and compose memos, produce guidelines, and develop standards that explain the legislation and its effects. Others prefer briefings and training opportunities, and they develop materials that can fit into the roll call schedules. "Whatever works" is the solution. What cannot be ignored is the need.

Other legislative changes may initially affect one agency but the eventual impact may bring about unanticipated changes in another. In North Carolina, as in many other states, after the victim's rights amendment was passed, positions for victim-witness coordinators were created by the legislature. That presence allowed prosecutors to conduct more interviews with victims and witnesses and to conduct them earlier in the process. Police soon found that the amendment also affected the policing domain. So what happened? There are now victim-witness coordinator positions in police departments using new procedures where previously there were none. The victim-witness staff in police departments conducts the earliest interviews and provides assistance until the case is referred for prosecution, when the prosecutor's victim-witness staff takes over.

When looking at factors that affect the police-prosecutor interface, resources cannot be ignored. The basic level of resources for police and prosecutors is usually determined by local budget appropriations, although district and state funding applies to some prosecutorial jurisdictions. Underfunded departments and offices work at a considerable disadvantage, and the results are obvious in the police-prosecutor interface. Too few resources directly contribute to backlogs in police investigations, delays in charging decisions, and even potential changes in prosecutorial priorities.

Prosecutors will always have less funding than law enforcement given the differences in relative size of the agencies and the types of services provided. However, when federal grant funds are made available to one of the agencies, usually law enforcement and not prosecution, then a resource imbalance is created and the work generated may have severe effects on prosecution, the courts, and prisons. Faced with an increase in filings by the police caused by the additional funding, the prosecutor will likely decline more cases to keep the system in balance. Otherwise, if the additional cases flow into the system, the quality of the dispositions will fall, and the courts will have a bigger backlog.

A good example can be seen in the impact of the millions of dollars that were poured into law enforcement drug control programs. The federal funds increased the size of law enforcement and its work to such a degree that many prosecutors were quickly overwhelmed. The high volume of drug cases forced them to redirect priorities to meet the increased drug caseload, sometimes at the expense of prosecuting other crimes. Even the size and population of the prisons changed as more and more drug cases produced more and more active sentences.[4]

When the federal government changes its priorities to focus on certain types of crimes or manner of policing, the money allocated to these programs may be in conflict with what is needed at the local level. Probably the funniest illustration of this occurred in the early days of LEAA at a meeting in the Southwest between police and prosecutors. One chief, whose jurisdiction was in desert canyon country, told the story of how a powerboat provided by LEAA was traded for some jeeps and four-wheel-drive vehicles provided by LEAA to another agency needing the boat. There are always lessons to be learned, but the basic problem remains; as long as funds are directed to be used for specific programs, the priorities of police and prosecutors are pretty well defined by the funding agency. The result is likely an imbalance in resources and work at the local level or an unwanted shift in priorities.

Does the imbalance create friction? It does in some cases. How about those complaints from police?[5] "My priority is 911 calls[,] not court cases."

"I report to the mayor[,] not the DA. The DA has a different agenda than mine." The prosecutors respond in kind: "The chief starts a new program without even asking if it will affect me." "If more police are funded without funding prosecution, who will do our work?" "We need automation, not police cars." "So what if the jail is overcrowded, let the sheriff build a new one."

The complaints call attention to the need for communication, coordination, and balance in the system. Some imbalance can be tolerated, but changes in one agency may have a substantial impact on other parts of the criminal justice system.

The Nature of the Police-Prosecutor Interface

Relationships between police and prosecutors are always "iffy" if for no other reason than the inherent differences in the goals of the two agencies. For police, it is to protect the public by keeping the peace, enforcing the law, solving crimes, and arresting offenders suspected of the crimes. For prosecution, it is to review police work for legal sufficiency, make realistic charging decisions, pursue the successful prosecution of defendants, and obtain reasonable and appropriate sanctions. How prosecutors view their reviewing authority over police arrests plays a large part in defining the relationships between the two agencies.

Police-prosecutor relationships are colored by a number of factors: the personalities of the leaders, their views about the role of prosecution relative to law enforcement, resource availability, and the nature of the local criminal justice environments. The personalities of the police chiefs, sheriffs, and prosecutors are important because the head of each agency is a public personage with a public following created in large part by the media. Additionally, sheriffs and prosecutors, as elected officials, represent political parties and constituencies. It is not uncommon to find the development of shared priorities or programs hindered by the simple fact that the parties don't like each other and do only the minimum to maintain a public face of harmony. During elections even this public face may be pushed aside if the principals are in conflict or are in different parties. In one jurisdiction, the atmosphere was so hostile that the sheriff refused to meet with the prosecutor and publicly proclaimed the prosecutor to be a power-hungry politician not interested in the rights of victims or the public.

The concern here is not in the personal likes or dislikes that may exist between the leaders of the agencies; rather, it is directed at how different types of police-prosecutor relationships can affect the discretion of the prosecutor. In the next sections, the effects of various relationships on the police-prosecutor interface are explored and the impacts on outcomes are addressed. In general, there has been a gradual expansion in the prosecutor's role and influence on the interface that is linked to federal support for new law enforcement and public safety programs.

The dynamics of the police-prosecutor interface can create distinctly different environments for criminal justice processing. Because prosecutors and police have the ability to shift from one type of relationship to another, the dynamics of the interface also change. For some prosecutors this means that the office experienced a major expansion of influence on police and policing. For others, it means that the prosecutor has stayed within the more limited, traditional role of making charging decisions and disposing of cases. In the U.S. criminal justice system, all the roles of the prosecutor are legitimate since prosecutorial discretion has not been reduced. It just has not expanded into the policing domain.

There are five major ways that prosecutors' offices can relate to law enforcement agencies. They can be classified as subordinate, neutral, antagonistic, managerial, and proactive. Each has a different set of procedures for operations, which affects the extent of the prosecutor's use of discretion. The relationships not only circumscribe the prosecutor's discretion but also affect the administration and organization of the office as well as its practices and procedures. The managerial and proactive relationships empower the prosecutor and extend his or her influence far beyond the traditional decisions of accepting or rejecting cases. They change the nature and scope of prosecution in profound ways.

Some jurisdictions exist where the prosecutor proudly performs as part of the law enforcement team whose role is to follow through after the police leave off; in other words, "My job is to prosecute the cases the police bring over." Under these circumstances the prosecutor's discretion is clearly defined and limited in use. The prosecutor accepts the arrest reports and prosecutes the police charges. How the cases are disposed, by plea or trial or dismissal, remains at the discretion of the prosecutor. As long as the disposition is satisfactory to law enforcement, there are few complaints. If the case is accepted for prosecution, the case is cleared.

This interpretation of discretionary power is not likely to be found in larger urban areas or in many urban/suburban areas. When it exists, it is more likely the product of small offices in fairly rural communities where the participants in the local criminal justice system are home grown. In some jurisdictions, the sheriff, chief of police, prosecutor, and judge have had more than one position in the system. The sheriff has gone to law school and is now the prosecutor; the judge has been appointed to the bench from the prosecutor's office; and the mayor was formerly the chief of police.

In these environments, the critical question is whether the prosecutor has a backbone. Will the office refuse to prosecute defendants if the evidence is insufficient, even though the offender is a troublemaker? Will the prosecutor subordinate prosecution priorities to those of the police chief or sheriff? Will the prosecutor support the police agenda even if it conflicts with that of the prosecution? Because relationships in small offices are personal as well as professional, these issues are extremely important, and perhaps most important when the prosecutor is a "solo," employing no assistant prosecutors, or has three or fewer assistant prosecutors, a category that includes almost three-quarters of all local prosecutor offices.

The nature of small offices lends itself to intimacy and tradition. However, it is not proper for prosecutors to cede authority to the police. When power shifts to law enforcement and the prosecutor has the view that the office should prosecute what the sheriff submits, then the judicial system has lost its checks and balances and the sheriff is driving the bus.

Sometimes prosecutors are neutral in the office's stance toward law enforcement. Active support of police activities is not offered and opposition is not tendered. In fact, the prosecutor is just not interested in integrating police interests with those of the office. Each agency simply "does its own thing." Police do policing; prosecutors prosecute. Nothing more is expected or desired.

The benefit of neutrality is that it doesn't restrict prosecutors from operating as deemed appropriate. Because the agencies are independent of each other, each defines the work to be done according to the prevailing statutory authority. The interface existing in this neutral environment is remarkably free from issues that might be important in other relationships.

In one jurisdiction where the police had embraced community policing, devoting substantial resources and money in developing the program, it was a stand-alone activity. The prosecutor neither supported nor opposed it and was only aware of its broadest elements. Attention was concentrated on screening cases for their ability to be sustained at trial and developing specialized prosecution programs and alternatives to prosecution that the prosecutor thought were needed.

Community policing and other police activities simply were not within the scope of the prosecution. If issues arose that mattered to prosecution, the prosecutor was always willing to meet with the chief to discuss them. Relations between the two agencies were friendly and professional. But no extra effort or change in prosecution priorities were made to accommodate community policing activities; nor did the police department expect accommodation. The result was a community policing program that was limited in its impact and a prosecutor's office that operated independently of its influence.

The key to maintaining a neutral stance depends heavily on the levels of professionalism in the two agencies. Imagine a dysfunctional prosecutor's office, one that is inefficient, understaffed, and has poor management. Could this office maintain a neutral stance if the level of professionalism in the police department was high? Certainly it could, since it would handle its caseload in the same inefficient manner, business as usual. But if the prosecutor's office was well managed and organized and it was the police department that was untrained, producing poor-quality arrests and incomplete paperwork, it would be difficult for the prosecutor to remain neutral since the community being served would see the performance of the prosecutor's office as being a problem. Too many cases would be declined or dismissed. This might drive the prosecutor to change the interface.

Under these circumstances, the prosecutor's most likely response would be to attempt to make changes to reduce the problems. One of two different postures could be adopted depending on the relationship with the department. An aggressive stance to force change is one option. Another is the managerial supportive tack. However, neutrality is not an option if the office is to operate with high-level prosecution standards.

The problem with neutral relationships is that the police are at a disadvantage. If a new police program needs positive prosecutorial responses like changing priorities or targeting special populations or cases, the program will likely not achieve its expected goal. In addition, prosecution goals are also weakened if police activities are not aligned with prosecution priorities.

Two good examples of this were observed in Missouri. There was concurrent jurisdiction between the city and county courts for some offenses. Where the police chose to file their cases had a major impact on county prosecutors. For example, DUI cases filed in city court by police were a benefit to the city because the fines went into its coffers. But serious DUI cases or those involving repeat offenders could not receive the harsher sanctions available from county prosecution if those cases were filed in city court.[6]

In another example, if police filed misdemeanor cases in city court, the use of habitual offender statutes available in county court to enhance the sanction was precluded. Police discretion in these two instances drastically restricted the power of the prosecutor to impose the maximum sentence possible for these cases.

Not all relations between police and prosecutors are smooth, and some are even antagonistic. Typically the result of these antagonistic relations is a separation of police and prosecution powers, and an ever-present sensitivity to any perceived attempt by either party to usurp the powers of the other. Police chiefs chafe from end-runs made by the prosecutor to the mayor, county council, or county executive to force changes in the police department. Prosecutors are threatened every time the chief meets with the press to complain about cases lost by the prosecutor or drunk drivers let go with a slap on the wrist when prosecutors reduce charges. Sometimes there is open conflict or even hostility between the two agencies, not that the public ever sees it. If a prosecutor wants or has to be aggressive, there are a number of ways of doing it without engaging in a public battle.

Nothing is quite like the power of the prosecutor to force recalcitrant police departments to perform differently. Consider a police agency that routinely submits incomplete reports and rarely responds to requests for additional information. Meetings with the chief have produced little except some intermittent memos instructing the sergeant to review case reports more carefully. The attitudes of detectives and police officers clearly indicate that their job ends with an arrest. All avenues for change have been thwarted. What's a prosecutor to do?

In the late 1960s, when the police rarely submitted criminal histories with their reports, one prosecutor posted a sign over the intake desk: "No cases will be accepted without criminal histories."[7] This was a clear statement of prosecutorial policy. The prosecutor was driving the bus. These types of conflicts have been greatly reduced as automated systems now make access to these particular records available throughout the system.

Another prosecutor was having a difficult time obtaining additional investigative information needed for proper charging decisions. After many futile requests to the police department, the prosecutor sent a letter to victims notifying them that the case was to be dismissed because vital information was not available from the police department. If they wished to discuss the matter further, the prosecutor supplied the name, address, and telephone number of the chief of police. Not nice for improving relations, but effective!

Discordant relations shed light on the power of prosecution to force some changes in police procedures even under the most adverse conditions. The prosecutor's primary target is police reporting since the police report is the initiating vehicle for prosecution. How can this report be improved when the law enforcement agencies don't see this as a priority problem? The options are few.

A common solution is based on the "do it yourself" principle (DIY): "If the police won't cooperate, then we will do it for them." This can be accomplished in a variety of ways. In one, the prosecutor's office designs its own case report forms for different types of crimes, identifying the basic information needed for intake and screening. The information from police reports is transferred to the form. Missing information is requested. This practice creates uniformity in reporting and is especially effective if the office deals with a large number of law enforcement agencies, each using different forms containing varying degrees of information.

Some prosecutors have used the same principle to mitigate the effects of poorly trained or disinterested detectives by employing a pool of investigators to do the follow-up work. This work typically involves locating and interviewing witnesses, serving subpoenas, and providing the trial attorney with backup investigative support. However, one has to be careful in ascribing the DIY principle as a criticism of all offices that employ large numbers of investigators. Many offices have good relations with police departments who detail investigators to prosecutors' offices. However, in the absence of detailed police personnel, and when there is a significant pool of DA investigators, then questions about police-prosecutor relations are in order.[8]

Relationships, even antagonistic ones, are a two-way street. There is always the possibility that law enforcement agencies will react negatively to prosecution priorities. The prosecutor is especially vulnerable if the ability to successfully prosecute certain types of crimes depends on the willingness of the police to enforce violations of those laws.

A prosecutor was elected on an anti-pornography plank that promised to prosecute to the limit persons arrested for operating "dirty book" stores. However, lacking the cooperation of police and county licensing boards, the agenda foundered. As this insistence on prosecuting pornography hardened, the prosecutor's reputation also suffered. When relationships are in conflict and the priorities of the agencies don't mesh, collaboration is unlikely and conflict is a continuing threat.[9]

On the other side of the street, the police department in a large city proposed a crackdown on prostitution and soliciting. Undercover police posed as "johns" and sweeps were made at night on selected city streets. But it was a Pyrrhic victory because the defendants were released on bail, or paid the fine and returned to the streets.

Few problems in antagonistic relationships are easily solved. Prosecutors have few weapons to make sure that police officers are in court when scheduled to testify. Other than asking for contempt citations, which judges may not be eager to issue, there is little prosecutors can do to get additional information from police officers or detectives who are busy working on the department's caseload. Most police officers are not interested in cases once a case has been cleared by arrest.

In the end, when the relationship between the two agencies is adversarial, the potential for any one of the agencies achieving its desired goals is unlikely. The two agencies will need to support each other for this to happen.

Today, it is probably safe to say that most relationships between the police and the prosecutor are managerial in nature, if for no other reason than the fact that isolation is out, conflict is difficult to sustain over time, and resources are scarce. The aim of a managerial relationship is to make the process between police and prosecutor efficient and productive so that the resources of the police are not wasted, and prosecutors have the information needed to move cases forward to disposition.

These are give and take relationships as the agencies develop coordinated programs and procedures to achieve some mutually agreed upon goals. The discretionary power of the prosecutor is expanded to enhance and strengthen the work of law enforcement and help it achieve its goals. The recognition that there is benefit to sharing goals and objectives gives discretion a longer and more effective reach into various parts of the criminal justice system than ever before.

Sometimes overzealous participation by prosecutors in police activities may produce questions about appropriateness and effectiveness. There are some prosecutors that are referred to as "closet cops." These attorneys are so enamored of police work that they "ride along" with patrols, keep up-to-date on detectives' investigations, participate in drug busts, and actively assist police at the crime scene. Depending on the level of participation, some of these activities may make the prosecutor a witness. That is not a good thing.

Prosecutors are needed at some crime scenes. They can be of enormous help to the police in preserving evidence and assessing its value and limitations. In like manner, the prosecutor's active assistance in drafting requests for search warrants and wiretaps may make the difference between a win and a loss in court. Inserting prosecutorial influence at these operational levels indirectly shows police what is essential or necessary for prosecution and what is not. The result, of course, is fewer cases declined for prosecution, fewer requests for additional information from police, and more quality dispositions.

Prosecutors may also be involved with federal and state law enforcement agencies, though to a lesser extent. However, attention needs to be given to those interfaces because managerial relationships can be more difficult. The priorities of these agencies may often be in conflict with local prosecutors who chafe at a lack of responsiveness to prosecutorial requests.

Too often the complaint is that the U.S. attorney's office will not prosecute cases under some dollar value or with minor sanctions. Only "big" cases are reserved for federal prosecution. The same type of complaint is heard from police. The FBI and DEA have guidelines about what they will investigate and pursue, which often bar them from accepting cases from local law enforcement agencies.

Joint Police-Prosecutor Programs

Joint police-prosecutor programs have substantially increased the influence of the prosecutor on law enforcement activities. The value of joint programs is that both agencies usually benefit from their involvement. The prosecutor brings information and expertise to the law enforcement program and at the same time police support the goals and objectives of the prosecutor. Prosecution adjusts its priorities so they mesh more closely with those of law enforcement to put the full weight of the office against specific crimes or offenders. In the absence of the joint program this might not occur. Two classic examples are the career criminal/repeat offender programs and drug task forces.

The repeat offender programs (ROP) and career criminal programs (CCP) penetrated the wall between police and prosecutor. Police saw how the prosecutor could reduce or minimize the chances that bad guys would slip through the cracks and return to the streets. But simply classifying an offender as a career criminal or repeat offender in the police department was no guarantee that the case would receive priority attention by the prosecutor or the courts. When the prosecutor joined forces with police, the story was entirely different.

Once cases were labeled as career criminal or repeat offender, prosecutors responded by making sure those cases received priority attention. Assistants were present at first appearance to oppose bail and argue for pretrial detention. Experienced trial prosecutors worked with the detectives to make sure the evidence was strong, extra trial preparation time was given to them, plea negotiations were limited, and sentencing enhancements were used whenever possible. The goal was incapacitation and the prosecutor used discretion to increase the probability of meeting that goal.

This type of selective prosecution doesn't depend entirely on the cooperation or participation of the police department. The prosecutor has the power to design and develop the same program even without police participation. Police participation adds to the breadth of the program, and specially designated police detectives usually increase the strength of a case for prosecution. However, the prosecutor can have an effective program without police participation. In the end, a coordinated joint program is superior if turf issues can be avoided.

The strategy of selective prosecution has gained wide acceptance. It is viable because the discretionary power of the prosecutor allows him or her to tap into a variety of programs that focus on a range of cases including, among others, child sex abusers, domestic violence, violent offenders, crimes against women or the elderly, auto theft, and drunk driving. When the programs are operated jointly by police and prosecutor, there is an added advantage of each agency reinforcing the goals and objectives of the other.

On a negative note, the discretionary power of the prosecutor also allows him or her to ignore police priorities and programs as well. Imagine how well a repeat offender program would work if the prosecutor did not give these arrests any different handling than the other cases in the office. The impact of prosecutorial disinterest could seriously hinder the success of police programs.

Joint programs typically designate special attorneys to work with specially designated detectives on particular crimes or criminals. Peter S. Gilchrist III, a former prosecutor in Charlotte, North Carolina, expanded this concept to include all offenses and offenders handled by the Charlotte police department.[10] The office was reorganized so that it aligned with the police department's organization. There was a homicide and violent crimes unit, a property crimes division, drugs, juveniles, and misdemeanors. Each unit worked with its counterpart in the police department. The assistants in each unit also developed protocols and guidelines for the prosecution of the targeted offenses and offenders. For the first time, protocols were developed for prosecuting auto thefts and burglaries in addition to those usually found for more serious felonies. A memorandum of understanding signed by the chief of police and the prosecutor formalized this relationship.

This type of "tenants by entirety" interface gives both sides tremendous advantage because it promotes specialization in both agencies. But it may not be feasible for all prosecutors since it requires sufficient numbers of attorneys to permit specialization and individual court docketing systems to minimize scheduling problems for the attorneys in each unit.

Joint programs are not the only vehicle that has increased the prosecutor's influence. One that also has gained wide acceptance is the multijurisdictional task force.

The original use of task forces was to disrupt and destroy organized crime, but in those days few local prosecutors were involved in the primarily federal operations. However, as the drug epidemic swept the United States, it infected local jurisdictions with the same features as organized crime. The establishment of multijurisdictional drug task forces (MJDTF), funded in large measure by the federal government, established local coordinated umbrella operations and changed once more the nature of the police-prosecutor interface.

Local prosecutors gained a legitimate role in defining the task force strategies since the laws violated are outside federal jurisdiction. Local prosecutors are more sensitive to changes in the jurisdictions served. Emerging drug trafficking networks can be identified and disrupted at this early stage, and priorities can be adjusted to reflect local community needs. Often, local prosecutors and police are better informed about local problems than federal attorneys and state law enforcement officials. As participants in the MJDTF, prosecutors can provide legal advice to the investigators. Local prosecutors can assist in developing and managing informants and are generally responsible for the plea bargaining process involving informants.

The difference between the prosecutor's role in a joint program and a task force is that prosecutors become the titular coordinator of multijurisdictional law enforcement activities. The role entails acting as a funnel for their coordinated activity, being the legal advisor to law enforcement in complex drug prosecutions, and prosecuting those arrested. The prosecutor is also a critical intermediary for aiding law enforcement in gaining access into the court system when they seek, authorization/approvals for wiretaps, search warrants, financial warrants, and the other tools needed to disrupt or destroy an organized drug distribution system.

Since the jurisdiction of the task forces is geographically broad, including multiple political entities—such as counties, cities, towns, and districts—many police departments participate in the typical task force. This reinforces the centralization of power in the prosecutor. As the clearinghouse and coordinator of activities, area-wide oversight to the process is provided. Thus prosecutors gain even more influence over law enforcement priorities and activities.[11]

Community policing draws attention to "quality of life" crimes. These are the nuisances and petty crimes that lower the quality of life for citizens and the ones that are seen more often than murders, rapes, or robberies. The offenders are usually young people loitering in front of stores, making some customers fearful of entering. Some are drunks who hang around liquor stores or the homeless who panhandle in front of restaurants. Included are the drug dealers who take over a park or a street corner. Hookers, vandals who break windows and create graffiti, and inhabitants of crack houses are part of the problem as well. These are the enemies of citizens' quality of life in a neighborhood.

Quality of life crimes are mostly misdemeanors or ordinance violations. Without special prosecutorial attention, these cases come in, have a hearing, and go out with a traditional slap on the wrist. With prosecutorial attention, these cases may drastically prevent future crimes and restore the quality of life to the community.

In one jurisdiction, a Hispanic neighborhood was up in arms about an influx of prostitutes on the sidewalks and street corners of the neighborhood.[12] Arrest was not a solution. The community demanded more than just arrests. The hookers needed to be removed permanently. The prosecutor went to the chief judge of the misdemeanor court and asked that sentences be imposed that were more than just fines; in fact, spending the night in jail was the preferred sanction. The prosecutor proposed that the court pay special attention to cases coming from this neighborhood, and an assistant prosecutor would be assigned to forcefully represent the state and request jail time for each defendant. In this instance, the prosecutor prevailed and the revolving door slowed down. The streetwalkers moved on or went inside, and the community was pleased.

Prosecutors can choose from a number of roles in relating to police as described earlier. Yet from the example above, it is easy to see how powerful these programs become when prosecutors actively join forces with police to reach the same goal. Imagine how limited the community policing results would have been if the prosecutor had not offered to help by vigorously prosecuting quality of life crimes and intervening with the court to respond to the neighborhood's needs.

In an evaluation of the impact of community policing on the criminal justice system, the many dimensions of the prosecutor's role became clear.[13] Of all the sites visited and surveyed for the evaluation, no police agencies reported opposition by the prosecutor to the program. This was to be expected since misdemeanor and ordinance violations are not normally high on the prosecutor's radar screen. Also, regardless of their views about the value of community policing, prosecutors would not openly oppose the program without considerable political risk to the office. More likely, the prosecutor made a few shifts in priorities to indicate support, but did not fully engage to maximize community policing results.

At another site, the prosecutor was a supportive but reactive participant in the community policing effort. The needs of the police efforts were addressed when the chiefs asked. However, active participation in the police department's planning or development process was not in the cards.

When prosecutors become active participants in the community policing program, the scope and effectiveness of the program is dramatically increased. Joint meetings between the two agencies at both the policy-making and operational levels have coordinated police activities with prosecution responses. For example, clearing a local park of drug dealers and users was accomplished by surveillance evidence, undercover buys, and raids by police. To avoid a return of this situation, the cleaned-up park was put under stricter enforcement by park authorities and patrolled by the neighborhood watch. The prosecutor helped by participating in the planning process, identifying the evidence needed to convict, and giving these arrests high-priority publicity.

Community policing programs underscore the arsenal of tools that prosecutors could apply to police programs. For community policing programs, supportive prosecutors have used the regulatory authority of other agencies, trespassing laws, and licensing and code enforcement statutes to enhance not just prosecution but the goals of the program by reaching beyond the narrow confines of criminal justice into the civil and regulatory systems.

The ability of police and prosecutor to work together depends on the extent to which the goals of the agencies and the program are shared. The expected solution for serious criminals is incapacitation. "Put the guy away for a long, long time" is an undisputed theme shared by all when referring to serious crimes and serious offenders. If, on the other hand, the prosecutor disagrees with the incapacitation goal, relationships between the police and prosecutor may be problematic.

For example, if a prosecutor believes that most drug addicts and abusers should be treated rather than punished, what would be the police's reaction after they make arrests? The goals of treatment and rehabilitation are much less likely to be shared than those of incapacitation and just desserts. Look at the initial resistance of police to the idea of employing victim-witness assistants in the police department. Police are not social workers!

Just desserts and incapacitation are goals that are most supportive of police-prosecutor relations. When treatment and rehabilitation or the idea of restorative justice is approached, it is a much harder sell for adoption by police.

As the influence of prosecutors reaches deeper and deeper into the criminal justice process, the opportunities for leadership and policymaking roles expand. At that stage the prosecutor can be proactive and innovative, pushing discretion to its limits. Sometimes this proactive form of prosecution extends the power of prosecution by using existing programs and procedures in new ways, in others, by packaging them into new forms. The basic aim of proactive prosecutors is to direct all the power and influence of the office to bring about changes in the criminal justice system, and to solve immediate problems and prevent future ones from arising.

The best examples of proactive relationships in the police-prosecutor interface can be seen in asset forfeiture, Weed and Seed programs, and community prosecution. Asset forfeiture is a strategy for disrupting drug trafficking. It provides a good example of how existing law and processes in the civil system can be redirected to focus on drug trafficking and related problems. The Weed and Seed program is an early example of prosecutors adding socioeconomic problems in the community to the police-prosecutor interface. But the most innovative steps were taken when a few prosecutors exploded the power of community policing by instituting generic versions of community prosecution.

Asset forfeiture is a powerful weapon in the fight against drugs. It is based on a clear set of objectives: to disrupt drug trafficking, take the profit out of crime, and pour the money or assets from these illegal activities back into the war against drugs.

What differentiates asset forfeiture programs from joint police-prosecutor programs or multijurisdictional task forces is that it is a strategy that uses other statutes in addition to criminal statutes to strengthen law enforcement goals. Joint programs and task forces did not substantially change traditional ways of policing or prosecution. Prosecutors and police were allowed to combine resources and thus strengthen programs and better achieve shared goals. However, they did not move much beyond the criminal justice system, and they were not innovative in the sense that new strategies were developed for either policing or prosecution.

Asset forfeiture is a strategy that says, let's take the illegal proceeds from drug dealing and racketeering and use those funds to fight crime or in some cases for other community programs outside of criminal justice. The ingredients needed to implement the strategy were supportive federal and state forfeiture statutes, coordinated police and prosecutor activities, the use of civil courts in addition to criminal courts, a means for collecting and distributing the proceeds, the protection of third-party rights, and community acceptance. It was these last two factors, in addition to the complexity of the program and the resources needed to operate it, that ultimately limited the usefulness and effectiveness of this strategy.

Forfeiture statutes vary widely by state. The underlying common statute is federal law that permits criminal and civil proceedings to seize the assets of illegal activities and forfeit them. This law also specifies a formula for the distribution of the proceeds. A percentage of the proceeds is retained by the Department of Justice; the remaining amount is then divided among the participating law enforcement agencies according to the level of participation. Local prosecutors' offices are not specifically included in these federal distributions, although some states have included them as part of state-seized proceeds.

There is wide variation among states in how cases are proceeded against, civilly, criminally, or in combination, and how the proceeds are distributed. Some states allocate all proceeds to libraries and schools. Other states allocate the proceeds to general funds, while others distribute most of the proceeds to state and local law enforcement agencies. Few states include the prosecutor in the distribution formula. Law enforcement agencies had the option to use federal forfeitures if the amounts were large enough to engender federal interest. But on the whole, there was little interest in this strategy.

In 1989 the Bureau of Justice Assistance (BJA) funded four demonstration projects under the auspices of the Police Executive Research Forum (PERF) to test the importance of this strategy in the war against drugs. The evaluation conducted by the Jefferson Institute confirmed both the complexity and importance of this strategy. Among its findings was that "the most effective organizations, as judged by net forfeitures, are those with access to a variety of resources and the widest jurisdictional responsibility, i.e. state agencies, law enforcement, and Attorney's General offices and multijurisdictional task forces."[14]

Because asset forfeiture usually follows civil proceedings, it introduced new civil proceedings to local law enforcement and prosecution. Some jurisdictions used police legal counsel as forfeiture attorneys. This practice raised questions among prosecutors about maintaining the checks and balances needed between law enforcement seizures and the adjudication process. Since most forfeiture dispositions are negotiated, the critical issue rested on the independence of the attorney negotiator. Police legal counsel were not good candidates because their department could benefit from forfeitures. The prosecutor was deemed a more independent source.

For this and other reasons, the prosecutor became either the coordinator and leader of task force activities or the sole director. Self-sustained units in a prosecutor's office did not generally fare well in terms of net forfeitures when compared to coordinated activities conducted by task forces. This is most likely because asset forfeiture involves complex operations. Effective programs need to have comprehensive and coordinated plans that include criteria for seizures and dispositions, asset maintenance and protection, guidelines for negotiated adjudications, disposition of the assets, and distribution of the proceeds.

In one sense the prosecutor was doing nothing different than required by his or her involvement in joint programs or other task forces; but in another sense the role assumed by the prosecutor expanded into police investigations of more complex financial and intelligence matters and involved civil courts.

The problem with asset forfeiture programs centered on the protection of third-party rights, which produced media and ultimately public opposition. Sensationalized cases of victim abuses were highly publicized. In one, a woman lost her apartment in a public housing complex because her adult son would not stop selling drugs from her apartment. In another, cash was seized from the automobile of a man who was stopped for a traffic violation. He claimed it was money for the purchase of a house. In another, an automobile was seized because a family relative borrowed the car and was arrested on drug charges. The owner of the car lost his means of transportation to work. The cumulative effect of these media exposés was to make public opinion about the use of asset forfeiture programs very controversial and overwhelmingly negative.

The complexities of operating asset forfeiture programs at the local level were many. Finding the needed talent such as skilled financial investigators; dedicated police staff for wiretaps, surveillance, and intelligence; property managers for seized assets; and attorneys experienced in prosecuting in criminal and civil courts was difficult and occasionally impossible, coupled with drains on existing resources. It is small wonder that asset forfeiture is limited today to mostly urban areas that have multijurisdictional task forces. However, its impact on the police-prosecutor interface was not lost. It decreased resistance to using other legislative, statutory, or regulatory tools to support criminal justice activities and promoted cross agency cooperation and coordination.

Weed and Seed programs were the forerunner of community prosecution since social services were added to the police-prosecutor interface and demonstrated the capability to mitigate some criminal justice issues that were rarely addressed effectively. Moreover, other influences and voices whose positions also had to be considered and sometimes accepted by police and prosecutor were added to the conversation.

Weed and Seed was a strategy targeting high-crime neighborhoods to "weed" out violent offenders, gangs, and drug traffickers through intensive law enforcement and prosecution efforts, and "seed" the neighborhood with prevention, intervention, treatment, and revitalization services. There are many forms of the Weed and Seed programs, but each was coordinated by the U.S. attorney in the district and involved law enforcement agencies, the local prosecutor, city and county officials, business leaders, service agencies, and other community representatives.

Starting in 1994, this coordinated strategy reinforced the interaction among police, social service agencies, the schools, community programs, and the prosecutor. From the police-prosecutor perspective, the reaction was mixed. Many prosecutors and police officials were opposed to becoming "social workers." They saw it as an unwanted and unnecessary change in roles. But funding was poured into these programs and public acceptance was favorable.

Police agencies tended to keep Weed and Seed activities separate from traditional policing by creating separate organizational units. Local prosecutors were given leadership roles in the program since all Weed and Seed programs were headed at least nominally by the U.S. attorney for the district. Often the operational leadership was delegated to the local prosecutor.

Weed and Seed continues today as part of the Bureau of Justice Assistance in the Department of Justice. Its appropriated funds have institutionalized the program and its basic aim has not changed. But its popularity in media attention waned as federal funds increased for community policing. Community policing had more immediate and visible results in terms of reduced crime, lower community fear, and increased public satisfaction. Weed and Seed's legacy for the police-prosecutor interface is that it opened the door for both agencies to see that crime was more than just a criminal justice issue and that social services could contribute in its reduction, prevention, and future avoidance.

Community prosecution is a neighborhood-based strategy designed to respond to special problems confronting neighborhoods or small geographic areas. It uses the power and authority of the prosecutor to help marshal resources from various agencies and community organizations in a coordinated attack on crime and crime-inducing problems. It is a strategy that recognizes that the "problems of AIDS, homelessness, declining inner cities, drug abuse and domestic violence to name a few, cannot be assigned to a single organization or institution that can act alone to achieve solutions."[15]

Community prosecution is based on four assumptions: (1) no single agency or organization can solve the complex, crime-inducing problems in our society; (2) the prosecutor accepts crime prevention and crime avoidance as legitimate prosecutorial goals and incorporates them into traditional operations and activities; (3) complex public safety issues are more effectively addressed in small geographic areas; and (4) the district attorney, as a locally elected official, is uniquely situated to spark initiatives, establish relationships, cement partnerships, and work as a member of the coalition for the common good.[16] Community prosecution takes Weed and Seed a step further by including any community concern in its scope and making the prosecutor an activist. To date, it is where the prosecutor is most proactive.

The purpose of community prosecution is to address problems in small geographic areas that have a negative effect on the quality of life in that area and ones adjacent. The crimes are not usually serious felonies but rather minor annoyances and irritations, the violations and offenses that degrade daily life. The prosecutor uses his or her political stature and legal expertise to tap into the vast resources of government agencies, use current rules and regulations, and most importantly, enlist local community service groups to resolve and fix these problems.

The progenitor of community prosecution was Michael Schrunk, district attorney of Multnomah County (Portland), Oregon. Portland's comprehensive community policing effort under the direction of then chief of police Charles Moose showed Schrunk how prosecutors could increase the effectiveness of community policing. This was accomplished by actively engaging in crime prevention techniques, by marshaling the statutes and regulations of local government to control problems, and by using the office of the prosecutor to influence other agencies and groups to join forces to reduce or prevent crime.

Schrunk's strategy was titled the Neighborhood DA program. A deputy district attorney (DDA) was assigned to a shopping center that was reeling from the effects of a nearby gulch where the homeless had jerry-rigged a wide variety of shelters. The first neighborhood DDA was paid for by business interests and was charged with identifying the major public safety issues and the key individuals, groups, and organizations needed to solve the problems associated with the situation. Among the problems were bathing in the adjacent motel's swimming pool, urinating in public, stealing from automobiles, shoplifting, and vagrancy, among others.

The Neighborhood DA program's success led the county council to fund additional assistant district attorney (ADA) positions that turned to other neighborhood problems, reflecting the different purposes to which public space is put. One ADA focused on the drug problem in a small area of the city where open dealing on the streets had led to unsafe conditions. Another was assigned to the downtown central business district to resolve problems arising from aggressive panhandling of patrons at sidewalk cafes or restaurants. Still another was assigned to a residential neighborhood that had lost its park and playground to gangs and drugs.

Much like with Weed and Seed, the police-prosecutor interface was expanded to accommodate other groups, and the prosecutor assumed the role of a facilitator rather than a prosecutor exercising inherent power. Schrunk facilitates while power is exercised by those to whom it rightfully belongs.[17] There is little conflict in this strategy because the goals of community policing and community prosecution are in sync.

The Middlesex County (Cambridge), Massachusetts, district attorney, Tom Reilly, extended the prosecutor's influence to crime prevention activities directed at the schools and juvenile offenders. In 1990 he was elected to an office reeling from staff cutbacks and increasing violent gang activity in the city of Lowell so intense that it threatened to destroy the schools as fearful parents kept their children home.

Reilly created and was the leader of the Community-based Justice (CBJ) task forces.[18] Composed of police, local school officials, municipal officials, social service professionals, and juvenile and youth case workers, the task force was to identify potential kids at risk, monitor the behavior of those in trouble, and decide the next step if they violated conditions of behavior. These decisions were consensual, based on input from all the CBJ participants.

The CBJ task force held weekly closed meetings throughout the year where specific youths whose behavior posed a threat to schools, neighborhoods, and communities were discussed. A priority prosecution list was drawn up and young offenders earned a place on the list by their own violent conduct. The members of the CBJ worked to reach a consensus about what was to be done to the youths. Decisions were made and the actions promised were recorded.

Police department reaction to the CBJ task force's mission was initially skeptical, even though the organizational relationship between the police and prosecutor was based on cooperation and coordination. The first supporters of the CBJ task force were school liaison officers, detectives, and patrol officers. Their successes in monitoring the behavior of violence-prone students ultimately resulted in the project gaining the department's full support. Reilly's role in this endeavor was much like that of the conductor of an orchestra. The prosecutor made sure that the right work was done at the right time and that the overall performance had its desired impact on the outside world.[19]

Sometimes police departments are reluctant to embrace new programs or strategies. Such was the case in Montgomery County, Maryland. State's Attorney Andrew Sonner was instrumental in convincing the county executive, Neil Potter, that community policing would counteract the drug epidemic. During 1991 a new police chief, Clarence Edwards, was appointed with a mandate from the county executive to make community policing a reality in Montgomery County.

At first, the assistant state's attorneys (ASAs) resisted involvement in community policing activities. A prosecutor wants to try cases, although most of the work is in plea negotiation. However, at their annual retreat, the ASAs proposed a "solution that would support community policing, provide more independence for prosecutors, expand career ladders, and move the office into community prosecution."[20]

It was proposed that the 39 trial assistants be divided into six teams of five to seven prosecutors. Five teams were assigned, one to each of the five police department districts; the sixth team reviewed felony cases and made charging decisions.

Because the resources of the two agencies were so disproportionate and the workload varied among police districts in both volume and type of crime, it was difficult to distribute the workload and take into account the experience levels and abilities of the ASAs among the districts. The most serious felonies still had to be assigned to the most experienced attorneys regardless of the police district assignment. Equally important, misdemeanor cases comprising the largest volume of the caseload could not be assigned to the district in which the offense occurred since the court assigned cases randomly to any district court in the county. The result was a reduction in the impact that this form of community prosecution could have on neighborhood concerns.

Unlike the neighborhood approach taken by Multnomah County and the school focus of Middlesex County, which allowed police and prosecutors to focus on the specific crime-related problems of small areas or juveniles at risk, the Montgomery County approach attempted to conduct community prosecution department-wide by organizing its resources (39 attorneys) to match the districts used by the police department. In this jurisdiction this approach was soon abandoned and the concept of neighborhood or small area problem solving was adopted instead.

As District Attorney Charles (Joe) Hynes of Kings County (Brooklyn), New York, said, "People must understand that there is more than just a law enforcement solution to public safety."[21] Hynes began community prosecution in 1991 when the office was reorganized into five geographical zones, each representing the population and crime mix of Kings County. Five felony prosecution teams were given responsibility for approximately 400,000 to 500,000 people in an area of 10 to 15 square miles each. The interaction of zone prosecutors with precinct captains, community leaders, and residents occurs at regularly scheduled meetings and allows the group to better prioritize and respond to neighborhood crime problems. In some zones, the focus is on serious crimes involving drug trafficking and repeat offenders. In other zones, it focuses on the prosecution of all crimes including violations, misdemeanors, and felonies, and the coordination of action plans among law enforcement, prosecution, prevention, treatment, and educational resources.

It is difficult to imagine community prosecution working in a borough of about 2.5 million people, but this decentralized organization and the "smaller" geographic zones introduced more flexibility into the law enforcement bureaucracy by delegating zone authority to police commanders and ADA chiefs. The new police-prosecutor interfaces allowed changes to priorities based on police and public concerns, and improved communication and coordination between the "newly designated" zone leaders.

A highlight of the Kings County community prosecution program was the establishment of a Community Court and Justice Center in the Red Hook section of Brooklyn, home to nearly 8,000 low-income or public housing residents. This court, funded primarily by the Fund for the City of New York, hears small claims and landlord-tenant matters, and provides services to both the victims of family violence and troubled youth. Some of the services include job training, legal education programs, substance abuse programs, and family violence counseling. At the heart of the program is mediation—individual, community, and peer-based. The Red Hook Justice Center recognizes the need for collaborative efforts to address complex problems. Hynes provides staffing for the community court. Public housing police and New York City police are actively involved in maintaining order and reducing crime in the public housing area, and the tenants and activists have a voice in the availability of services and their quality.

Community prosecution activities have expanded thanks to government support. With each new program, the character of the police-prosecutor interface changes and expands to include other participants. In every case, the police have had their powers enhanced by prosecutorial support, but more importantly, they have gained access to recourses other than arrest and prosecution. The prosecutor has emerged as a "facilitating leader," one who holds but does not exercise power. Rather, he or she facilitates its exercise by those to whom it rightfully belongs.[22]

Conclusion

The police-prosecutor interface has changed dramatically over the past 30 years, a very short time period compared to our 200-plus years of existence as a nation. In the beginning of the American experience, the coroner and sheriff were the offices imbued with discretionary power. The prosecutor, if he did exist, was merely a court functionary. It took the Jacksonian democratization of the 1830s to give the prosecutor elective status and discretionary power.

Until the creation of LEAA about 130 years later, the police-prosecutor interface barely existed. With the national interest on crime and the war against drugs, federal money allowed for experimentation and innovation.

Most importantly, it led to the adoption of a systems view of criminal justice and the recognition that the separate components were actually intertwined. The interfaces between the police and prosecutor were tweaked and stimulated to make changes. These changes, at least some of the major ones, have been described in this chapter. They include joint programs, multijurisdictional task forces, community policing, and the use of other regulatory rules to aid law enforcement and the community. The proliferation of task forces allowed prosecutors to enhance police work over many jurisdictions. Police and prosecutors have added the goals of prevention and avoidance to their traditional ones of law enforcement and crime reduction. Finally, the role of criminal justice fits into the larger framework of social justice.

But back to reality! These monumental shifts in the relationships between police and prosecutor have not yet affected the vast majority of law enforcement agencies and prosecutor offices. Absent crisis situations, little change takes place. The status quo almost always survives. The first step needed is to improve managerial relationships based on the shared goals of incapacitation and just desserts found so often in repeat offender–type programs. Sharing goals and objectives provides police with enhanced ability to control crime and maintain public order and the prosecutor with stronger cases more likely to reach an appropriate disposition. Until this relationship is established, especially in the smaller offices, further expansion of police-prosecutor interface activities is unlikely.

A lot of the change in the police-prosecutor interface depends on the availability and direction of federal funds. Increasing the number of law enforcement positions available for community policing by funding Community Oriented Policing Services (COPS) programs may create an imbalance between the work resulting from increased arrests and the prosecutor's ability to handle it. But at the same time, since the crimes are typically misdemeanors, prosecutors may be able to absorb the additional volume without difficulty.

However, funding for drug courts has shifted the emphasis from incapacitation to treatment and rehabilitation. If these goals are not accepted by law enforcement, prosecutors may expect opposition from law enforcement based on charges that they are "soft on crime." But since the drug courts operate under the sanction of the courts and with the active participation of judges, the prosecutor may be insulated from these charges. It will be interesting to watch.

Finally, at some future time, technology may catch up with the needs of the criminal justice system. For the police and prosecutor, the operational benefits of technology may extend to report writing, evidence collection, and drug labs. Its management benefits may also be found in improved communication among offices about pending cases and the location of defendants. At the present time, the level of automation and technology used in the criminal justice system barely supports the communication needs between the police and prosecutor.

CHAPTER THREE

Controlling the Gate to the Courts

From the public's view, once an arrest has been made, the criminal case is loaded into a veritable meat grinder, that is, the judicial system, only to emerge at an unspecified time with a disposition of some kind, unless, of course, the case has media interest. That certainly was the situation for Enron's Kenneth Lay, Martha Stewart, and O. J. Simpson. Yet compared to the total number of cases disposed of daily in the courts throughout the United States, these celebrity cases are relatively rare. These cases do not represent the vast majority of crimes and accused persons that are processed by the courts, most of which will receive dispositions that do not involve an active sentence, that is, incarceration. What happens after arrest is all but invisible to those in the general public. Even TV's *Law and Order* barely focuses on the day-to-day charging and disposition procedures of the prosecutor.

Once a defendant has been arrested by the police and an arrest report is forwarded to the prosecutor's office, the prosecutor takes charge. The first task is to evaluate the reports forwarded by the police department. If there is insufficient information for a charging decision, a request for additional information is typically issued. Otherwise the reviewing attorney has limited choices: (1) accept the case for prosecution and file the charges supported by the report; (2) decline to prosecute the case; or (3) divert the case to applicable programs, for example, drug treatment.

The charging authority is the prosecutor's alone. No one, neither the courts nor the legislature, can force a prosecutor to accept a case, decline to prosecute a case, or place charges that are not warranted by the facts.[1]

The prosecutor's charging decisions are the most important ones made in the criminal justice system since those decisions cannot be reversed by others. Of course, the prosecutor can change those decisions if new information about the case surfaces. As a result, the prosecutor's decisions made at charging affect the courts, defense counsel, jails, prisons, alternative programs, and most certainly the defendant.

Consider a simple case of larceny where the shop owner caught a young woman stealing a bracelet. She had no prior record, was employed part-time, and was terrified after the police were called and she was arrested.

Prosecutor A was in the midst of a public awareness campaign about shoplifting during the holiday season. His posters around the county proclaimed, "Shoplift and see the jail." The young woman was charged and prosecuted with the office calling for incarceration rather than probation. The defendant received three days in the county jail given that it was her first offense.

Prosecutor B, on the other hand, was not engaged in a similar community awareness campaign about shoplifting. This was just another misdemeanor case. The fact that the defendant was young and had no prior record caused Prosecutor B to be wary of creating a criminal record, much less pursuing incarceration. Instead, the defendant was placed in a diversion program coupled with making restitution to the shop owner and doing 100 hours of community service. If these activities were completed successfully, the charges would be dismissed. If she failed to complete the program or offended again, the charges would be formally filed.

Same crime, same defendant, but different decisions and different outcomes! Prosecutor A gave priority to this minor offense since the office's current priorities reflected the community's values. The judicial system was used to obtain the maximum punishment available. Prosecutor B gave priority to the characteristics of the defendant and used diversion to avoid creating a criminal record for a first-time offender. The same factors were considered, those concerning the offense and the offender, but the weight assigned to each factor radically changed the outcome of the case and the penalty.

Many critics would argue that the system is unjust and arbitrary because similar crimes committed by similar defendants result in different charging decisions and different dispositions. In the quest for uniformity these same critics overlook the fact that differences in decisions to accept, reject, and divert abound for a number of reasons. The quality of police work is very important. Poor investigations lead to cases being declined. Inexperience on the part of the assistant making the charging decision may produce inappropriate charges. Even under the best circumstances and correct decision making, the results will differ because of different priorities between prosecutors and the communities they serve. However, the most common criticism leveled is that prosecutors are simply arbitrary and capricious in deciding which cases to accept and which to decline.

Yet research has demonstrated just the opposite. A major study of prosecutorial decision making showed that prosecutors are far more rational and objective than the critics believe. In fact, computer models can accurately predict what prosecutors will do based on just a few factors.[2]

The charging decisions made at intake are the most powerful in the criminal justice system. The prosecutor serves as a form of checks and balance against insufficient police investigation and reporting. The prosecutors control the gate to the court system and thus have the opportunity to implement prosecutorial policies and set priorities for prosecution.

By controlling the gate to the court, the prosecutor's discretionary power has broad impact. It defines the workload of the court, alters defense counsel's caseload, substantially affects the type of cases probation officers handle, and even partially determines the populations of detention facilities.

There are still chief prosecutors who ignore the importance of this discretionary power at intake in exchange for the excitement of trials and convictions. The most experienced trial assistants are in the courtroom while less experienced assistants are reviewing cases at intake. If those experienced trial assistants were assigned to intake, better decisions would be made by reducing the overall caseload while at the same time ensuring stronger cases and better dispositions. Accepting weak cases that will only be dismissed later in the adjudication process does a disservice to the defendant and wastes the prosecutor's and taxpayers' resources.

To Charge or Not to Charge

Most cases referred by the police for prosecution are accepted by the prosecutor. Estimates of declination rates vary from as low as 2 percent to more than 50 percent, with a median of about 15 percent.[3] The wide range is the result of prosecutorial charging policy coupled with the quality of police work.

These estimates apply primarily to felony cases and serious misdemeanors since the potential sanctions include loss of freedom. Few prosecutors screen less serious misdemeanors, traffic, or moving violations before the first court hearing. These cases are typically prosecuted on the original arrest charge in the lower courts.

Whether a case is accepted or declined depends primarily on two main factors. The quality of law enforcement's investigations and reports is foremost. Every prosecutor's office receives cases from multiple law enforcement agencies including the sheriff, police departments in the jurisdiction, and even from other agencies like Fish and Wildlife officers. Some of these departments are well trained and have sufficient officers and detectives to assemble good reports before submission to the prosecutor for screening. This situation is optimal and the ultimate goal of every prosecutor.

The second factor is based on the prosecutor's evaluation of the evidentiary strength of the case. If prosecutors find that evidence has been tainted or constitutional issues exist—for example, improper search and seizure procedures—the case is weakened. If witnesses are not identified or will be uncooperative, the case is weakened further. There are three choices: reject the case outright by declining to prosecute; ask the police for additional information; or use the prosecutor's investigative staff, if they have any, to gather missing information or additional evidence.

Obviously, it is in the police department's best interest to have the arrest cases prosecuted, but it is the responsibility of the prosecutor to make sure that prosecutions are valid and supported by the evidence. Since these decisions are usually made by individual attorneys,[4] the arresting officer may seek assistants who share the same priorities with respect to the seriousness of the offense or offender. Some may even attempt to influence new or inexperienced charging assistants.

This practice is called "assistant shopping" and produces inconsistent charging decisions and inappropriate outcomes. For example, an arrest was made in a case involving simple possession of marijuana. The evidence for possession was very weak since the drug was not found on the offender's person, but in the car, which contained two other passengers. Knowing the arrest was weak, the arresting officer sought an assistant in the office known to have zero tolerance for drugs. The assistant charged the case. A more experienced assistant might not have.

In some instances, police will try to influence an inexperienced assistant by suggesting that a declination of the case based on weak evidence would send a message to the street that the prosecutor was soft on drugs or alternatively, that a rejection would harm a larger investigation that was about to pay off. Some senior detectives suggest that prosecutors always win in cases like this one because judges and juries take a hard line against these offenses or offenders.

The simplest remedy for assistant shopping or intimidation is to use only experienced assistants to make charging decisions. Unfortunately, not all prosecutors see this advantage. The preference is to assign experienced assistants to the courtroom, not to intake. Since experienced assistants would rather try than screen cases, both the prosecutor and the experienced assistants are happy. There are several alternatives to correct this conundrum. First, schedule experienced attorneys to rotate through trial and intake. Second, have an office procedure that states "you charge it, you try it," which basically says that if an assistant files a bad case, that assistant will have to try the case if it goes to trial. Finally, the intake desk is a good rehabilitation assignment for assistants who are physically and mentally spent after a bruising trial. In any event, assistant shopping must be controlled and the prosecutor must be a manager as well as an attorney.

Resources and Costs Limit Prosecuting Every Case

Budgets and people add another dimension to accepting cases. In most jurisdictions, the criminal justice system simply does not have sufficient resources in the form of prosecutors, indigent defense counsel, judges, or even space to prosecute every case.

Underfunded agencies create backlogs in the courts and serious public safety problems. In the 1980s, with the rising drug epidemic, jails became so overcrowded that cities like Philadelphia had to release offenders convicted of less serious crimes before their sentences were completed so the jails could accommodate the growing number of pretrial detainees. The detainees, in turn, spent longer and longer time waiting for trial, further reducing the number of jail beds available for sentenced prisoners.

If the courts are heavily backlogged and the prosecutor's office is understaffed, prosecutors have to decide if there are certain types of cases that should not be prosecuted, or should be transferred or diverted to other alternative programs.

To reduce caseloads, some prosecutors simply will not prosecute certain lesser offenses like bad check cases or citizen disputes. Others tighten the requirements for prosecution. For example, simple assaults or shoplifting involving thefts of less than $10 may be declined. If crimes can be handled either in city courts or county courts, prosecutors may send them down to the lower court.

The most creative strategies to alleviate overcrowded courts and insufficient money focus on using remedies other than criminal prosecution, which may be just as effective. These remedies may include using civil and regulatory legislation to enforce laws, abatements, citations for code enforcement, or licensing violations, especially if fines result. Alternative programs such as mediation, dispute resolution centers, and citizen complaint bureaus can also reduce the number of cases accepted for prosecution.

Budgets are always a consideration. Some prosecutions may be too costly either in terms of investigative time or budget. Complex cases such as white-collar crimes or death penalty cases may have to be transferred to the state's attorney general for prosecution because they require investigative efforts far beyond the local prosecutor's resources. In unusual circumstances, prosecutors may "borrow" staff from another prosecutor's office to temporarily work a very complex case.

There are times when cases incur costs that cannot be met, or simply are not worth the expenditure. This is an issue when cases require the extradition of defendants or travel for out-of-state witnesses. Just recently, the Boulder, Colorado, district attorney admitted that the thousands of dollars expended on extraditing John Mark Karr, a suspect in the JonBenet murder case, from Thailand to Boulder substantially cut into her budget. The hard reality is that prosecution requires resources, and some cases may have to be rejected, even if reluctantly.

Diversion programs have gained wide acceptance not only because such programs give added flexibility to sanctioning but also because they share a common ingredient. Persons responsible for offenses can be held accountable without imposing criminal sanctions.

Diversion can be court-ordered or operated under the prosecutor's control. The hammer held by the prosecutor over diversion is the ability to bring the case forward for prosecution if the offender does not meet the conditions of the diversion program. Typically, offenders are given a specified number of hours for community service programs and a dollar amount of restitution to be paid to the victim.

Diversion takes many forms. In its simplest application the prosecutor tells the offender and the offender's counsel that the case will be held in a "stet file," sometimes the bottom drawer of a filing cabinet, and will be dismissed if the defendant stays out of trouble for a specified length of time—for example, two years. Drug courts are a more complex form of diversion.[5] These courts operate under the supervision of the sentencing judge with the support of a drug treatment and rehabilitation program and with prosecution oversight. Community service and restitution are popular alternatives to prosecution since offenders are held accountable but without being incarcerated.

Some diversion programs in medium to large offices may be operated before any court action. In Polk County, Florida, the former state's attorney, Jerry Hill, operated a mediation program manned by volunteers with oversight provided by an assistant state's attorney (ASA). If a defendant is eligible for mediation, he or she does not experience the prosecution process until after the dispute has been successfully mediated, at which time the court dismisses the case.

Mediation is very popular for cases involving citizen complaints about neighbors trespassing or having animals on the loose; consumer fraud, for example, dry cleaning damage; environmental pollution; bad checks; and property damage or other loss.

Treatment and rehabilitation programs are increasingly being used to help offenders with problems like anger management, poor parenting skills, drunk driving, domestic violence, or other personal problems. Most of these programs are community-based and are operated by groups in the community since specialized skills may be required or the prosecutor's caseload may be large.

In 1972, when LEAA funded the National Center for Prosecution Management to publish the first handbook for prosecutors on the value, benefits, and use of diversion programs, the National District Attorneys Association shelved it because it was too controversial for prosecutors.

Charging Policies and Their Impact on Prosecution

Although dismissals and diversion can account for up to 30 percent of dispositions in the court,[6] the majority of cases are accepted for prosecution. The charges filed are based on office policies that define criteria for accepting cases and the prosecutor's assessment of the priority for prosecution.

Charging policies reflect the variety of prosecutors' views on the role of prosecution in ensuring justice and equity in the criminal justice system. Some prosecutors take a laissez-faire view of charging responsibility: "I trust my assistants to make the right decisions. They know what I would do." This may be true for solo practitioners or those running very small offices, but in medium to large offices it can create excessive variation in charging otherwise similar cases. It permits any attorney to make charging decisions according to a personal interpretation of what the chief prosecutor would do, or what the assistant would do if occupying that position.

Beyond this short-sighted view of charging policy are more sophisticated approaches that have substantial impact on the types of cases allowed into the court system, the methods used to bring cases to final disposition, and achievement of appropriate sanctions. For simplicity's sake, these charging policies have been classified as legal sufficiency, system efficiency, and trial sufficiency (see Figure 3.1). The names not only differentiate charging policies but also give insight into the routes best suited to reach a disposition.

The least restrictive charging policy is legal sufficiency. Here the criterion for accepting a case for prosecution is whether it is legally sufficient—that is, have the elements of the crime been satisfied? Has the crime been committed within the prosecutor's jurisdiction? Is the defendant a person the prosecutor can legally prosecute (some prosecutors do not have

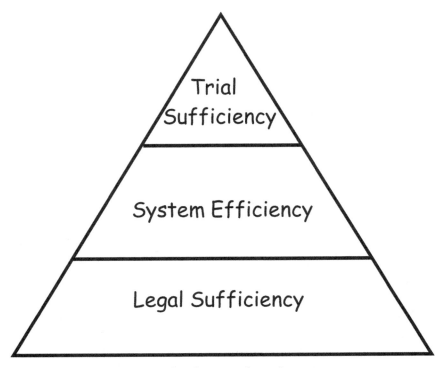

Figure 3.1   The Charging Pyramid: Mix and Match.

jurisdiction over juveniles)? Are the elements of the crime present? These may involve issues like proof of the ownership of stolen property or lack of permission to use property. The elements of an offense are defined by statute. If the case is deemed legally sufficient, then it is accepted for prosecution.

This charging policy is narrowly focused. It overlooks some of the most important aspects of case review and results in the loss of many cases in the courts because important evidentiary problems were not considered. It opens the door for cases that may have serious constitutional defects such as bad searches, improper lineups, or problems with Miranda warnings. It does not consider witness testimony or credibility or breaks in the chain of custody of evidence. It does not consider the defendant's criminal history. It merely accepts cases if the elements of the crime are present; that is, it is legally sufficient.

Because only the elements enter into consideration, the charging policy doesn't require an experienced trial attorney at intake and screening. In fact, in some offices third-year law students or even nonattorney staff perform this task, hopefully with an assistant prosecutor reviewing and approving the draft recommendations. The results of this approach are seen later in high dismissal rates as judges correct mistakes that could and should have been caught at intake. High rates of pleas to lesser offenses are usual as weak cases are negotiated down and out.

Charging decisions made under the policy of system efficiency raise the acceptance bar by requiring that cases be strong enough to survive probable cause hearings, sometimes called preliminary hearings, and consider the overall condition of the system including backlogs and time to disposition. If these criteria are not met, the case will either be declined or dismissed if the charges are already in the court. This policy recognizes that in addition to screening, speedy dispositions will make the system more efficient. In other words, the prosecutor understands that reducing time to disposition will free the staff to handle other cases.

Since cases are expected to survive probable cause hearings, the experience level of the screener is increased. Now assistants have to be able to predict the probability of cases surviving preliminary hearing and place charges that would be negotiable with the defense and the defendant. The aim is to dispose of these cases quickly. The best speedy disposition is a plea of guilty to the original charges at arraignment.

In Winnebago County (Rockford), Illinois, State's Attorney Paul Logli created an intake unit that was manned by two seasoned assistants. The assistants reviewed the cases, made charging decisions, and referred those that were most likely to plead guilty to one or more of the charges sent to the plea negotiation unit. The remaining cases were assigned to trial assistants. After testing the idea, Logli eventually merged the plea negotiation unit into the screening unit to further increase its efficiency. The rule is to dispose of the case in the least amount of time with minimal use of prosecutor resources and achieve an outcome that is both reasonable and appropriate.

Trial sufficiency is the most restrictive of the charging policies and the most difficult to implement. Here cases are accepted if there is sufficient evidence to sustain them at trial, and they are charged at a level that can be proven at trial. Plea negotiation is not allowed prior to trial because it contradicts the trial sufficiency standard—namely, that the case can be sustained at trial on the original charge. A plea to the original charge(s) is acceptable until the first day of trial. Every case entering the office is evaluated according to these standards. If the charges placed cannot be sustained at trial, then they are either rejected or held pending further information requested from the investigating agencies.

If the case is strong, there is no real reason to go to trial. Defense counsel understands this as well. Trials are expensive in resource terms and are time consuming. Only those that are 50–50 should be in trial. If it's a lock, get the plea to the original and negotiate the sentence. Even strong cases can be lost at trial. A trial is essentially a "crap shoot." Unexpected things occur. Putting "twelve in a box" introduces significant uncertainty.

The high standard set by this charging policy makes intake and screening the most important function in the office and the screening assistants its most critical attorneys. In essence, with the exception of a plea to the original, pleas to a lesser offense are off the table and dismissals are relevant if the case falls apart on the way to trial. These cases are scheduled for litigation to achieve a reasonable and appropriate sentence. The attorneys will be judged by the dispositions of these cases. Case review at intake examines every element of the case to assess its strengths and identify weaknesses that can be overcome.

Obviously, the persons making these judgments must have trial experience, especially since this charging policy discourages making changes in charges later on. In addition, the policy considers dismissal a disposition that should be rare and the result of a major change in the evidence or poor work by the intake assistants. The high standards set by this policy also produce much higher rejection rates than those of the other standards discussed. This result can potentially pose problems with police-prosecutor relations.

This is a difficult charging policy to implement office-wide unless the prosecutor has carefully thought through its management and operational implications. Perhaps the most successful prosecutor to do this was Harry Connick, the former district attorney of Orleans Parish, Louisiana (and more notably, entertainer Harry Connick Jr.'s father).

Connick took office in 1972 and vowed to change it from a poorly rated prosecution office that relied on correcting poor charging decisions through negotiated pleas to an office accepting cases only if they were sustainable at trial. Plea bargaining was banned and his most experienced trial assistants were installed in the intake unit. In addition, any dismissal or change of charge had to be authorized by one of the three top assistants in the office.

In the first year, the office rejected 50 percent of police cases at intake. Gradually this rate decreased as the law enforcement agencies became educated about the new standards and reporting requirements. Police relationships were mollified when Connick established career criminal and repeat offender units in the office to give priority to these cases. For the next 30 years of his tenure, Connick did not deviate from this policy. The prosecutor's office became a model for tight management controls over the assistants' decisions and for the criterion for acceptance of cases for prosecution that was as restrictive as it could be.

For most offices, this policy is too demanding to be applied to every case. However, its standards fit well with the concept of selective prosecution, which gives special attention to top-priority crimes or offenders and allows the rest of the cases to be handled under different policies.

These three policies are employed in felonies and occasionally in misdemeanor filings. For felonies, the most policy-intensive area, a charging pyramid can be constructed to indicate the proportion and type of cases that fit the various charging policies. Most offices today use some combination of charging policies for intake decisions.

Legal sufficiency is the least restrictive policy at intake. On average, 85 percent of cases will be accepted at intake, the bottom of the pyramid. Additional cases will be declined with a system efficiency policy, the middle of the pyramid. The cases that have a low probability of passing a probable cause hearing and the 10–15 percent that could pass the probable cause hearing but are facing a congested court system or a resource-constrained prosecutor will be declined. Finally, only 50 percent of the cases originally presented at intake will survive the trial sufficiency policy, the top of the pyramid. As cases are dropped from consideration, the demands on the prosecutor are reduced and the resources can be better directed to serious crimes and offenders where cases have good evidence.

Misdemeanor cases are high volume within the courts and the prosecutor's office. While there are offices that have misdemeanor policies and even misdemeanor intake, they are relatively few. More likely these consist of a stack of files that typically contain a police report which is handed to a junior assistant. The assistant goes to court, usually reading the report for the first time when the case is called by the clerk. Cases generally follow a simple assembly-line process to disposition. Usually the charges at prosecution are those cited by the police. It would not be unusual for defense counsel and the assistant prosecutor to confer as the docket is read as to a reasonable and appropriate disposition—including dismissals.

Traffic court is even more of an assembly line. Defendants are usually not represented by counsel, the police are the only witnesses, and the outcome is very predictable. In most cities the city attorney plays the role since ordinance violations other than traffic are addressed as well.

These are the prosecutor's charging choices. One standard can be used for all cases; the prosecutor can have one for misdemeanors and another for felonies, and perhaps a third for traffic and ordinance violations. The choice is dependent on the prosecutor's resources, the nature of the legal environment, and to some extent the desires of the community.

Setting Priorities for Prosecution

Not all cases presented for prosecution can or should be accepted. Not all cases accepted have the same priority for prosecution. Some are more important than others and some require more preparation time or resources than others.

Most local jurisdictions have bare-bones budgets including priorities for education, health care, and economic development. The local criminal justice systems, even with state and federal aid, simply do not have enough resources to enforce every violation of the law. Prosecutors not only have to choose which laws to enforce but also how to apply office resources to the cases accepted. Serious crimes, especially those involving violence, are assigned to experienced assistants, while public order crimes like drinking in public or barroom brawls are given to less experienced attorneys. This is one way prosecutors set priorities for prosecution.

The sanctions attached to crimes play a large part in setting priorities. Consider a list of sanctions that begins with fines or restitution and ends with life imprisonment or death. It is clear that the sanctions attached to each offense are important. Most motor vehicle and ordinance violations have low priority because the sanctions available include fines, points, court costs, and perhaps restitution or driver's education.

The list of sanctions for misdemeanors includes fines, court costs, and restitution as before but probation and jail for typically a year or less now top the list. Felonies, on the other hand, add further sanctions since incarceration and in some cases even death are included.

Even though sanctions are attached to the seriousness of individual offenses, usually by statute, other factors influence the priority of cases for prosecution. The evidentiary strength of the case and the nature of the defendant's role in the offense are major factors as well. For example, a defendant who has a long history of criminal activity, threatened the victim with a gun, and is arrested with stolen property would likely receive a prison sentence. A defendant who is young, without a criminal history, and is seen leaving an unoccupied house with stolen property will be treated quite differently.

These three factors set the priority given to cases for prosecution. All three reflect the values of the community and likely those of the elected prosecutor by defining the seriousness of the offense. Some cases involve crimes so heinous or so notorious that there is no question about the priority for prosecution: the O. J. Simpson case; the Manson case in California; Jeffrey Dahmer, the Milwaukee man-eater; the Muhammad-Malvo sniper case in the Washington, D.C., metropolitan area; John Hinckley and the assassination attempt on President Reagan, and the list goes on. When sanctions are severe and/or the crimes so bizarre, Court TV will cover the trial.

Public interest and media attention may influence decisions about accepting such cases, but in the everyday working world of the courts, the bulk of the cases in the criminal justice system rarely receive special attention. The decisions made at intake, whether to accept the case and what charges to place, are based on the nature of the offense, the defendant's record, and the evidentiary strength of the case.[7]

The seriousness of the offense is best defined by the extent of injury inflicted or the value of property lost or damaged. Top priority is assigned to cases involving violent crimes like murder, rape, robbery, and aggravated assault. The seriousness of the injuries or the numbers of persons injured increases this priority. Thus, a defendant arrested for assaulting a jogger will get more prosecutorial attention if the victim is severely injured or dies as opposed to escaping uninjured. A defendant who guns down seven customers in a convenience store will be prosecuted more vigorously than a defendant with a gun who took money from the convenience store after physically assaulting the clerk and leaving him unconscious.

Cases where there is a high potential for injury also will be given priority. Armed robberies, arson, and carrying dangerous weapons are good examples of potentially dangerous situations with a high risk of injury even if none occurred. Such cases usually result in additional charges being introduced or upgrading the principal charge.

The amount of property loss or damage also affects the priority of the case for prosecution. Examples include estimates of losses due to burglary, larceny, motor vehicle theft, fraud, and bad checks. These amounts are usually specified in the law. As the amount of loss or damage and/or the number of victims increases, so does the priority of a case for prosecution.

This is why the prosecution of Kenneth Lay of Enron, who was convicted of fraud and conspiracy, a fraud that impacted thousands of people, was so notorious. Likewise, though with less media attention, the prosecutions of bank managers or stock fund managers who embezzled millions of dollars that rightfully belonged to a large number of people are given more attention than shoplifters who steal an item worth less than $10.

If the seriousness of the offense is trivial, criminal prosecution may be too harsh a response for the offender and a "waste of prosecution time" for the courts. Typical examples include disputes between neighbors over trespassing or damage to property, claims about dishonest business practices, or even passing bad checks. These cases are good candidates for other responses, which call for accountability and reparation but not necessarily criminal prosecution.

Prosecutors also can make rules about which cases will not be prosecuted. For example, drug possession cases will not be prosecuted if less than one ounce of marijuana is involved; cases involving solicitation, gambling, or larceny of less than $50 will not be prosecuted. In addition to having the discretion to state what will not be prosecuted, prosecutors can also suggest other remedies, which may include filing cases in small claims court or using mediation or dispute resolution programs. Some cases at this level of seriousness often settle themselves after a cooling-off period.

Special advocacy groups pose a different problem for prosecutors assessing the seriousness of the offense. A group familiar to most is Mothers Against Drunk Driving (MADD), which demands zero tolerance, priority prosecution, and significant punishment of drunk drivers. There are a myriad of advocacy groups. There are the advocates and opponents for gun control, birth control, environmental pollution, child abuse, and a host of other social problems. As vocal activists with access to the media, they can focus pressure on the prosecutor's decision to accept cases or on what is a reasonable and appropriate disposition.

The prosecutor's problem is balancing the public's interests against those with a narrower focus. A prosecutor in West Virginia was denounced by PETA for not prosecuting the owner of a chicken farm whose conditions were deemed unsafe by PETA. In declining to file charges, the prosecutor said there were other, more pressing crimes to prosecute. This balancing act is not without risk for elected officials.

In addition, the seriousness of the offense has to be balanced against the resources available to the prosecutor. If environmental groups are pressing hard for criminal sanctions against a major polluter of the drinking water in a community, the prosecutor may not have enough staff and investigative resources to handle this complex case. However, because the pollution has the potential for inflicting more damage if left unchecked, other options will be sought. The state's attorney general may take over the case or provide the office with additional resources on a temporary basis. Other state agencies dealing with environmental pollution or public health issues may take jurisdiction. In this case both civil and criminal remedies may be acceptable paths to justice.

The Defendant's History and Actions

Clearly the seriousness of the offense in terms of injury and property loss or damage plays a large role in establishing the priority for prosecution, but charging decisions are also affected by the offender's criminal history.

The defendant's criminal history and activity or involvement in the crime are important considerations in the charging process. A long record of aggressive offenses makes a case more likely to be accepted and charged than one that involves a youthful or first-time offender who only acted as a lookout or driver.

Career criminals, repeat offenders, sexual abusers or predators, and, of course, defendants with histories of violent crimes are given high priority and are not likely to have those cases dropped no matter how insignificant. As one prosecutor put it about career criminals, "I would prosecute them for spitting on the sidewalk." Long criminal records provide prosecutors with an opportunity to argue for pretrial detention and to add enhancements to the charges that increase the sentence.

Another set of cases guaranteed to be accepted for prosecution includes those involving offenders who have violated the public trust or community values. Such crimes may include embezzlement of public or private funds, illegal activities for personal gain or wealth, and sexual molestation of children and youth, to name a few. Because the justice system upholds the norms and values of society, the prosecutor will prosecute those who violate them.

Prosecutors take a more lenient stance when reviewing cases involving first-time offenders or youthful offenders. Placing criminal charges against those persons is frequently a life-altering and damaging event since it makes future employment problematic, reduces insurability, and shuts the door on future opportunities. Thus it is more difficult to evaluate these cases.

Careful consideration is given to declining the case or referring it to some type of diversion, which if completed would leave the offender without a criminal record. If there was no injury and the damage was minimal, the offender had no prior record, and the role played by the defendant was secondary, this might be a good candidate for diversion. But if the offender had a significant criminal history and was a principal in the offense, the prosecutor may decide that enough is enough and accept the case for prosecution. That said, the views of one prosecutor may not be shared by another. It is always the prosecutor's prerogative.

Evidentiary Strength of the Case

The evidentiary strength of the case makes the difference between accepting and declining to charge. Most cases are declined for a lack of evidence. If there is insufficient evidence, some cases may be held until the police can provide additional proof.

If brought forward with weak evidence, cases usually do not survive a defense motion to dismiss. The effect of charging weak cases quite simply is a waste of time and manpower for prosecutors, defense counsel, and the court, not to mention the stress on the defendant.

Evidentiary strength has three dimensions: physical evidence, testimonial evidence, and legal considerations about whether constitutional or statutory protections have been violated. Problems with physical evidence usually arise if the chain of custody is broken. If the movement of physical evidence is improperly documented as it changes hands, then it cannot be conclusively linked to the defendant. Defense claims that O. J.'s bloody glove was planted by the police is one example where the claim could not be rebutted conclusively. Sometimes these weaknesses can be overcome by the presentation of other evidence, sometimes not.

Crime scenes can also be contaminated. This can happen if the scene has not been properly sealed by the police. Investigators may accidentally disturb and even destroy evidence. Trampling the grounds of a crime scene is not good police procedure. Footprints and tire tracks are particularly susceptible to this issue.

Cases can be lost if evidence is missing from the police property storage room after it was collected at the crime scene or is lost in crime labs. If the chain of custody is broken for a sample submitted for DNA testing, the results could be challenged. If this evidence is crucial for a case and it is flawed, prosecutors have few options other than dismissal.

Testimonial evidence from the victim and witnesses are essential to conviction. Here the priority issues focus on the cooperation of the victim and witnesses. The credibility and competence of witnesses will be tested in court, and corroborating testimony is usually necessary. Victims of crime and witnesses to crimes are often fearful of reprisals, especially if the crime is gang-related. Rape victims may fear testifying and simply move away or refuse to cooperate with the prosecutor. Maintaining victim cooperation can be a tough job for prosecutors, but without that testimony the state may find it impossible to convict.

It's true that prosecutors can subpoena witnesses—including victims—to appear in court, but they can't force them to testify. Prosecutors can also prosecute cases even if the victim refuses to press charges. Most often, however, if the victim or witnesses are reluctant, the case will be declined or dismissed. The situations where this occurs are many and varied. In domestic violence cases, the victim often has a change of heart and refuses to testify or does not see the incident as a "crime" but rather as a family matter.

In cases involving citizen complaints, the parties may end up settling the dispute out of court. In other instances, the victim may also be a "guilty party" and, therefore, reluctant to testify. For example, "Johns" caught in a prostitution raid are not likely to be star witnesses for the prosecution.

In one case involving a drunk-driving negligent homicide a witness's testimony was crucial for the prosecution. Unfortunately, the police "forgot" to tell the prosecutor that the eyewitness was a drug addict whose brain had been burned out by speed. In another case, the witness was a cellmate of the defendant while in pretrial detention and was looking for a reduction in sentence for testifying for the prosecution. The witness clearly had a major credibility issue. One prosecutor noted that the perfect witness is a middle-aged nun with 20/20 vision and excellent hearing. Eyewitness testimony is much more inaccurate than often believed.

To ensure credibility, witness testimony needs corroboration. To use an old adage, two sets of eyes are better than one. If the testimony cannot be corroborated by others or by other physical evidence, then the situation falls into a "she says, he says" argument with neither side proving the case except perhaps the defense who can introduce reasonable doubt. Research on prosecutorial decision making indicates that the strength of the case improves significantly if more than one police officer can testify to the facts.

On some occasions, prosecutors have to deal with confidential informants (CIs or snitches) who offer to testify against others in the hope that charges against them will be dropped or at least reduced. If not already incarcerated, CIs usually seek long-term commitments from police and/or prosecutors granting the CI immunity against some offenses or reduced charges in others.

In Illinois, some of the prosecutors that participated in multijurisdictional drug task forces (MJDTF) drew up contracts with CIs specifying duties, the amount of drugs that were to be seized, or a minimum number of busts that had to result from the information given in a specified time period. The contract spelled out what the prosecutor would do if the conditions were met, and what would happen if they were not met. The CI, the prosecutor, and the law enforcement agency signed the contract.

Constitutional issues must be considered in weighing the evidentiary strength of a case. It may be impossible to survive problems created if Miranda warnings were not given. Improper searches made, inappropriate lineups held, and violations of wiretap procedures all can make critical evidence worthless. Sometimes problems arising from these violations of constitutional protections can be overcome by offering a reduced charge in exchange for a guilty plea; other times the problems are insurmountable and the case has to be dismissed.

Standards for evidentiary strength play a large role in defining an office's charging policy. Some offices accept cases that are legally sufficient even if the evidence is marginal. Other offices accept cases only if they have enough evidence to sustain them at trial. Between these two extremes are offices that accept cases that have enough evidence to prove probable cause and usually end in a negotiated plea.

The above discussion has focused on the strength of evidence needed for felony and serious misdemeanor cases. A different scenario applies to lesser misdemeanors, moving violations, and violation of ordinances. Although these cases typically represent the largest proportion of cases prosecuted in a jurisdiction, screening differs from felonies since (except for serious misdemeanors) police reports contain little information about the incident, not enough for a review of the facts.

Visualize a speeding ticket; it identifies you, your vehicle, the date and time you were stopped, and the reason why. You and the police officer sign it. What is there to review except that it is complete? A complaint filed by police for a barroom fight or a bad check or shoplifting also contains minimal information, just enough to establish that an offense occurred and an arrest was made.

Because the information is limited and the offense is less serious, in many offices complaints are reviewed by nonattorney staff for completeness. Some offices also allow nonattorneys to make recommendations about whether to decline or dismiss. These cases are already in the system so usually the action is to dismiss.

Some cases are rejected outright (or dismissed in court) if they have major deficiencies, which can be as minor as missing or illegible vital information. It is amazing to see reports or citations lacking basic information like the location of the offense, date and time, or the nature of the violation. Some complaints cite the wrong statute; others are for offenses or offenders over which the prosecutor lacks jurisdiction.

If adjustments have to be made to the original police charges, they are usually in the form of plea offers. The prosecutor will reduce a speeding ticket for a guilty plea, or dismiss a larceny charge if the defendant makes restitution, or dismiss a destruction of property charge if the defendant makes repairs and reimburses the owner for damages.

In incidents involving disputes, arguments, and fights, it is not unusual for police to make arrests simply to avoid an escalation of the incident. In well-run prosecution offices, the intake desk routinely calls the arresting officer to determine whether to pursue the case further.

There is a lot of discretion exercised in the assembly-line processing of misdemeanors and violations. Since nonattorney staff conducts most of it, it is important that attorneys review and approve their recommendations. In well-run offices this happens; in less than well-run offices, the authority is inappropriately delegated to nonattorneys.

For the vast majority of cases, evidentiary strength is a major factor. Yet, despite the best screening at intake, some cases will be accepted for prosecution and later fall apart. When this happens, it is in the prosecutor's interest to either become more liberal in the plea offers or to dismiss the case.

Other Issues in Setting Priorities for Prosecution

Most people agree that some cases should or should not be prosecuted for reasons that go beyond the law. The offense can be serious, the offenders may have a criminal history, and the evidence may be sufficient to convict, but the circumstances are such that it is not in the "public interest" to prosecute to the full extent of the law. These decisions are based on a consideration of what is in the public interest or in the interests of justice. Just what does this mean? Consider a few examples.

A husband and wife were arrested for fraud. They had a family with young children. If the prosecutor went ahead with the case, the children would be placed in foster homes. This could be avoided if the prosecutor decided not to file charges against the wife in return for a guilty plea by the husband to all the charges.

A renowned case was that of Jonathon Pollard, accused of passing U.S. intelligence secrets to Israel. Pollard was charged, tried, and convicted, but the charges against Pollard's wife were dropped so Pollard's family could remain intact.

Violations of laws that the community opposes may also be declined. Probably the best example of nonenforcement occurred when Prohibition was the law of the land. Violations concerning the sale and consumption of alcohol were winked at and largely ignored until, finally, Prohibition was repealed.

Community values and norms play a large role in the selective enforcement of laws. One community may be horrified and outraged by adultery, pornography, or consensual sex between same-sex adults. It may demand the immediate prosecution of all those involved in these crimes. Yet another community may view these incidents as falling into areas of personal privacy and choice among consenting adults. This community would be irate if police and prosecutors arrested and charged these activities as crimes even though the laws exist.

An off-duty police officer was caught in a drug bust. In a sting operation conducted against prostitution the undercover officer was caught having sex with the girl he was setting up. In this example, the issue is official misconduct for which there are internal law enforcement agency remedies.

Public prosecution would achieve no additional purpose in punishing the officer, but it could erode respect for the agency.

Although the "public interest" is an amorphous term, it is important because it allows the prosecutor to decline cases when prosecution would only cause more serious harm or damage to other public interests than the punishment of an individual.

Public interest may also justify a higher priority for prosecution than otherwise might prevail. Practically guaranteed to be accepted for prosecution are cases involving offenders who have violated the public trust or community values. These offenses may include corporate crimes, insider information trading, embezzlement of public or private funds, fraud and scams for personal gain or wealth, and sexual molestation of children and youth, to name a few. In upholding society's values, both the justice system and the prosecutor let the public interest be a factor in setting priorities for some prosecutions.

The Link between Charges and Sentences

Three strikes and you're out! This familiar baseball saying has been translated by 25 states to refer to felonies. Three felonies and you're in prison for a very long time, sometimes for life without parole. While the definitions of "three," "strikes," and "out" vary among the states, all the statutes share a similar aim: to incapacitate an offender for a long time so the offender cannot continue this proven felony activity. In addition to the three strikes laws, some 34 states have habitual offender laws that may result in imprisonment for life after a specified number of convictions. Adding habitual offender charges to a crime will severely increase the sanctions that the court can impose in addition to the sentence attached to the underlying offenses.

Criminal statutes generally include the sanctions that can be imposed upon conviction, or the maximum allowable sanction like a fine of $10,000 or 24 months in prison, or both. Sentencing guidelines also describe the range of sanctions that can be imposed based on the record of the offender and the seriousness of the offense.[8]

If the statutes linked a sentence to every crime, then charging would be a relatively straightforward process. But legislatures have also passed laws that allow some crimes to be enhanced, thereby complicating the charging decision. Each state defines the offenses it believes should count as a strike. Most common are violent crimes like murder, rape, robbery, and aggravated crimes like assaults, burglaries, and child abuse. There is great variation among the states and, of course, great controversy about the use of three strikes laws. However, there are situations where three felony theft convictions trigger a habitual offender statute or three strikes law.

Since 1980, the U.S. Supreme Court has upheld the right of the states to legislate three strikes laws, essentially ruling that the enhancements are not disproportionate to the offenses. These laws have been a major weapon in incarcerating repeat offenders or career criminals for offenses that rarely produced active sentences. For example, the most likely sanction for burglary is usually probation. But certifying the defendant as a habitual offender increases the probability of his receiving a sentence with active time. If the goal is to seek incapacitation, adding enhancements to the charges certainly helps.

Adding capital murder charges to a homicide is the most severe enhancement possible because it calls for the death penalty. The leveling of this charge also starts a complex and costly undertaking that eats up court time, staff resources, and budget. It also automatically puts into play a string of appeals after conviction with the imposition of the death penalty. Accordingly, decisions to place these charges are made only after lengthy review and discussion in the prosecutor's office.

Mandatory minimums mandate minimum sentences for the conviction of certain crimes. Common offenses subject to mandatory minimums include the possession of a gun during the commission of a crime, usually a felony, and selling or distributing drugs within a specified number of feet from a school or the possession of drugs over a specified limit, for example 500 grams of cocaine. Some statutes also include the number of prior convictions.

One would think that prosecutors would favor mandatory minimums because those minimums mandate incarceration for crimes that prior to the minimums could have received lesser sentences. This is not necessarily the case. Mandatory minimums generally do not receive favorable reviews because the prosecutor's discretionary power to tailor sanctions to fit individual cases is constrained. In the long run, the ability of the prosecutor to negotiate dispositions that are more reasonable and appropriate than those mandated by the law is more limited.

Enhancements increase the discretionary power of prosecutors by allowing prosecutors to increase or decrease the severity of sentences by modifying the original charges. Mandatory minimums and three strikes legislation, however, reduce the prosecutor's discretionary power by taking flexibility out of the charging process.

By 1999, 25 states were studying or using some form of sentencing guidelines that specified a range of sentences for various offenses, typically felonies, and often abolished parole. Sentencing guidelines are essentially a grid, with one column classifying offenses into categories like drugs, property crimes, robbery, assault, and so on and the rows classifying the criminal history of the offender according to his or her criminal record—for example, no prior record, prior record but no active sentences, prior record with active sentences. Inside each cell in the grid is a range of sentences from which the judge can select.

The sentencing judge has the discretion to go outside the range based on mitigating or aggravating factors. But in doing so, a written record of the reasons must be provided. No one single matrix exists because the states have developed and implemented guidelines consistent with that state's statutes.

Sentencing guidelines had a powerful effect on charging decisions because if the offense fell under the guidelines there was little uncertainty about what sentence the defendant would receive. The guidelines gave the prosecutor the ability to "charge bargain." For a plea of guilty, the charge might be reduced to one not covered by guidelines or at least to a different cell on the grid.

If sentencing guidelines are available, prosecutors often refer to them in the charging process to make sure that the "punishment fits the crime." If the prosecutor wants jail time as a possible sentence, the guidelines are checked to make sure that the charge selected includes the possibility of jail. If a lesser charge is selected that does not include jail, then the prosecutor's view of what is reasonable and appropriate is ruled out of the sentence.

The charge chosen may also affect the defendant's eligibility for other programs, especially diversion programs. Many of these programs have eligibility criteria, some of which are linked to the seriousness of the charge. Prosecutors who want to direct the offender into these programs take these entrance criteria into consideration when charges are filed.

The level of charges, felony or misdemeanor, and the charges selected define the type of sanction that would be acceptable to the prosecutor. So the level of the charge placed on the case cannot be untangled from the prosecutor's expectations about the likely outcome of prosecution.

The decision of what to charge is not the end of the charging process. There are other decisions that prosecutors can make that affect the way cases are prosecuted, increase the chances of getting preferred outcomes, and reduce workload in the office. The most common considerations include decisions about jurisdiction (juvenile or adult), the level of ADA experience that will be needed, when the charges will be filed, and where the case will be prosecuted.

Prosecutors are not restricted to trying cases in the local jurisdiction. Criminal cases arising in one jurisdiction may be prosecuted in a number of venues. A case can be transferred to the office of another local prosecutor or prosecuted by municipal prosecutors, the state's attorney general, or the U.S. attorney, if agreements are reached.

Although each venue has its own jurisdictional requirements, there is enough overlap between the offices that makes some transfers possible and often beneficial to prosecution. Every offense that shares concurrent jurisdiction with one or more prosecution systems is, theoretically, eligible for a change of venue. These opportunities have given the prosecutor additional strategies in achieving preferred dispositions.

In some instances it is more efficient to consolidate a number of cases into one prosecution than to conduct them separately. Think about a person charged with passing bad checks all over the state, or burglars who practice their trade throughout a metropolitan area containing several counties or towns. If one defendant can be prosecuted by more than one jurisdiction, it just makes more sense to consolidate the offenses and have them prosecuted by one office.

This action also strengthens the plea negotiation position of the prosecutor. Now he or she can offer to have the charges in the other jurisdiction dismissed if the defendant pleads to charges pending in the prosecutor's jurisdiction. Consolidation may also make the defendant eligible for sentence enhancements under habitual offender statutes.

While consolidation sounds worthwhile, its weakness lies in the quality of communication systems among the jurisdictions. In practical terms, how does one office discover that a defendant under their review has other cases pending in another jurisdiction? With few exceptions, there are no statewide criminal justice information systems that prosecutors can query.[9] Unless staff phone or e-mail other offices to check for pending files against specific defendants, there is little chance that consolidation will take place.

Colorado is an exception to this statement. The state has developed and implemented a system called "ACTION" that allows its 22 prosecutor offices to communicate with one another and with the state's central database. It is now routine procedure for the staff to check incoming cases against the central database to determine whether there are other pending cases in other offices. This is a major advancement for prosecution!

Some cases may be prosecuted either in state courts or municipal courts. These concurrent jurisdiction cases typically involve ordinance violations, some misdemeanors, and in some cases, traffic and moving violations. Generally procedures are agreed upon by the county and municipal prosecutors as to which offenses are prosecuted in each court system and the police and magistrates are informed. For example, all ordinance violations will be prosecuted in municipal courts and all misdemeanors involving injury or property loss or damage will be prosecuted in state courts.

Concurrent jurisdiction cases may create conflict between the two court systems partly because the sanctions in municipal courts are usually substantially less than sanctions available for violations of state statutes. If the local prosecutor wanted stiffer penalties for certain crimes, the case would be filed in state, not municipal court.

However, municipal courts need revenue from fines and fees, which often goes into the general fund and provides the local government with substantial income. As a result, city prosecutors may be reluctant to transfer "high fine" cases like drunk driving to the local prosecutor and lose the revenue generated.[10]

In an office in Missouri, there was a continuing problem with driving under the influence (DUI) cases. DUIs filed in municipal court could generate fines for as much as $500. But the county prosecutor had given top priority to prosecuting drunk drivers under state law. If they were tried in his office, the sanctions imposed could be far more severe than a fine, even to the extent of prosecuting some defendants as habitual offenders.

The conflict between the two courts was clearly defined: one sought to keep the high revenues, the other sought stiffer penalties. Police who were not following existing guidelines stating that DUI cases should be filed in the state courts exacerbated the problem.

Some prosecutors have tweaked existing systems of justice other than their own as creative solutions to problems unanticipated by legislation or the courts. Most interesting was a jurisdiction in the Northwest where the city attorney and the district attorney had designed a successful technique to quickly respond to juveniles who were disruptive in school and destroyed school property.

Under the original system, the school year would be over before the district attorney could have a case ready for prosecution. It would take juvenile court months before it decided, first, whether the case should be adjudicated, and then, what action should be taken. Swift, sure, and certain justice was out of the question.

The city attorney, however, was not bound by these restrictions. The city attorney could file a complaint citing municipal ordinance violations and order the parents and the students to appear in court by a specific date, usually within days of the incident. The parents could be held accountable for the child's actions and fines and restitution could be imposed. Swift, sure, and certain justice was now attainable.

In some states the attorney general has criminal as well as civil jurisdiction. If a local case has consumer protection or interstate trade implications, then based on this broader scope, it may be transferred to the attorney general or to a statewide grand jury for further investigation before charges are placed. In a few instances, the attorney general may take over a local prosecution, but these events are rare. Usually these situations occur when the local prosecutor is not prepared to prosecute this kind of case or there is an issue of public corruption that requires an involuntary takeover. These occasions are so exceptional that prosecutors rarely consider the option.

Federal prosecutions by the U.S. attorney's office (USAO) are another story. Federal legislation tends to impose harsher and more severe penalties than state statutes, so transfers to the USAO are often desired for serious or complex cases.

For example, federal law allows for the death penalty in cases like drug trafficking, while some states like Michigan and Massachusetts do not permit the death penalty for any violations of the law. Federal law may also have mandatory minimums that do not exist at the state level, thus making federal prosecutions more desirable if incapacitation is the goal.

The problem lies in getting the USAO to accept and prosecute the state's cases. Some federal guidelines prohibit prosecution of cases below a certain dollar limit. This particularly applies to complex drug and organized crime cases. Some district courts may be overworked and backlogged. The case is not in the interests of the public; there are other cases pending that have a higher priority. The decision to accept a case for prosecution may be negotiable, but it belongs to the U.S. attorney and cannot be changed.

Back in the 1970s, San Diego's district attorney, Ed Miller, had a number of cases that could have been prosecuted federally but were rejected by the USAO citing a lack of staff. Ed Miller proposed a different approach. Why not have his assistant district attorneys (ADAs) "cross-designated" as assistant U.S. attorneys (AUSAs)? In this manner, he could prosecute his cases in federal courts with his assistants. The courts and the U.S. attorney approved, and this became the first recorded use of local prosecutors designated to prosecute in federal courts. Later the concept was used in reverse, when some AUSAs were designated as state and local prosecutors to assist in the prosecution of complex cases, usually drugs, in state courts.

In the end, it is primarily the prosecutor who decides where cases are to be tried. Sometimes these decisions are not always for the best. Take the O. J. Simpson case. Los Angeles's district attorney, Gil Garcetti, had the choice of trying the case in Brentwood where the murders occurred or downtown where the central office was located. The demographic makeup of the two jurisdictions and defense counsel's strategy of making race the issue, not the murders, tipped the scales in favor of acquittal. Brentwood was wealthy and white; downtown Los Angeles was poor and predominately black and

Hispanic. A jury in Brentwood might have forced the defense to use other strategies with different results. It was just a questionable choice of venue or, at best, the unluckiest.

Conclusion

On the surface it may seem that making charging decisions is a complicated process involving the consideration of the facts of the case, the defendant's criminal history, the credibility of the witnesses, the strength of the evidence, the availability of statutory enhancements, and the best place for the case to be tried. In the main, however, what seems complicated is rather simple if the prosecutor has a charging policy and it is transmitted to the staff.

Once the assistants and staff know the office priorities for prosecution, charging decisions reflect these priorities. This is why it is important that the prosecutor's policy reflects community values. It is also important that charging decisions are consistent with the charging policy and that they are uniformly made by all the charging assistants. Anything less introduces undesirable variation into the justice system.

The prosecutor's charging decisions start the court's adjudication process. It is this discretionary power that controls not only the gate to the courts but also, more importantly, supports the values and norms of the community by defining what behavior will not be tolerated and holding offenders accountable.

CHAPTER FOUR

The Final Accounting:
From Filing to Disposition

Every case filed has to be accounted for by receiving a disposition, and that outcome is recorded in the public record. Some cases will slip through the cracks and linger in a state of limbo, even for years. Such cases are rare, thus the focus turns to the routine ways that prosecutors bring cases to disposition and how discretion is used to obtain dispositions that are reasonable and appropriate. While discretion is granted to all prosecutors, how it is used differentiates one office from another and often produces different outcomes, some acceptable and others not.

Consider a case of breaking and entering. The defendant was caught at the scene in possession of stolen property. A search of the records showed a few prior arrests for auto theft, shoplifting, and larceny but nothing violent. In Prosecutor A's office, the defendant pleaded guilty to a lesser charge of breaking and entering and received a sentence of probation. In Prosecutor B's office, the defendant pleaded guilty to the original charge and was sentenced to 18 months in prison followed by two years of probation. Why did this happen?

A number of factors explain the difference. But knowing these factors does not make prosecution uniform. The court has only a limited number of ways to dispose of cases. They include:

1. Pleas of guilty
2. Trials by judge or jury
3. Dismissals
4. Diversion and alternatives to prosecution[1]

Nationwide, about 65 percent of felony cases are disposed by a guilty plea, a large number are pleas negotiated by prosecutor and defense counsel, and 32 percent are dismissed or disposed of through some other method, including deferred adjudication and transfers to other court jurisdictions. Only about 3 percent are disposed by trial.[2]

Much as defendants and victims want a day in court, there are simply not enough courtrooms or judges to try every case. On average, judges conduct about two jury trials a month or 24 a year.[3] If there is one judge and 100 felony cases, not all could be tried. So dispositions by a plea negotiation or dismissal are the only realistic ways to dispose of cases.

In the normal course of criminal justice, there is a familiar rhythm to prosecuting a case and reaching a final disposition. The most sought after disposition from the prosecutor's perspective is a plea of guilty to the original charges. This requires good screening at intake and a case with strong evidence resulting from thorough police work.

Even under these circumstances negotiated pleas still occur. A defendant may plead guilty to the original charge to receive other concessions such as a reduced sentence, avoiding being tagged with a mandatory minimum sentence, serving incarceration in a local penitentiary rather than one out of state, or simply not losing a driver's license or having car insurance rates increased. While many prosecutors would like pleas to the original charges, they are often forced to negotiate to avoid overloading the court with jury trial demands. Defense counsel understand the situation as well.

There are problems associated with negotiated pleas. Some assistants lack the talent for negotiation or are simply poor managers of caseloads. Other problems are created by defense counsel, who refuse to negotiate or even enter into conversation with the assistant or defendant about any prosecution offer. Some stem from the presiding judge's philosophy. There are some judges who are so opposed to plea negotiation that they refuse to accept a plea agreement. Other judges prefer to do the negotiations themselves, notwithstanding the recommendations of the prosecutor or defense counsel. Finally, not to be outdone by these difficulties, there are the defendants who, after extensive time in the prison library, consider themselves qualified to be their own lawyer, usually with very poor results.

Navigating through these shoals to reach reasonable and appropriate dispositions can be tricky. However, it is possible if certain guidelines and rules that help all the parties in the negotiation process are followed. One important fact is that each case has a market value. In other words, everyone in the courtroom knows the range of punishment the judge is likely to impose at sentencing. This becomes the market value of the case and provides the basis for negotiating an acceptable plea.

For example, the sentences imposed on the breaking and entering case cited above could have been a reflection of two different court cultures: one where the market value attached to the case was probation, and the other where the market value was imprisonment. Although it is the judge who imposes the sentence, it is the responsibility of the prosecutor and defense counsel to anticipate what the judge will accept if a plea is negotiated.

Bench and jury trials are another story. It is quicker and easier to have a bench trial, but defendants are often wary of having a single judge being both judge and jury unless the judge is known to be soft on the particular offense involved. "Judge shopping" is a way of life in these situations, although it is not always successful.

On the whole, bench trials for felony cases are not the norm for most jurisdictions, although courts can be found that use this method more frequently than jury trials. These courts tend to be unified courts, as in Pittsburgh where the same court process handles both misdemeanors and felonies.[4] With the large bulk of the caseload being misdemeanors, bench trials are a practical response. In courts that are not unified, jury trials of misdemeanors in the lower courts may not even be available.

Thanks to television and the movies, jury trials are familiar to everyone. So too are the uncertainties that surround them. Jury trials place the most demands on the resources of all the parties, including prosecutors and the court. Yet assistant prosecutors dream of that venue. To have a jury trial is to reach the pinnacle of prosecution; to have a reasonable and appropriate outcome is to reach the pinnacle of the professional. But as Brooklyn district attorney Eugene Gold cautioned, "The chances that every one of my 500 attorneys will ever try a case in front of a jury are zero."

The hard reality is that most courts are overloaded and there is enormous pressure to reduce the volume of work by any means possible. This brings into play diversion or deferred prosecution, which is now an acceptable dispositional route, and dismissal, which may or may not be acceptable.

Diversion programs reflect the newest dispositional choice. By offering alternatives to prosecution, diversion in its many forms has the great benefit of diverting cases out of the criminal justice system and into other, more acceptable, programs. Diversion takes many forms, not all of which may be available in a local community. It can embrace drug treatment, mediation, community service, restitution for bad checks, parenting courses, or anger management programs. The makeup of the community and the willingness of the prosecutor and courts to use diversion are the main factors in creating alternatives to prosecution.

The benefit of these alternatives is flexibility. The circumstances of the defendant and the crime enter into decision making about whether noncriminal sanctions would produce better results in preventing future offenses than the negative effects of traditional punishment.

Dismissals, however, are harder to value. Cases are dismissed for a number of reasons, some of which can be interpreted as a reasonable and appropriate disposition and others not. On the one hand, if the evidence originally reviewed at intake has changed and the case is no longer appropriate for prosecution, the case should be dismissed. On the other hand, if the case should never have been accepted at intake, prosecutorial resources have been wasted. Depending on the circumstances, dismissals can tell you a lot about the quality of prosecution. Unfortunately, unlike conviction and guilty plea rates, dismissal rates are not recorded in a form that identifies the reason for dismissal.

Some dismissals are temporary. They may be called dismissals with leave or dismissals without prejudice. These dismissals allow a prosecutor to reopen a case and prosecute the original charges if the defendant does not satisfy the conditions imposed as part of a diversion or deferred prosecution program: "If you don't complete the program, I will prosecute you."

Dismissal's most prevalent use, however, occurs when the defendant fails to appear at a court hearing and a bench warrant is issued. Dismissing these cases with leave clears the court's docket of a large volume of "pending" cases that can be reactivated if the defendant is arrested.

There is one more judicial action that is not a disposition but has a major impact on the prosecutor's ability to bring cases to reasonable and appropriate disposition. It is the decision to continue a court event. Continuances prevent potential dispositions since the event can be rescheduled for a myriad of reasons.

Every day a judge sits in a courtroom with a list of cases to be heard on the calendar. Now the judge knows and everyone else knows that all the cases on the calendar will not be disposed or moved on to the next logical place in the system. To do that the judge must hold a court hearing for each of them or violate "speedy trial" rules and other court-imposed schedules. The easiest and fastest way to "hold this hearing" is for the defendant and the defense attorney to request a continuance for some reason legitimate or otherwise. Granting the continuance satisfies the court's hearing requirement, removes the case from the calendar, and reschedules it for another day.

But each time a case does not move forward to the next step toward final disposition, it incurs tremendous costs to the criminal justice system in terms of wasted time and effort. Police sit in court, usually drawing overtime pay, waiting to testify. Prosecutors and defense counsel prepare for hearings that will have to be repeated later, calling for more preparation, and victims and witnesses are turned off by the whole ineffectual process, sometimes never to appear again. Cases rarely ever improve with age. That is why defense counsel rarely complains about delays.

Continuances are easy temporary holds. Even dismissing a case or taking a plea of guilty takes more court time than a continuance. So the pressure is always on the court to grant them. The sad fact is that prosecutors can do little to change the ways of a judge or an overloaded court except not to contribute to its happening by always being prepared for each hearing.

Finally, there are always some cases that fall through the cracks and never seem to reach disposition. Records show cases that have lingered on for four to six years, always being shoved to the bottom of the pile when attention is brought to them. Most of them are held pending because the defendant has fled the jurisdiction and a bench warrant has been issued for arrest. Others grow old and cold because of poor case management on the part of the prosecutor. These cases generally are "dogs" and probably should not have been accepted in the first place. Still other cold cases are created by judicial inaction, defense counsel problems, and victim and witness reluctance to testify. Defense counsel routinely waive the speedy trial requirements of the law.[5]

It is difficult to get prosecutors and the court system to pay attention to old cases, given the press of more active work. But in the long run, their existence calls into question the equity and fairness of the system.

The roads to disposition vary from jurisdiction to jurisdiction and even from one courtroom to another. There is a local legal culture in each court. The culture defines the rules and procedures that the local court system uses and characterizes the tone and tenor of justice. Some court systems are modern and well managed, others are dated and inefficient. Each, however, provides an environment within which cases are processed.

Within these local legal cultures are individual judges. Since the power of the judge to make disposition decisions and to sentence defendants is absolute, the prosecutor's discretionary powers have to be tailored to meet the views and philosophies of individual judges. As a Missouri prosecutor once said, "You have to know how far you can push and when you have to back off." It takes a clever person to play these situations to advantage.

Somehow, despite all the differences in community standards and expectations; legislative environments; court cultures; judicial, prosecutorial, and defense philosophies; policies and priorities; and procedures and programs, cases are disposed, justice is dispensed, and defendants are sanctioned with varying degrees of equity and efficiency.

The Dynamics of Adjudication

It's a strange word, adjudication, used only in reference to the courts and judicial decisions. It is rarely found in normal conversation. The adjudication process is unfamiliar to most people except those interacting with it. Parts of the process are known because of notorious cases that the media spotlights and from Court TV videos. Most people know about trials and grand jury indictments but few understand the process that moves cases to dispositions. So in the interest of clarity, we present a brief synopsis of the process and the flow of cases (see Figure 4.1).

This simplified version of the process shows that there are six basic steps in the adjudication process, each serving a different purpose. The first three focus on the accusatory stage, the last three steps constitute the trial process.

First appearance usually occurs within 24 hours of arrest. Here the defendant:

- Is notified of the police charges
- Has bond or bail set, or is remanded to jail
- Has his or her indigent defense status reviewed and may be assigned a public defender if he or she is eligible

This court hearing has only one purpose: to determine whether the defendant should be released on bond/bail or remain in jail while the prosecutor decides whether to prosecute and what charges to place.

The grand jury or the preliminary hearing, and some jurisdictions have both, has a single purpose: to decide whether there is enough evidence to support a prosecutor's charge that there is probable cause that the defendant committed the crime. If there is, an accusatory instrument is issued. For a preliminary hearing, it is a bill of information signed by the judge; for the grand jury, it is an indictment handed up to the judge. If there is no probable cause, then the case is dismissed and the defendant is released.

At arraignment the accused defendant is arraigned on the charges, which are read to him or her by the judge. The defendant is asked to plead guilty or not guilty. This hearing sets in motion the disposition process.

Figure 4.1   Case Processing Flow.

Pretrial conferences are typically scheduled after arraignment. In these administrative hearings, defense counsel, defendant, prosecutor, and the judge indicate whether:

- The defendant wants to plead guilty.
- Defense counsel will file motions.
- There are special considerations or requests that the judge should be aware of.
- The defendant will demand a trial.

Then, a court date is set for disposition by a guilty plea, a trial, or a motion to dismiss.

After a conviction, sentencing occurs. This may be immediately after conviction if the offense does not carry with it a sentence of more than a year in jail or prison. For example, in traffic court with a traffic ticket, the finding is made immediately. For serious cases, however, the judge listens to the sentence recommendation of the prosecutors and defense counsel, and orders a presentence investigation (PSI) by the probation department.

This simplistic rendering of the adjudication process shows the steps in the process but hides the many variations on the theme that make one court process totally different from another. All courts follow the same basic road to disposition, but every court has its own local legal culture within which the discretion of the prosecutor, the quality of law enforcement, the rules of the court, the type of judge, and defense counsel create procedures that make each local legal culture somewhat unique.

Compare these two court systems to see how local legal cultures can vary. In Court A, relations between the police, prosecutor, and public defender are terrible. The police hardly ever follow up on the prosecutor's requests for additional information; the prosecutor believes that the police are incompetent and poorly trained as witnessed by inadequate reports. The court does not have a chief judge with any authority to exercise control over the other judges, each of whom set their own rules and procedures for handling cases. The public defender does not routinely communicate with the prosecutor about cases of mutual interest. In this dysfunctional situation, one would not expect to find a smooth processing of cases through the adjudication process. Conflict is more the name of the game, creating backlog and delay.

Court B is a model of cooperation, communication, and good management. Police produce good reports and supply strong evidence when referring a case to the prosecutor. The state's information is immediately forwarded to the public defender or private defense counsel, and after meetings between the assistant prosecutor and the assistant public defender, a reasonable and appropriate disposition to the case is agreed upon. The defendant agrees to plead guilty at the next court date.

The same basic process underlies both courts; but what a difference the local legal culture can make in moving cases swiftly to a reasonable and appropriate disposition.

Plea Negotiation in Practice

Reaching a guilty plea is anything but simple. Imagine negotiating a kayak through white-water rapids. The most important things to do are to maintain balance in the midst of swirling waters and stay away from dangerous rocks. The dynamics of pleading guilty are very similar because it too is beset by forces that push and pull the case to what, hopefully, is an appropriate disposition.

There are four principals in the negotiating process: the prosecutor, defense attorney, judge, and defendant. Without question, each, respectively, has different goals:

- To prosecute the state's case and obtain a reasonable and appropriate sentence
- To defend the defendant by ensuring that due process and the rights of the accused are protected
- To decide whether the defendant is guilty, and if so, impose a sentence
- To beat the rap

Unless the defendant pleads guilty to the original charge, which is the best outcome from a prosecutor's perspective, there will be a process of negotiation before a satisfactory plea agreement can be drawn up. Somewhere between the most severe sanction that can be imposed and the most lenient is an outcome that will satisfy the prosecutor, defense counsel, and defendant. When this is identified and agreed upon, disposition is achieved.

This process is usually referred to pejoratively as plea bargaining. Many if not most people view it with dismay and consider it arbitrary, unjust, and probably the result of some backroom deal. In the adversary system of justice, such negotiations are natural and expected. Negotiated pleas, properly controlled, allow the criminal justice system to operate fairly and efficiently.

The biggest advantage flowing from the negotiations is that it allows the prosecutor and defense counsel to tailor a disposition fitting to both the crime and the offender. When laws are violated, the statutes usually define not only the offense but also its sanctions. Typically they are expressed as caps or ranges: "Violation of this law will result in a fine not to exceed $5,000 or one year in jail, or both." Somewhere within this range is a plea that is acceptable to all the principals including the defendant.

Properly managed, dispositions through negotiated pleas also keep taxpayer costs down while reserving time and space for those cases that should go to trial. Plea negotiation represents an efficient use of public funds and increases the capacity of the system to adjudicate more cases.

Negotiations include not just reductions in charges but other considerations. They may concern the location of the prison to which the defendant would be sentenced—one close enough so that family and friends can visit, for example. The charge may be changed so that it does not bring into play a mandatory sentence, a loss of a driver's license, or an increase in insurance rates. Treatment programs may be recommended as an add-on to probation. Both the prosecutor and defense counsel bring different information to the table reflecting different perspectives. This provides a better understanding of the type of sanction that would best fit the defendant and, as a result, a better quality of justice.

Despite views to the contrary, the negotiation process is generally rational and consistent. The parties do not sit down and just pull sanctions from the air and negotiate for an acceptable one. Statutes usually specify a range of punishments as well as lesser offenses that can be charged. Also, each local jurisdiction has established a market value for most crimes, which represents the "going rate" for sentences and sanctions. It is determined by the offense, the criminal record of the defendant, the views of the judiciary, and, to some extent, the tolerance of the community.

For example, burglaries committed by first-time offenders typically carry a sentence of probation. Rarely would a judge sentence an offender to prison under most circumstances. If the same offense is committed by a drug addict, now the market value may change. It may call for probation with conditions that the defendant enroll in and attend drug treatment programs. If the defendant has a long criminal history, the sentence most likely will include prison time and perhaps the selection of a prison that has an extensive drug treatment program. Knowing the market values keeps everyone's expectations reasonable.

If the market value includes a range of expected sanctions, which are known to defense counsel, prosecutors, and the court, then the process of negotiation depends on finding an acceptable one within this range. Research supports this hypothesis.[6] In this study, sheriffs, prosecutors, and defense counsel were asked to review 30 cases that had been designed to cover all combinations of the seriousness of the offense, the defendant's criminal history, and the strength of the evidence. Each group was asked to state its priority for prosecution and "a reasonable and appropriate sanction" for each case.[7]

The analysis confirmed that a system of market values existed and was known by law enforcement, prosecutors, and defense counsel. Most of the time prosecutors and defense counsel value cases similarly. If they can reach agreement about a reasonable sanction, then guilty pleas are likely. If agreement cannot be reached, then trials are a more likely outcome.

The shaded cell in Table 4.1 illustrates the acceptable area of potential agreement between the prosecutor and defense counsel. The prosecutor would like the defendant to serve some active time between one to five years, with one representing the minimum acceptable sanction. Defense would like probation or nothing more than two years. Somewhere between one to two years in prison (the shaded areas) is an acceptable disposition. A compromise, possibly 18 months in prison followed by two years' probation, might work. If agreement cannot be reached, for example, defense counsel insists on no jail or prison time, then this case will most likely go to trial.

Although market value adds a degree of certainty to negotiations and keeps it reasonable, the negotiation process is also affected by a number of other factors:

- The qualifications of the principals are considered. Some are professional and experienced, others are not. Some assistant prosecutors are poor negotiators and communicators. Some defense counsel refuse to even discuss the case with prosecutors.
- The stability of the expected sanctions or sentences are of concern. They may change quickly if the community becomes frightened or intolerant of new crimes they previously had not encountered and demands harsher responses. Conversely, if the community becomes more tolerant of certain crimes, the sanctions may be considered too severe. For example, the drug epidemic resulted in a rash of harsh sentences for possession of marijuana. Now, with the emergence of drug courts and advocacy groups calling for its legalization, some of these sentences have favored treatment over incarceration.

Table 4.1   Plea Negotiation Matrix

Prosecutor	Defense
5 years incarceration	Not acceptable
1 year jail	2 years incarceration
Not acceptable	Probation

- The amount of overcrowding in the jail or prison system is a factor. Jails are designed to hold pretrial detainees until their cases are disposed and inmates who are serving short-term sentences. If the pretrial detention population explodes, there are fewer jail beds for convicted inmates. This typically happens when the courts are backlogged and can't dispose of the pending caseload. If the situation gets bad enough, the jail may be forced to release some of the inmates early to free beds for pretrial detainees, as it had to in Philadelphia during its drug epidemic years. If overcrowding enters into the decision about pretrial detention, then the impact on negotiations can be significant. If you, the defendant, are out on bail, would you likely be in a hurry to bring the case to a speedy disposition?

With few exceptions, negotiated pleas are a way of life in most courts. Yet there are prosecutor's offices that still have unrealistic expectations about what cases should not be negotiated. Either the crime or the defendant are so bad that only a plea to the original charge would suffice or barring this happening, the case should be tried on the original charges. In other instances, the office may be unaware of the fact that the court is overloaded and does not have the capacity to try any more cases than what it already has on the docket.

In one office the prosecutor was complaining that the court was unable to keep up with the trial calendar. One assistant alone had about 50 cases on her trial docket. With only three judges available for all criminal cases, even her trial docket could never be disposed, never mind the trial dockets of the other assistants. There was simply not enough trial capacity. The assistant was asked how many cases were tried the previous year by all the judges. She said 23. That means, for her alone, about 27 of her 50 cases could not go to trial. Her problem now became one of deciding which 23 were the most trial worthy and which 27 should have plea offers prepared.

Sometimes the prosecutor is between a rock and a hard place. In a different jurisdiction, the prosecutor had a pending caseload of 52 capital cases involving the death penalty and more arriving almost daily. A reasonable estimate, not counting any additional capital cases, was that it would take five years to clear the existing backlog because death penalty cases are the most complicated and time consuming of all cases. There were few choices. The caseload could continue to build by not making changes; the court could be petitioned to seek additional judges to handle the existing capital cases, knowing that budgets were already stretched tight; or there could be offers to remove the death penalty charges in exchange for a guilty plea and sentencing to life without parole.

The realities of the local criminal justice system often contradict the vision of how the criminal justice system should work. Statutes, rules, and regulations do not provide sufficient discretion to produce reasonable and appropriate dispositions—in other words, to do justice. Criminal cases have three basic components: the offense, the defendant, and the evidence. Laws standardize the sanctions for offenses, but they do not allow for equalizing results among similarly situated defendants.[8] To achieve just outcomes, the sanctions standardized by law must be tailored to consider the nature of the defendant and the evidentiary strength of the case. Plea negotiation inserts a balance between the statutes and the individual circumstances of cases.

Laws providing for mandated sanctions offer a clear illustration of the dilemma faced by prosecutors when the defendants meet the statutory criteria but not the justice one. For example, during the 1970s, Michigan had a statute requiring a mandatory prison sentence for possessing a firearm while engaged in a felony.

One prosecutor described making a charging decision about a young girl with no record who was caught shoplifting, which is a felony. Upon the defendant being searched, a gun was found in the bottom of her purse. Although the gun statute was quite clear about the conditions needed to qualify for the mandated sentence of prison, charging this crime in this case was not in the interests of justice.

This is not a rare occurrence; examples of the inequities of mandated sentences abound.[9] But the dilemma is not only relevant to offenses with mandated sentences. It is present throughout the process because sanctions need to be tailored to specific individuals and specific cases if justice is to be served. This tailoring is at the heart of the negotiation process. Negotiations are the means for obtaining acceptable dispositions to individual cases.

There are some prosecutors and judges who oppose plea bargaining, arguing that a case should be tried on its legal merits without concessions.

There have been two famous examples of imposing a ban on plea bargaining; one in Alaska, where the attorney general imposed a statewide ban, and one in Orleans Parish (New Orleans), where a local prosecutor imposed a ban in the office for some 30 years.

When Alaska gained statehood in 1958, the state adopted an attorney general prosecution system and established a Department of Law, headed by the attorney general, with the responsibility to prosecute all violations of state law. The attorney general appointed 13 regional district attorneys to implement his policies and procedures. In 1975, Attorney General Avrum Gross ordered a ban, first, on charge bargaining, and later, when that proved ineffective, on sentence bargaining as well. His goal was "to restore public confidence in the system, increase the number of trials, improve the litigation skills of prosecutors, and return prosecutors to their traditional roles of evaluating evidence and trying cases instead of negotiating."[10]

Impact evaluations in 1978 and 1991 indicated that both charge and sentence bargaining became rare events during the first 10 years of the policy. During the late 1980s "charge bargaining reappeared, but prosecutors continued to avoid sentence bargains." Since cases were not ending in negotiated pleas or trials, the question was, what was happening to them?

The data showed that before the ban prosecutors refused to prosecute 4 percent of the cases; after the ban, the declination rate increased to 44 percent. Because charges could not be changed under the ban, police reports were subjected to closer scrutiny and cases that were only marginally strong were declined.

The study also showed that by limiting the prosecutor's charging discretion and banning negotiations, discretion was shifted out of the courts to the probation office, which conducted presentence investigations and made sentence recommendations to the judge. As one defense attorney said, "We don't prepare them for trial, we prepare them for the presentence investigation."

Statewide bans on all forms of plea bargaining are difficult to implement and control because the criminal justice system needs discretion to tailor justice to the circumstances of the offense and the criminal. This is an essential part of our criminal justice system. If discretion is restricted, as happened in Alaska, the need for it is not eliminated. It doesn't go away. It merely shifts elsewhere; in this case, to the probation office.

While it is difficult to abolish plea bargaining on a statewide basis, it does not follow that it cannot be done within a local jurisdiction. Orleans Parish (New Orleans), Louisiana, offers an excellent example of how plea bargaining can be restricted by shifting the elements that produce negotiated pleas to the very front of the adjudication system—namely, intake—rather than transferring them outside the office or farther down the process.

In 1974, when Harry Connick was elected district attorney for Orleans Parish in Louisiana, a policy to reduce plea bargaining was outlined and implemented. His experience points to the many dimensions of negotiating pleas, the challenge prosecutors face in controlling the use of discretion, and the need to integrate this strategy into all aspects of prosecution, not just the trial process.

New Orleans in 1974 was a smaller jurisdiction than it is today with 10 judges in the criminal court, each having a docket or calendar, and 60 assistant district attorneys. The system processed about 6,000 cases annually. Defense counsel were provided primarily by the Orleans Indigent Defender Program (OIDP), which employed 22 attorneys and was supplemented by court-appointed attorneys who were not paid because funds were not appropriated by the state. The courts were heavily backlogged, and for one month a year, each judge was freed from court duties to clear his or her docket.

Connick's goal was to reduce plea bargaining, defined as pleading guilty to a lesser charge or dropping some of the charges for less severe sanctions. When Connick took office 85 percent of all cases were plea bargained. One year after his election, less than 10 percent of all cases were the result of negotiated pleas, and by 1976 pleas to reduced charges were 3.6 percent of all dispositions. How this was accomplished illustrates the complexity of the plea process, the need to recognize the importance of the agencies interfacing with the office, and the stiff internal management and organizational requirements needed to enforce the ban.

Normally, negotiations are conducted after the defendant has been charged and before a trial is scheduled. In New Orleans, the entire negotiation process was essentially conducted during the intake stage so that there was nothing left to negotiate later on. Connick's policy stated that once a defendant was charged, the charges could not be changed except under exceptional circumstances and only then after the prosecutor or his top deputies approved the change. Trial assistants could not amend the charges nor could they dismiss a case. This policy, of course, put all the emphasis on intake and screening, which Connick staffed with the most experienced assistants.

This ban endured for the 30 years that Connick held office. The management skills needed to maintain the policy were substantial. The relationship with law enforcement agencies, which did not like to see cases rejected, improved after a career criminal unit was started to specially prosecute these cases and the office's communication with the department increased. Even the judges aligned with the policy once it was demonstrated that the policy would not increase the number of trials or add to the backlog. In fact, the backlog was reduced because a high percentage of cases were declined and never entered the system.

For the most part, these two examples of bans on plea bargaining are rarities as witnessed by the National Center for State Courts' statistics that show 65 percent of cases disposed by pleas. This is because the benefits of plea negotiations are many:

- Law enforcement agencies are spared the onus of being witnesses in trials and of incurring overtime costs waiting to testify.
- Prosecution saves extensive case preparation time, and even witness costs, if defendants plead guilty.
- Defense counsel can represent more clients if they are not in trial.
- Court costs are diminished if pleas occur early, dockets can move faster, and jury costs are avoided.

- Probation's work may be reduced if presentence investigations are decreased.
- Pretrial detention costs retreat after defendants are sentenced.
- Sometimes even the defendants and their families benefit from not having a public airing of the circumstances of the offense.
- Victims and their families may find some relief from the swift resolution of cases and the sanctions imposed.

Only correctional and treatment systems may see negative effects if the sanctions imposed increase their populations.

The Judge's Impact on Plea Negotiation

Defendants have two trial choices, by a judge or by a jury. Either choice introduces uncertainty about the disposition. Bench trials, or trial by a judge, places the entire case on the shoulders of a judge. The judge's verdicts undoubtedly are influenced not only by the evidence in the case but also views about the relationship between crime and punishment and the marketplace created by the judge's past decisions. Jury trials, on the other hand, require the unanimous agreement of the diverse views of 12 people.

So which to choose? From a defendant's perspective the answer is that which will most likely produce a not guilty verdict or dismissal. The defense attorney knows which judge is assigned the case and knows whether this is a "hanging" judge or one who will be lenient and persuaded by legal arguments. If the assigned judge doesn't fit the bill, then perhaps some "judge shopping" is in order.

Nothing can diminish the most important power of the judge, the power to impose sentences. Like the prosecutor, the primary goal of the court is to bring cases to disposition as quickly as possible with the least use of resources. But unlike the prosecutor, the court is also required to maintain objectivity and balance in the proceedings, protect the legal interests and constitutional rights of the defendant, and make rulings that are fair and balanced. The judge is the referee of a contest between two adversaries, the prosecutor and defense counsel.

Much of what takes place in the courtroom depends on the judge and how business is conducted. The ability of prosecutors or defense counsel to control or influence judicial behavior is very limited. If relationships between the judge and the other members of the courtroom workgroup are less than satisfactory, prosecutors or defense counsel are forced to find other ways to mitigate the damage that might be done to obtaining satisfactory dispositions.

Typically, the major difficulties created by judges stem from lack of objectivity, policies about granting continuances, docket management skills, the extent to which the plea negotiation process is obstructed or supported, and views on sentencing. When any or all of these factors are negative, the checks and balances needed by the justice system may suffer. If possible, the defense attorney may attempt to transfer the case to another judge, one more supportive or more flexible than the present judge. This is "judge shopping" in a generic sense.

Judge shopping can take a number of forms depending on the local court system and its procedures. Prosecutors or defense attorneys can't just ask the court to transfer the case because the judge is too liberal or too conservative to judge the case. Thus, judge shopping has to be based on more subtle maneuvers.

In North Carolina and some other states, judges "ride circuit." This means that they will be assigned to one location in their judicial district for possibly six months. Now in smaller jurisdictions with only two or three judges handling criminal cases, the judge can have powerful consequences. If the judge has a reputation for being lazy, incompetent, or biased, prosecutors and defense counsel alike seek ways to avoid having cases tried by this judge. If the judge's rotation is about to end, it is not uncommon for defense counsel to request a continuance knowing that the next hearing will be in front of the new judge.

It is a little different in large offices with a large pool of judges. Even though judges may be rotated between criminal and civil courts, judge shopping is more limited. In large offices, if cases are assigned randomly by the computer to individual judges, changing the assignment is not easily done. The reasons for the requested change have to reflect special circumstances. Some maneuvering is possible but in a limited sense. For example, a defendant may have several cases pending before multiple judges, which can be consolidated and assigned to a single judge.

Sometimes, the behavior of the judge is so inappropriate that the prosecutor can request that the judge recuse himself or herself. In 2004 a Virginia commonwealth attorney filed an eight-page brief detailing allegations that the Virginia judge handling the second murder trial of John Muhammad conducted an independent investigation of the Muhammad's jailers, questioned their powers and procedures, altered Muhammad's jail file, and repeatedly suggested that a key document had been doctored.[11] As a result of this clear violation and the publicity that ensued, the judge stepped down.

In Missouri, one county prosecutor stated that he regularly moved to change a case from one judge to another if he believed that the assigned judge was biased. Although it did not make the prosecutor a favorite with the affected judge, he did not fear retribution for using this tactic.

These are extreme and infrequent examples. Although judge shopping is always a consideration and the opportunity will be seized if needed and if possible, most cases move from step one to step two in an orderly although sometimes circular fashion. The length of time that it takes to bring cases to closure is almost entirely under the control of the judge, since only the judge can grant motions for a continuance. Some judges are notorious granters while others maintain rigid control over the number of continuances that are allowed.

Another less time-consuming action is to dismiss the case. If the prosecutor requests a dismissal or if the court hearing indicates that the case fails to meet evidentiary standards, dismissals are quick. A single form signed by the prosecutor and the judge is all that is needed to end the case.[12]

It may sound from the above recitation that judges are motivated by one goal only: to clear the daily calendar. While this may be true, it is not the point. The point is that there are incentives for judges to grant continuances, and this is one of them. The problem with granting continuances is that the case does not move from step one to step two but merely repeats step one at a later date. Continuances represent work avoidance, not case progress.

The liberal granting of continuances affects the prosecutor in a number of ways, all negative. Each case calendared has to be prepared. If the scheduled hearing is for probable cause, the evidence and testimonies of the police, victims, and/or witnesses has to be prepared and documented. With a continuance, the case file is set aside until the next scheduled court date when the procedure is repeated. As a result, continuances represent unnecessary and costly work for the prosecutor. These cases can easily consume from one to almost six staff-years of unproductive attorney time.[13]

There is little prosecutors can do about some continuances. For example, a savvy defendant buys time by looking for an attorney and has the case continued until one is retained. Or the courthouse lawyer who is still "looking for Mr. Green" will be granted continuances almost as a matter of course.[14] In the pretrial stages, like preliminary hearings, arraignments, and administrative settings for motions or pretrial conferences, prosecutors have few hammers to move cases forward. This process is controlled almost exclusively by defense counsel and/or the courts.

While the prosecutor views continuances negatively, the defendant benefits, especially if out on bail or released on recognizance (ROR). Even if the defendant is detained, the place of detention will likely be in a local jail near friends and family and not in a state penitentiary. And time served in jail will be credited as time served if given an active sentence. When the choice is between pleading guilty or taking the chance that the case may fall apart and be dismissed, the decision is often not a difficult one for the defendant.

In one office, the court with few exceptions had a very liberal continuance policy, and the public defender used it to advantage. The state's attorney could do nothing except make sure that the assistant was always prepared for every hearing, including trials. Telling the judge the state was unprepared could not be used as the basis for yet another continuance for the defense.

In yet a smaller office the prosecuting attorney used an Excel spreadsheet to record the number of continuances granted daily by every judge. He kept a running total of the number of continuances granted for each pending case. He prepared monthly reports for each judge. If the judge was considering a request for a continuance, the trial attorney told him how many had already been granted on the case. This was about the most proactive prosecutorial attempt to control and reduce continuances observed. The prosecuting attorney in this case was a great case manager and not afraid of the judges. The prosecutor's relations with the judiciary remained reasonable and cooperative, not paranoid or political.

The delays and extra work caused by continuances push the prosecutor to add incentives for early pleas. Less work will be squandered if a defendant pleads guilty at the preliminary hearing or upon arraignment. Considerably more work will be required if the same defendant pleads guilty on the first day of trial. But here again uncertainty reigns. Some defendants believe that the best offer will come from the prosecutor later in the process because the case will break down. So they wait until the day of trial.

To counter this mentality prosecutors use a number of incentives to encourage an early plea. The most common is "No reduced plea after a certain date or hearing." This policy says that the offer being presented now will be withdrawn after a certain date or hearing, and the defendant will be prosecuted on the original charges. Hampering the effectiveness of this tactic are the views of the judge. Some judges believe that if the original charge has been reduced in a previous offer, then it should be available independent of any date or hearing. On the day of trial this judge will allow the defendant to plead to the reduced charge, and there is nothing the prosecutor can do about it.

Or is there? In Wayne County (Detroit), Michigan, the late prosecuting attorney William Cahalan was one of the first prosecutors to try to implement a no reduced plea (NRP) policy in what was then Recorders Court for the city. He was warned by some judges that they would not honor his policy. Mindful of this, he ordered that if a plea offer had been made and rejected by the defendant, the case file would be stamped NRP in large, red, capital letters visible to the judges and indicating its rejection. He also informed his staff that the first time a judge indicated that he would not honor the NRP conditions, he was to be informed and he would personally argue against the judge's decision in open court. Well, that time did come, and the media had the pleasure of seeing the prosecuting attorney with his entourage march into the courtroom and announce to the judge that he was ready right then to personally try the case on the original charges. If the judge wanted to let the defendant plead to a lesser charge, then the public should be aware of his decision. Guess what? There were no problems with implementing a no reduced plea policy after that. Backbone and politics do count!

Being prepared is also important. A county prosecutor in Missouri has a "first offer is the best offer" strategy. Here, the first offer made to the defendant will be the most lenient one. If it is not accepted within a specified time frame, then a second offer is made that is harsher. This continues until the day of trial when the defendant is tried on the original charges. Of course, this strategy will fail if the prosecutor is bluffing and is not ready to try the case on the original charges on the day of trial.

For the most part, dismissals are final dispositions, and it is to the prosecutor's benefit to publicize those that are "wins" because they save everyone time and money. Most notable are dismissals of cases in one jurisdiction because the defendant pleaded guilty in another jurisdiction. Take the example of a successful federal prosecution of a drug dealer that produced a long, long sentence to prison. Why should the local prosecutor proceed with his case, which he has been holding until the federal case was disposed? Better to dismiss it and move on to other, more urgent ones.

Even within a single jurisdiction, if one case is disposed and there are others pending, it may be in the public's interest to dismiss the other charges if the sentence already received is appropriate. Take a simple case of forgery and uttering. One defendant could have 40 outstanding bad check cases. If he pleads guilty to 15 of them, there is no benefit in pursuing the rest (it would not increase his sentence), so the best option is to dismiss them. Not only does the prosecutor gain a conviction, but she saves the public's scarce tax dollars.

The Dynamics of the Courtroom

A cynic once said that the only things judges do are direct traffic and maintain order in the courtroom.[15] To be sure, a layperson sitting in the courtroom would find a judge's day somewhat confusing. The judge sits in a courtroom and watches a clerk entering data into the computer system, occasionally passing papers to the judge and possibly the attorneys. Defense counsel and prosecutors take positions at the appropriate tables, shuffle papers, and make unintelligible statements to the judge, who responds in a similar manner. Perhaps a witness is called to testify to something. After a while the whole process is repeated when new defense attorneys arrive for a new case. Different prosecutors may arrive as well, but that depends on how the office is staffing the individual courtrooms.

From an observer's vantage point not much makes sense because these hearings represent only bits and pieces of the overall process of adjudication. Unlike television coverage of trials, the daily work of a courtroom is essentially taken up with moving cases from step one to step two, from step two to step three, or from step three to step four. Although much of the activity involves dealing with the minutiae of cases, it cannot take place without the presence of a judge to make sure that the laws, court rules, and procedures are being followed.

In the local legal culture, the courtroom workgroup establishes relationships that are far more complex than those developed between police and prosecutor, or defense counsel and prosecutor. Part of this is due to the fact that each participant in the courtroom has relationships with the other participants in addition to the judge. How the judge responds can set up a three-way dynamic, which may or may not bring about timely dispositions.

Some judges are by nature good case managers, accepting the responsibility for moving cases; others are not. The importance of being a traffic cop is valid. Judges who recognize the duty to act as a traffic cop can easily put an end to defense counsel or defendants "playing the system." The major tools are pretrial conferences or administrative settings. Conducting these hearings lets the judge check the status of cases and resolve issues that may delay or hinder movement to the next step or create more continuances.

Judges can exercise more administrative power over the adjudication process. Judges can refuse to grant any more continuances; judges can force laggard defense counsel to communicate with clients about plea offers and the next step. As observers of behavior in the courtroom, judges can tell the prosecutor when assistant prosecutors need to have additional training in order to competently handle certain types of hearings.

In one office prosecutors were assigned to geographic areas and were responsible for prosecuting all crimes occurring in the area, including homicides. Unfortunately, this practice resulted in attorneys who had little or no homicide trial experience trying homicide cases. This problem was conveyed by the judges to the prosecutor, who responded by creating a separate homicide unit composed of experienced attorneys.

In another jurisdiction, the judges in misdemeanor court routinely evaluated the decorum and performance of newly hired assistant prosecutors and then reported those evaluations to the prosecutor, who could then target more training in areas where it was needed.

Whether judges are liberal in granting continuances or are poor case managers has a significant effect on delaying cases transiting the court system. Since case delay usually favors the defendant and, therefore, is opposed by prosecutors, the relationships between the prosecutor and the court are important. Under favorable circumstances where cooperative relationships exist, case delay is minimized and plea negotiations occur early in the system. For the defendant, the negotiation process allows the prosecutor and the defense attorney to tailor a disposition suited to any special circumstances. Lack of cooperation effectively restricts these efficiencies.

The prosecutor-court-defense relationship guides case processing, but the roles that each plays during negotiations and sentencing determine the final outcome. Only a judge can impose sentences. It follows, then, that prosecutor and defense counsel must consider the judge's views on crime and punishment when estimating what sentence will be imposed. Every court has its hanging judges who incarcerate early and often, and liberal judges who use incarceration as the very last option. Every court also has judges who are moderate and objective. Both prosecutors and defense attorneys know what to expect as the cases reach the final stages of disposition.

In some courts, judges are opposed to plea bargaining on the grounds that it is unfair and discriminatory. With these judges, prosecutors have to move carefully, recognizing that the negotiated plea has to be justified on the grounds that it is reasonable and appropriate and fits the defendant and the crime. In other words, the plea to a reduced charge must be justified as will enhancements. Otherwise the court will not accept the plea. The prosecutor has the power to negotiate a plea, but the judge has the power to reject it and accept a plea to the original or a lesser charge. Sometimes the judge's interference can be limited if the prosecutor places charges that are reasonable and acceptable to defense counsel. Sometimes it cannot. This creates a difficult situation for both prosecutor and defense counsel.

The involvement of judges in negotiations is not unusual, just controversial. Some judges take such an active role in negotiating sentences with defense counsel that the prosecutor merely steps aside and listens. Other judges are so opposed to plea negotiations that agreements are rejected even though all the parties have agreed. An even more difficult situation occurs, however, when judges interfere with the negotiation process.

There are mixed blessings when judges step outside their role and actively participate in the negotiation process. With the active participation of the judge, a large degree of certainty is injected into the process. Judges, for example, will state to both prosecutor and defense counsel that if the defendant will plead to a simple assault, then the sentence will be community service and an anger management course.

On the other hand, if the prosecutor and defense counsel are having difficulty in negotiating a plea that is acceptable to both parties, the judge's interference raises questions about the objectivity of the judicial function. For example, the defendant may offer to help the police solve other cases if the judge will sentence the defendant to minimal jail time. The offer is under consideration. However, the judge does not buy into the deal and thinks the defendant's record makes him less than reliable and even a danger. The judge vetoes the deal and tells both sides what sentence will be imposed.

The prosecutor is particularly concerned if the judge and defense counsel discuss the sentences or sanctions that the judge is willing to impose. Sometimes this is done in chambers; other times it may be done in open court at a pretrial conference. Sometimes, when the prosecutor and defense counsel are conflicted, communication may be between defense counsel and the judge, with no input from the prosecutor. The most the prosecutor can do is to try to minimize the effect by charging at the highest sustainable level. But even this action can be subverted by the judge who accepts a plea to a lesser charge.

For all of these dysfunctional courtrooms, there are many that are well run. Here relationships among the judges, prosecutors, and defense attorneys are professional, and procedures for good case management are the rule, not the exception. In these environments, cases flow smoothly to disposition.

Sentencing: The Final Rendering

Once a defendant has been convicted, it is time for sentencing. It is at this point that the many goals of a criminal justice system can be viewed. Some sentences are imposed to prevent crime and deter criminal activity. Others provide an opportunity to treat and rehabilitate those unlucky enough to be arrested. Some seek to incapacitate offenders and protect the public from future criminality. Many punish the offender for unlawful and illegal behavior in accordance with the circumstances of the offense and offender.

To give balance to the sentencing process, the judge may consider the recommendations of a number of voices representing the different points of view. Usually, prosecutors and defense counsel present sentencing recommendations in court. A probation officer may be asked to conduct a presentence investigation (PSI) if a prison sentence is possible. More recently, with the passage of victims' rights legislation in 49 states, the voices of victims can be heard through victim impact statements. The sentencing judge decides the sentence based on the facts of the case and the history of the offender.

One should be aware that the sentencing judge may not have all the available information about a case or sufficient information to make just and equitable sentencing decisions. Just reading police and other investigative reports provides only basic information about a case from a law enforcement perspective. The most complete information about cases is provided in trial settings since the prosecutor and defense counsel present the evidence.[16]

But for the majority of cases disposed by guilty pleas, the amount and type of information provided to judges for sentencing may be substantially less than that held by the prosecutor or defense counsel. Sentencing may be reduced to a recitation of the facts of the case and the defendant's criminal history and behavior. The information presented typically is only enough to satisfy the judge that the defendant is guilty and the plea is given voluntarily.

If incarceration is a possibility, the court needs more information not only about the offense but also the defendant's criminal history and lifestyle so the court can evaluate the defendant's risk to society if probation is ordered. Generally the court orders a presentence investigation (PSI) report from the probation office with recommendations for sentencing.

Although relatively few victims opt to prepare victim impact statements, if they do, the court's attention is directed to consider the harm done to others as a result of the defendant's actions. The facts as known to the judge then become the basis for the sentencing decision.[17]

Why Do Sentences Vary?

Judges impose sentences that may be defined by the Constitution, federal and state statutes, and local ordinances. Typically statutes put "teeth" into the law by stating the sanctions that may be applied if proven. But the teeth are usually stated in a "not to exceed" format, such as: "Violations of this act will result in fines up to $10,000 and imprisonment of up to 10 years." Under the cap is room for a lot of sentencing variation.

Over the years, many attempts have been made to control variation in sentencing. Some have legislated uniformity through sentencing guidelines that have now been adopted by about 20 states.[18] Other attempts have been through mandatory minimums, which seek to ensure uniformity at the bottom line. California's "three strikes and you're out" legislation also serves this purpose. State judicial systems have also worked to increase uniformity in sentencing among judges through education, workshops, and conferences.

Yet despite all these and other efforts, when local court systems are compared, wide disparities in sentencing are apparent. The main reason is that courts reflect the local environments. What sentence do you think a defendant who pleaded guilty to a burglary would receive in Kings County (Brooklyn), New York, as compared to rural Randolph County, Missouri? A fair guess would be probation in New York and jail time in Missouri. The two communities have vastly different priorities because of existing crime patterns.

There is higher tolerance for crime in large urban areas such as Brooklyn that would not be tolerated in smaller communities where crimes of violence are less frequent and the community is outraged by crimes that Brooklyn sees all the time and would likely ignore. For example, at one time Brooklyn had a "50 stitch rule," which meant that assault cases would not be prosecuted to the fullest extent unless at least 50 stitches were needed for the injuries sustained. On the other hand, prosecutors in Minnesota were plagued by an epidemic of snowmobile burglaries, which emptied summer homes of valuables in winter, a problem unknown in New York City.

Variation in sentencing exists even within a courthouse due to the wide variation in judicial philosophies, administrative abilities, and roles in the adjudication process. All of these factors end with a simple fact: when an individual case is being evaluated by a judge for sentencing, there is significant uncertainty as to what sentence will be imposed.

This is not to say that the differences in sentencing are like a teacher throwing papers on the steps and assigning grades according to which step they land on. As we have noted, almost all judges and participants in the courtroom adhere to a market value system that defines a range of reasonable and appropriate sentences for various types of crimes and criminals.

One element of successful dispositions is that the defendant is held accountable for the criminal behavior and receives a punishment that is reasonable and appropriate for the circumstances of the case. The question, of course, is how does one define reasonable and appropriate? The answer is not readily apparent. From the prosecutor's perspective, the definition depends on the evaluation of the seriousness of the offense, the strength of the evidence, and the nature of the defendant. In other words, all these factors collectively determine the sanctions that should be sought.

For example, deterrence is a factor in the decision to prosecute a man arrested for soliciting. It is hoped that public shaming will deter such behavior in the future, if not for the offender, then for others. Treatment and rehabilitation modalities would offer the defendant an opportunity to control their behavior while incapacitation would seek jail time to prevent offending while incarcerated and to discourage offending in the future. The concept of just desserts requires that the circumstances of the incident be considered in addition to the man's status with regard to family and work being evaluated to reach an appropriate disposition, which may include pretrial diversion.

Achieving reasonable and appropriate dispositions requires that the prosecutor be able to operate with different modalities that can exist side by side in the office. This is why prosecutors' offices may have diversion programs for first-time offenders, may make recommendations for sentences to include treatment programs for drug or alcohol users or abusers, and may have violent offender units to make sure that predators are incarcerated for as long as possible. Unfortunately, for a variety of reasons not all prosecutors are open to this expansive view.

Both prosecutors and defense counsel have differing expectations about what constitutes a reasonable and appropriate disposition and sanction. Although the probability of the prosecutor getting the expected outcome is high, it is not certain. No one can predict with certainty what sentences judges will impose if the defendant pleads guilty or is found guilty. Thus, negotiations and the dispositional routes selected hinge on what each party thinks is a likely sentence. This is not as simple as it sounds, although the local legal environment's market will give some clues.

Sentence Recommendations

Either the prosecutor or defense counsel or both can recommend sentences, if permitted in the state's statutes and the judiciary is open and receptive. Each proposes an acceptable sentence for the judge's consideration and states the reasons why it is justified. These reasons usually focus on the number of victims, the seriousness of the injuries suffered, the value of the property lost or damaged, the attitude of the defendant, and other mitigating or aggravating factors.

If the disposition is the result of a negotiated plea, then the prosecutor and defense counsel speak with one voice, or the prosecutor "stands mute," allowing defense counsel to make the recommendation.

There are two glitches in this procedure that can disrupt the sentence recommendation process and create inequities in decision making. One is the prosecutor's attitude about making sentence recommendations and the extent of his or her involvement at this stage. Some prosecutors have backed away from making sentence recommendations on the grounds that sentencing is the judge's responsibility and the prosecutor should not intervene. The prosecutor's position is that the negotiated plea offers mutually acceptable conditions to both sides and a high degree of certainty with respect to the sentence that will be imposed. The judge is responsible for setting the sentence. Taking this hands-off approach, however, can shift more influence to defense counsel, who may become the sole voice in front of the judge.

In a broader sense, not making recommendations weakens the prosecutor's role as an advocate for the state since he or she is not presenting the state's position at the sentencing hearing. Since all offenses are against the state rather than the victim, the prosecutor has the responsibility to argue for a reasonable and appropriate sentence. The prosecutor is normally the most knowledgeable person about both the offense and the defendant.

The other glitch occurs when judges become active participants in the plea negotiation process by revealing the sentence to be imposed if the defendant pleads guilty, by accepting pleas to reduced charges that the prosecutor has previously rejected, or by conducting the negotiations directly with defense counsel. These actions short-circuit the negotiation process and may work against the interests of either the prosecutor or defendant.

For example, a defendant is willing to plead to a crime that carries with it the potential for some prison time only if both the prosecutor and defense counsel recommend probation and treatment programs. If the judge intends to sentence the defendant to a short prison term followed by probation and announces so, then the plea negotiation is over. In this case, a trial may be in the offing.

Sentence recommendations are valuable because the positions of both sides of the case are made clear, and the judge's knowledge about more aspects of the case is increased. If the recommendations are not forthcoming, the quality of the judge's sentencing decision is open to question.

Presentence investigations (PSIs) conducted by the probation office gather information about the defendant and the defendant's lifestyle so that any risk to society can be assessed. Much of the information gathered is not included as evidence because it is "extralegal." Judges are not bound by PSI recommendations.

The investigation basically examines the defendant's socioeconomic background, education, work history, family stability, friends and colleagues, mental and social stability, recidivism, drug use, and other factors that affect their potential risk to society. Depending on the seriousness of the crime, PSIs are often detailed and lengthy. Usually PSI recommendations focus on some type of probation (and/or treatment programs) or incarceration.

Because PSIs, conducted by the probation office, gather information from a variety of sources, the investigations are time-consuming and can create serious delays in sentencing. Recognizing this, some prosecutors provide PSI investigators with complete case files including police reports and evidence that was not used in court. Other prosecutors update the information contained in the case file by contacting the detectives involved in the case for any additional information they may be privy to, like "talk on the street" and "rumor has it." These informal pieces of information keep information about the defendant up-to-date.

One unusual use of presentence investigations was found in Middlesex County (New Brunswick), New Jersey. Judge George Nicola was leading a project to expedite the disposition of drug cases, which were inundating the court. He established three tracks for drug cases based on the likelihood of being disposed by trial, plea, or dismissal, and whether the defendant faced incarceration or not.

Each defendant charged with a drug offense subject to active time was interviewed by a probation officer before his or her court hearing. In addition, probation officers were immediately assigned to cases that did not include incarceration. They prepared a "mini PSI" for the judge, which could be used at arraignment to expedite the disposition of cases and referral to diversion or treatment programs.

Shifting the PSI to the front of the adjudication process brought information to the court early that normally would have waited until a disposition had been reached. The results were substantial increases in early, expedited dispositions.[19]

In the mid-1970s victim impact statements (VIS) were first introduced in the United States. To date, some 49 states have legislation that gives victims rights in criminal proceedings and allows input at sentencing. VIS lets victims describe in writing the harm done or the losses suffered as a result of the crime.

The use of VIS is controversial. Research into its effects shows mixed results. The purpose of VIS was to add another voice to sentencing, which traditionally had been silent, and to allow victims to gain a therapeutic release. Traditionally, victims are largely ignored by the criminal justice process and do not play an important role unless the prosecutor calls the victim as a witness for the state.

This limited role of the victim is understandable because we have defined the prosecutor's responsibility as representing the state, not private citizens. Private prosecution allows the victim to prosecute the offender for injury and loss. Private prosecution was the process used by the English during colonial times. But in the colonies, the idea of private prosecution soon gave way to public prosecution because it was not workable as a means for keeping developing communities and regions safe and secure under barely subsistence conditions.

Private prosecution individualized justice because it allowed any victim to bring a complaint against any person who victimized him or her. Public prosecution defined justice in terms of wrongs against the state and the welfare of the state. The role of the prosecutor was to prosecute offenses against the state, not to prosecute grievances by individual citizens.

This distinction is at the heart of the controversy over the role of the victim and whether that voice is appropriate for the U.S. system of criminal justice. On the plus side, VIS is touted as a valuable way for judges to have information about the severity of harm done to the victim. But those opposed question whether this information is appropriate for sentencing decisions that are based on deterrence, incapacitation, rehabilitation, and retribution.[20]

What influence should be given to victim suffering when the question is whether the state should reduce the defendant's opportunity for future crime by imprisonment? How should the loss the victim suffered be viewed when at issue is whether the defendant appears to be a good risk for rehabilitation? Does the suffering of one victim deter a defendant from committing more crimes?

While the victim's plight should not be ignored, its value to the state's criminal justice system is marginal. Opponents of VIS argue that shifting the focus of sentencing from the offender to the victim adds an irrelevant aspect to sentencing. The state is prosecuting the defendant, not the victim, and the focus should be on the defendant.

Perhaps more importantly, VIS and bringing victims into the sentencing process also has the potential for creating different classes of victims, "leading to stiffer sanctions for those who offend against particularly eloquent, loved or upper class victims." By allowing victims' voices a say in sentencing, "VIS's potentially create a situation in which sentencing length may be determined by the eloquence and social standing of the victim rather than the severity of the offense and the specific underlying facts of the crime."[21]

Some have proposed a simple solution to this valid criticism, that is, allow the victim to make a statement *after* sentences have been imposed. In this way, the victim would be heard but the influence on sentencing would be eliminated.

There is no denying that comprehensive services to victims are essential and should be routinely provided. The question is whether these services should be located outside the criminal justice system so as to maintain the integrity and existence of the basic assumptions about criminal justice and its relationship to the state.

Restorative justice focuses on crime as an act against another individual or community rather than the state. Today the term encompasses a growing social movement to institutionalize peaceful approaches to harm, problem solving, and violations of legal and human rights. The victim's role in criminal justice has taken on added importance in the restorative justice movement. Restorative justice is a broad term that encompasses many forms, but with some common elements:

- Victims have an opportunity to describe the full impact of the crime on their lives and to hold the offender accountable.
- Offenders can tell the story about the crime and how it affected them. The defendant is given an opportunity to make things right with the victim, typically through some form of compensation like money, community service, self-education, and expressions of remorse.

In criminal cases, the means for restorative justice is through mediation, which involves a face-to-face meeting, in the presence of a trained mediator, between the victim of a crime and the person who committed it. Mediation is an accepted diversion program in many prosecutor's offices, although it generally focuses on less serious misdemeanors like trespassing, neighbor disputes, dogs running loose, and vandalism.

It is when the restorative justice movement expands to include more serious crimes and to involve the entire community in the process of rehabilitating the defendant and making reparations for the victims that it conflicts with the traditional criminal justice system. It introduces some serious questions and calls for substantial systemic changes.

Some questions the movement introduces include: Who is a victim? Is it a single person, a community, a business? Who gets to decide? Is it legislators, judges, local government officials, community alliances? Who decides who gets to participate from the community and how? What are the criteria for choosing?

Are all victims equal for a given act? Are the very young or very old to be treated differently? What if the victim is less than upstanding?

Who decides who an offender is? With what criteria? Who decides whether a defendant is likely to express remorse and change his or her lifestyle? What type of restoration is best suited for each situation and each offender?

The attempt to develop a restorative justice program for offenders convicted of driving without a license or on a suspended license in Spokane,

Washington, produced good insight into these questions and the resistance of the formal criminal justice system to the proposed concept.[22]

The concept of restorative justice and its emphasis on offender accountability is one that permeates many diversion, mediation, and dispute resolution programs. In that sense, it is not foreign to the criminal justice system. What is foreign to our system is the concept of victims influencing sentencing decisions and the offender's acceptance of responsibility for his or her actions and being remorseful also impacting sentences.

There has always been a place in our society for social justice, but it is outside the bounds of the criminal justice system and the adversary system of checks and balances. The relationships between victims and offenders and the restorative powers of accountability and remorse are better served in social service settings than in the criminal justice world.

Conclusion

The relationships between police, prosecutors, defense counsel, and the court define and differentiate local criminal justice systems in such a way that criminal justice varies from one courthouse to another, and even from one courtroom to another. In these environments, the dynamics of disposing cases not only cause changes but also affect the ease with which dispositions are obtained.

Each of the participants in adjudication plays a role that ultimately affects the outcome of cases and the sanctions imposed. The quality of law enforcement and its priorities, professionalism, and resources in large measure set the stage for successful prosecutions. But it is the stances taken by the prosecutor, defense counsel, and judges that define how cases are disposed, the routes they take, and the barriers that are erected along the way. In the end, however, it is the judge who imposes sentence, and the judge's philosophy about crime and criminals, tempered by legislative mandates, that determines the type and severity of the sanctions imposed.

CHAPTER FIVE

Falling Apart

In the previous four chapters the focus was on the decisions prosecutors make to bring cases to disposition and the stages of the adjudication process where the prosecutor was most influential. These included intake and screening; charging; the accusatory process, including indictments and preliminary hearings; the disposition routes to guilty pleas or trials; and post-conviction activities.

As cases traveled these routes to disposition, individual forces affected the outcome, like the quality of police investigations; the policies and priorities of the prosecutor, judges, and defense counsel; the structure of the courts; and community values. This view of the decision-making process seems straightforward, but it is a sanitized version not often mirrored in the real world. In that world, different environments exist that profoundly affect the decisions made and the outcomes obtained. The impact of some or all of these external forces in different environments has yet to be examined.

In real life, the combinations of factors produce different criminal justice environments. These environments give local criminal justice systems different identities; more importantly, the patterns of dispositions are quite different from those found in other court systems. As a result, defendants convicted in one jurisdiction may be acquitted in another, and in still others the case may have been declined for prosecution.

Describing the impact of these forces and associated dynamics is not an easy task because so many forces may come into play. Still, it can be simplified by looking at cases that ended in unexpected ways and in which the prosecutor did not achieve the hoped-for reasonable and appropriate disposition or sanction. Many seem to think prosecutors are invincible and defense attorneys have little or no chance to obtain an optimal result for the client. The truth is that if prosecutors reject weak cases and require the police to investigate with vigor and provide a complete and high-quality report, the odds are against the defense. However, the decisions made at intake are far from perfect. Police departments appear to be more interested in arrests than convictions. The prosecutor may be up against a judge whose decisions lean toward the defense, and occasionally a very good defense attorney is at the table poking little holes into the case. All of these issues and more can leave the prosecutor with a case that is springing leaks.

When cases break down, they are usually the result of an unfortunate mix of people, events, and decisions that create ill-advised responses. Rarely can blame be attributed to a single agency or entity. However, the prosecutor invariably plays a major role because of the ability to exert checks on some parts of the system and make changes during the different stages of the disposition process.

In the early stages of adjudication, police are initiators in bringing cases forward and later may serve as witnesses in court. Defense counsel appear only after an arrest, and the court exercises control after charges are filed. Only the prosecutor transcends all stages of adjudication—charging, pretrial, trial, and postconviction.

The adversarial system of justice is premised on the assumption that this approach will provide checks on abuses of power and in the end produce an outcome that reflects a balance among competing interests. When checks and balances are absent, or the prosecutor's decision making is questionable, or even when misconduct occurs, cases may be headed down the wrong route for an inappropriate disposition.

Following this overview, the road to disposition is traveled by five cases as unfortunate decisions are made that produce undesirable outcomes. In each of the following chapters, the dynamics of the forces affected by the case are analyzed to determine the extent to which the prosecution could have chosen alternative responses or taken other actions that might have increased the chances of obtaining a reasonable and appropriate disposition in the quickest time with the least use of resources.

Each case shows different perspectives of local systems of criminal justice in action. Priority attention is given to determining the extent to which the prosecutor's decisions and choices were contributing factors in the outcome. The extent to which the prosecutor shares or creates the unanticipated outcomes is evaluated. Since prosecutorial misconduct plays a role in the cases, it is useful to take a brief look at that problem.

Prosecutors Cross the Line

Like all human beings, even prosecutors make mistakes. From a professional, ethical perspective, the most serious is the abuse of fiduciary powers. The frequency of these mistakes can be gathered from each state's bar association, which maintains a list of lawyers who have fallen under professional scrutiny and the range of punishments that were invoked. Most serious is disbarment, which frequently is caused by an attorney's embezzlement or misuse of a client's funds. In the public sector, it is often due to undisclosed exculpatory evidence or biased or prejudicial behavior. Moving down the sanctioning scale are suspensions of licenses for varying lengths of times, then censures or reprimands, which include warnings and cautions about inappropriate behavior.

Investigations of inappropriate behavior by bar associations typically are initiated by a complaint and are conducted in secret by a grievance commission. If the attorney is cleared, then generally his or her record is cleared also so that no one knows of the complaint. In contrast, if grounds are found for the complaint, the case is heard by a judge who makes a finding, which may be appealed by either the state grievance commission (acting in defense of the complaint) or by the attorney charged and/or his or her attorneys. The findings of the court and its sanction are available to the public, although those usually have to be accessed through the bar association if there is no media publicity attached to the event.

Many attorneys survive because they operate in a world that tolerates their behavior and rarely criticizes their decisions. Law enforcement agencies accede to their political power; defense counsel behaves well during plea negotiations; and the media are generally uneducated in the niceties of ethical behavior in law and professional responsibilities. Conditions harboring inappropriate behavior frequently may be found in smaller jurisdictions that have relatively few judges and defense counsel, infrequent serious violent crimes, and a "good old boy" atmosphere.

So why do prosecutors get into trouble? A lot of it can be traced to a combination of factors that include egos, power, and stubborn arrogance. The main culprit for elected officials is ego. The daily doses of political power induce a state of arrogance. Somewhere in the course of their march to elective status and its affirmation by reelection, they become infected by a belief that they are either above the law or can make better decisions than those required by standards, rules, and guidelines, which define professional behavior and responsibility. The old saying "power corrupts and absolute power corrupts absolutely" applies especially to elected officials.

Other factors influencing misconduct can be as simple as personal problems such as drug abuse, alcoholism, gambling addictions, or simple greed. Sometimes it just reflects a person's complete inability to grasp the concept of ethical and responsible behavior.

This was an issue in the Duke rape case, which is discussed in detail in chapter 7. The basic problem was the failure to disclose exculpatory evidence, evidence that could point away from the defendant. The laws that require providing full discovery of the prosecutor's case to defense counsel were developed to avoid precisely this problem. Unfortunately, it's all too common. Two federal prosecutors were found to have withheld exculpatory evidence in the corruption trial of Senator Ted Stevens. The prosecutors were suspended and the case was dismissed. The prosecutors had their disciplinary action reversed for improper administrative actions but were not cleared of wrongdoing. Certainly a dismissal was not the reasonable and appropriate disposition the U.S. Justice Department sought.

In Oregon, a well-respected chief prosecutor was the target of a charge of unethical behavior brought by the Oregon Bar Association. The prosecutor was charged with refusing to plea bargain with 15 defendants who were represented by a particular law firm. The defendants were required to find new representation before a plea bargain could be offered by the prosecutor. With new counsel the plea offers were forthcoming. However, complaints were filed with the bar association. The trial board that heard the case agreed that the prosecutor was overzealous in the execution of his office and ordered a six-month suspension of the prosecutor's law license. Subsequently, a review board agreed with the findings of the trial board, but instead of the six-month suspension the requirement of a public reprimand was approved.

Hiding exculpatory evidence and attempting to punish legal counsel are not the only ways prosecutors can find the way to hot water. In a bar in North Carolina the prosecutor had an argument with another patron and used racial epithets and other profanities. Many observed the subsequent confrontation between the two parties, which ended with the prosecutor's ejection from the bar. When word of the incident got out, a group of local attorneys petitioned the court to have the prosecutor removed from office. The judge ruled that the prosecutor's behavior was prejudicial to the administration of justice. The case was appealed to the state Supreme Court, which affirmed the removal decision.[1]

In Maryland, a prosecutor made "extrajudicial" statements to the press that violated professional standards. The court ruled that the prosecutor committed professional misconduct by discussing a defendant's confession and plea deal with the press, and by offering opinions regarding the guilt of two other defendants. This route to hot water is perhaps all too common. The media is after a story, and impromptu comments on developing cases can be a serious problem.

The final example comes from the state of Michigan. The prosecutor was one of the profession's leading lights on the development of diversion programs and prosecuting white-collar crime. In an appalling lack of judgment, he "borrowed" more than $30,000 from a fund dedicated to undercover operations. This was a major breach of the public trust and cost the prosecutor nearly four years in prison.

A study by the Center for Public Integrity[2] examined 11,452 cases in which charges of prosecutorial misconduct were reviewed by appellate court judges. It found that since 1970 at least 2,012 cases cited prosecutorial misconduct as a factor when dismissing charges at trial, reversing convictions, or reducing sentences. It also identified 223 prosecutors around the nation who had been cited by judges for two or more cases of unfair conduct. Only two had been disbarred in the past 33 years for mishandling criminal cases.

The study also found that misconduct covered a wide range of activities. These included making inappropriate or inflammatory remarks in front of a jury to mischaracterizing or mishandling physical evidence, hiding evidence or failing to disclose exculpatory evidence, threatening or badgering witnesses, using false or misleading evidence, or harassing or displaying bias against the defendant or defendant's counsel, among others.[3]

The Cases

In the following chapters, five cases are used to illustrate how cases can unravel and do not reach what the prosecutor would call a reasonable and appropriate disposition. Three cases are infamous and two may acquire comparable reputations given the outcomes.

Two cases are excellent examples of political forces and the media causing lapses in prosecutorial judgment. One is the 2011 prosecution by New York district attorney Cyrus Vance Jr. of Dominique Strauss-Kahn (DSK) for the sexual assault, attempted rape, and sexual abuse of a hotel cleaning woman. The other reviews the investigation and prosecution of three Duke University lacrosse players charged with raping a stripper hired to perform at a private party. Actions taken by North Carolina district attorney Michael Nifong during this highly charged case resulted in disbarment.

The third case concerns the 1996 murder of JonBenet Ramsey in Boulder, Colorado, which is still unsolved despite intensive investigations and huge outlays of taxpayer money. The police-prosecutor interface plays a major role in the case, as does the powerful role of the prosecutor to accept or reject cases or to do neither. The local legal and social environments also play a role.

The fourth case examines the 2011 prosecution of Casey Anthony, acquitted of killing her three-year-old child but found guilty of four misdemeanor counts involving lying to police officers. This is an excellent example of problematic charging decisions and a defense lawyer who would not yield. Here the prosecutor tries to prove a difficult case but misses the chance to take a more reasonable and appropriate disposition, probably without the risk of a trial.

Finally, the last case is reserved for the trial of O. J. Simpson for the brutal murder of his wife and her friend in 1995, which produced a veritable circus of questionable behaviors and an acquittal on grounds never charged. It also shows what happens when the prosecutors are not in the same league as the defense attorneys. However, the prosecutors had options far before the case went to trial in choosing the legal environment in which to operate and establishing a properly supported case management system to support the trial assistants.

Each of these cases reflects different types of root causes for being unable to achieve the desired reasonable and appropriate disposition. However, there is a reason why only 3 percent of cases are disposed at trial. A trial exposes all the weaknesses in the prosecution's case and gives the defense plenty of opportunity to create reasonable doubt among the jurors. These weaknesses generally are the result of inept police investigations, poorly collected or protected evidence, bad police-prosecutor relations, misguided or overzealous prosecutorial decisions, uncontrolled defense tactics, questionable judicial objectivity, and the overwhelming influence of the media.

While none of these cases had a result that the prosecutor intended, many had issues to litigate. In those circumstances, the prosecutor should probably prevail 50 percent of the time. The really strong cases should be settled by plea negotiation long before trial. However, the many fingers of blame in these cases show the critical importance of high ethical standards, good management throughout the criminal justice system, but most of all, the education of the stakeholders, the public, and media about the dynamics of a process created by discretion, policy, and priorities.

CHAPTER SIX

DSK: A Rush to Judgment

In the spring of 2011, Dominique Strauss-Kahn (DSK) had it all. He enjoyed international fame and approbation as managing director of the International Monetary Fund (IMF) and was considered likely to win the 2012 election for president of France. Often known simply by his initials, DSK was wealthy, secure, and headed for an even brighter future. The flames that destroyed his future and perhaps changed his country's future were ignited, strangely enough, by a rush to judgment initiated by experienced investigators and the elected prosecutor in one of the largest and most historic prosecution offices in the United States.

Not only was the Manhattan district attorney's office misled by the complainant, Nafissatou Diallo, the 32-year-old hotel maid from Guinea who charged DSK with rape and assault, but the ultimate unraveling of her testimony hinted at a more serious criminal conspiracy with others who coached her in presenting a credible story until finally, six weeks later, she admitted her lies. During this interval, DSK resigned from the IMF, proclaiming his innocence, and saw his hopes for winning the title President of France vanish despite a turnaround in the evidence that was to lead to a total dismissal of all charges against him.

The Facts

On Saturday, May 14, 2011, at 1:30 p.m. the New York Police Department responded to a call from the Hotel Sofitel alleging that a guest in the hotel had sexually assaulted a maid who had entered to clean his room, thinking it empty. A naked man had appeared from the bathroom and forced her to have oral sex. The man was identified as Dominique Strauss-Kahn (DSK), the managing director of the International Monetary Fund (IMF) and a political power in France. His whereabouts were unknown since he had checked out of the hotel.

By sheer coincidence, DSK was waiting at the airport for his flight to Paris, scheduled to depart at 4:40 p.m., when he noticed his phone was missing. He called the hotel to inquire if they had found it. The hotel staff informed the police investigating the case of the call, and the police asked the NY Port Authority police to detain him. DSK was removed from the plane 10 minutes before its scheduled departure and was taken into custody. He was held at the Rikers Island jail pending investigation.[1]

On Sunday, May 15, a lineup was held and the maid, Nafissatou Diallo, identified him as her attacker. Additional evidence, including her work clothes and semen, was collected from the room and submitted for analysis. DSK was arrested and charged with four felonies and three misdemeanors. On that same day, Diallo was recorded calling an imprisoned man and discussing the potential rewards that might come to her.

On Monday, May 16, DSK was arraigned in criminal court on the arrest charges. The judge denied a bail request from his attorneys and remanded DSK to Rikers Island pending a grand jury investigation.

Two days later, on May 18, the case was presented to the grand jury. DSK chose not to testify. The grand jury handed up an indictment that same day. Also on this day DSK submitted his letter of resignation as managing director of the IMF.

The following day, May 19, DSK again applied for bail, which was granted with conditions. The conditions included bail set in the amount of $1 million in cash and a $5 million bond. In addition, DSK surrendered his passport and was placed under house arrest at a rented townhouse where he was confined with an ankle bracelet and subject to electronic monitoring at his own expense.

On May 23 the forensic test results showed that evidence from Diallo's work clothes matched the DNA samples taken from DSK.

Two weeks later, on June 6, DSK was arraigned in Manhattan's Supreme Court on the indictment.[2] He pleaded not guilty to several first-degree felony counts including criminal sexual act, attempted rape, and sexual abuse, and his counsel filed for discovery. The case was adjourned until July 18.

Investigations continued until June 30, when the victim's lawyers notified the prosecutor that their investigators had uncovered major problems with Diallo's credibility and that they no longer believed much of what she told them. As a result, on July 1, the court released DSK on his own recognizance after a hearing in Supreme Court where prosecutors acknowledged the weaknesses of the case. The prosecutor retained DSK's passport and travel documents.

The following day the July 18 court date was rescheduled for August 1 to give both sides more investigative time, then rescheduled again to August 23.

During this period, Diallo filed a civil lawsuit in Bronx County Court on August 8 seeking unspecified monetary damages for a "violent and sadistic attack" and "intentional infliction of emotional distress." As *Time* magazine noted, "Timing is unusual because civil complaints almost never get filed while criminal charges are still pending."[3]

Finally, on August 22, the district attorney filed a Recommendation for Dismissal in Supreme Court.[4] The following day, August 23, the case was dismissed and all charges were dropped. On September 5, DSK returned to France.

From the initial report on May 14 to the final dismissal of all charges, this case existed for 14 weeks and 3 days. It took only five days to indict the defendant on the charges and another six weeks before the prosecutor's office formally admitted to its substantial evidentiary weaknesses. The last half of this case's short life was consumed primarily by procedural formalities.

Analysis

The controversies arising from this case focus mainly on the exercise of prosecutorial discretion at intake and in the accusatory phase of case processing. Only two decisions materially affected this case—namely, the decision to take the case to the grand jury for indictment before a comprehensive investigation was finished and the decision to oppose bail. For both decisions, more than one choice was available. The effect of the ones chosen are now known; unknown are the outcomes that could have resulted had other choices been made.

The first question involves intake and charging, whether the case should have been accepted for prosecution, and why so quickly? Given the nature of the case, the lack of corroborating evidence, and the fact that it began to unravel only a week after the offense, why was an indictment sought within four days of arrest even before a preliminary investigation was completed? Could the district attorney have been influenced by other forces than prosecution in proceeding so quickly? In other words, could other alternatives have been chosen that would have avoided or mitigated the damage to the victim, the defendant, the prosecutor, costs to the criminal justice system, and even the international reputation of our system of justice?

The weakness of discussing cases after the fact is that the outcome is known but the reasons for it usually are hidden. This problem is overcome by identifying the other choices that were available and within the prosecutor's discretion. The expected effects of those options can be compared to those that were actually chosen. This type of examination may allow one to reach a more balanced conclusion about the outcome, and about whether and to what degree the prosecutor's responses contributed to the final disposition of the case.

In this event, one could not have predicted the ramifications of a sexual encounter May 14, 2011, in the Hotel Sofitel in New York City when Ms. Diallo let herself into the room occupied by Dominique Strauss-Kahn, announced "housekeeping," and encountered a nude male emerging from his bathroom. What happened next created a criminal offense that everyone agrees is difficult to prosecute because it usually lacks corroborating evidence and relies on the credibility of the victim and defendant. It also created worldwide interest and exposed the reputation of the New York criminal justice system to ridicule, at least in France.

DSK admitted to having oral sex with Ms. Diallo, claiming it was consensual. She, with varying explanations, admitted that the act occurred but under extreme force. After waiting for more than an hour, she reported the incident to her supervisor, who notified the police. At about 1:30 p.m. the NYPD arrived, secured the crime scene, and took Ms. Diallo's report. Semen found on the floor and wall was retrieved, and later testing identified DSK as its owner. He admitted to ownership but claimed the act was consensual.

The decisions of the police to initially detain DSK are reasonable. Under the circumstances, with the suspect ready to depart for France, which makes extradition of its citizens difficult if not impossible, coupled with the seriousness of the charges, the police had no other option.

What outraged DSK's French countrymen was the media coverage, including television coverage, when the police brought the defendant in for a lineup and booking. This practice is commonly known in the United States as the "perp walk." It produced unanticipated outrage among the French viewing the public shaming of one of the country's most distinguished personages. The police, media, and few in the criminal justice system were unaware of the impact of this frequently used procedure on the defendant's home country, in this case France.

In the United States, the system of justice is adversarial. It assumes that those charged with crimes are innocent until proven guilty. It challenges the state, through its prosecutors, to prove guilt beyond a reasonable doubt, and in some cases, provides defense counsel to represent the accused in court if they cannot afford to pay. The basic premise is that by creating adversaries—namely, pitting the defense against the prosecution—the "truth will out." The judge and sometimes a jury serve as arbiters and rule on the facts and evidence presented at trial.

In contrast, France has an inquisitorial system of justice, as does Italy and Spain, among others. In this system, there is no presumption of innocence.[5]

An examining judge conducts the investigation of the facts of the case, questions witnesses, interrogates suspects, and orders other investigation as needed. Prosecutors and defense counsel may ask questions, but the goal of the inquiry is to determine whether there is a valid case against the suspect, a process that may consume months.

During this investigation, the privacy of the suspect is generally respected and held confidential until the person is formally accused, charged, and arrested. The assumption of "innocent until proven guilty" is not relevant in inquisitorial systems, which seek the acquisition of truth about cases under investigation.

If the examining judge finds enough evidence, the accused is bound over for an adversarial trial. A trial judge and jury who determine guilt or innocence replace the examining judge. Most serious or complex cases go to trial where, based on the substantial examination of evidence, convictions are generally the rule. Cases where the evidence is weak tend not to reach the trial stage.

These differences help explain, in part, France's public outrage against the actions taken by police and the prosecutor as a result of U.S. media identifying the defendant and subjecting him to instant notoriety. They also point to weaknesses in our U.S. system that make a "rush to judgment" possible, and the disastrous consequences it may provoke.

Adversarial systems, based on the presumption of innocence of the suspect until proven guilty, employ an array of checks and balances to ensure fairness and minimize any tendency to let one component of the criminal justice system ride roughshod over another. Those checks and balances are especially important in the early processing steps from arrest to charging. Prosecutors have the power to check the police, and courts can temper the results of both sets of decisions if the police and prosecutors step out of line. If pressure to speed up the investigative process prevails, undesirable results may occur.

The relevant questions focus on the prosecutor's decision to file charges after only a preliminary investigation, despite the stated policy of the office to prosecute only those cases where the defendant was guilty "beyond a reasonable doubt." So why the haste to file charges when the case was based on preliminary investigations and weak evidence? This case shared many of the same characteristics as those involving public corruption. The prosecutor might have a weak case but would rather have the case decided in the courts rather than rejecting the case outright. The DSK case involved a very public and powerful figure accused by someone who appeared to be a relatively powerless victim of color. Not knowing anything further, it is a somewhat natural response to address the power differences by moving aggressively to charge, to teach the elite a lesson. Another possibility is that achieving a conviction in a high-profile case can bring political benefits of widespread publicity flowing to a newly elected prosecutor. That is a double-edged sword since an acquittal can yield widespread negative publicity.

The decision to go for an indictment in such a short period of time (four days after the incident) with little evidence to support the case except the victim's testimony was dangerous since typically the resolution of "he said, she said" cases rest on the credibility of the two persons involved. Despite this, the prosecutors justified their request for an indictment in their Recommendation for Dismissal memo stating, "Investigation between the time of the incident and May 18 revealed no red flags in the complainant's background."[6]

Prosecutors noted that the hotel had employed Ms. Diallo for three years without incident. She had no criminal history; and although she had used a false visa to enter the United States, she readily admitted it. The forensic evidence was consistent with a nonconsensual sexual encounter and supported the claim that a sexual encounter had happened, but did not resolve whether it was consensual or forcible.

Priority for prosecution always involves the seriousness of the offense, the criminal background of the offender, and the strength of the evidence. DSK did not have a criminal history, at least in the United States, and the evidence was thin at best. An assistant district attorney would usually ask the police for more evidence before formally charging or asking for an indictment.

With the evidence collected so far, there was no compelling reason to seek an early indictment unless it was to continue the pretrial detention of the defendant. If this were the case, the prosecutor's priority for having more investigative time before filing charges would have to yield to speedy trial conditions established to protect abuse of pretrial detention.

Pretrial detention cannot be viewed as a "freebie" jail sentence available to law enforcement or prosecutors. "Doing sheriff's time, or prosecutor's time" is just plain unethical. Bail has two objectives: one is to prevent a defendant from fleeing the jurisdiction while pending charges (the risk of flight); the other, to reduce the risk of the defendant being a danger to the community if released pending trial (preventive detention). DSK had surrendered his passport by this time so the risk of flight was minimal.

Prior to the 1970s most jurisdictions treated bail as an either/or situation (cash or jail). After that, bail reform movements and the National Standards and Goals for Pretrial Release and Pretrial Diversion[7] focused attention on the viability of alternatives to incarceration while pending prosecution.

New York City was one of the leaders in the bail reform movement. The Manhattan Bail Project, initiated by the Vera Institute of Justice, found that defendants with jobs, ties to the community, and family roots were good candidates for release on their own recognizance and would lessen the financial burden on the jails.[8] In 1978, the New York Association of Pretrial Services Agencies was founded to develop, sponsor, and advocate for nonincarcerative alternatives for the disposition of criminal cases including monitoring, supervision, and employment programs, among others.

The pretrial release conditions that DSK's attorneys initially requested and were denied by the lower District Court were not unusual though extremely high in dollar value.[9] It had already been determined that DSK did not have diplomatic immunity and his passport had been seized. Clearly, given his background, international stature, and public recognition, the likelihood of him being a danger to the community was not an issue. Still, the fear of flight persisted and the prosecutor prevailed in his argument for denial of bail. But he did so at his own peril.

When bail was denied on May 16, the judicial clock started running. To keep DSK in custody, the prosecutor knew that he had to obtain a grand jury indictment within 144 hours or DSK would be released on bail, probably with some of the conditions that his defense counsel and the court agreed to. Now the conflict between custody and investigation emerged. Six days is a very short time to investigate a case with inherent evidentiary problems, no corroborating witnesses, a claim and admission by the defendant that the event was consensual, no conclusive evidence of forcible rape, and victim whose credibility had not been established in any meaningful way.

Ironically, once the felony indictment was obtained, five days after his initial detention, the Supreme Court judge approved bail with conditions similar to the ones that DSK's defense counsel had been denied at the initial arraignment. If the goal of prosecution had been to deny pretrial release to the defendant, it did not succeed. Worse yet, it erased any opportunity for the prosecutor to protect himself if subsequent investigation weakened the evidence.

Could the prosecutor have chosen another accusatory route that would have bought more time? Perhaps that route would have provided a few additional days but with more potential risk to a successful outcome. In New York, felony cases may be brought forward either by grand jury indictment or by Supreme Court information. This latter accusatory instrument is a written accusation by a district attorney and serves as a basis for prosecution. In this case a bill would have to be filed within 10 days or the defendant would be released.[10] Not much advantage here.

For a defendant, the advantages of the Supreme Court information are not being indicted by a grand jury, the opportunity for defense counsel to negotiate terms and conditions of release, possibly a negotiated guilty plea, and a probable cause hearing at which defense counsel will hear some of the prosecutor's evidence. For the prosecutor, the same advantages also hold in addition to extending the time to release from jail if the information is not filed within 10 days. In general, bills of information are used if time is needed to negotiate a plea of guilty.

If the district attorney thought the case was a "slam-dunk," the choice of a grand jury indictment would be strategically more valuable than the bill of information where the ensuing probable cause hearing would not only expose some of the evidence but also heighten media attention. But the case was far from being a slam-dunk based on a four-day superficial investigation of the victim and the circumstances.

More surprising, in light of the essential need for further investigation by prosecutors experienced in sex crimes and "he said, she said" cases,[11] the case was transferred from the sex crimes bureau to other experienced assistants in the office.

The quick indictment and transfer of the case out of the sex crimes unit served to undercut the priority for a more complete investigation. It also contradicted the stated charging policy of the office. In their Recommendation for Dismissal memo they avowed that they would not try any case if they did not believe that the defendant was guilty beyond a reasonable doubt. "If we do not believe her beyond a reasonable doubt, we cannot ask a jury to do so."[12] Having said that, in the same breath, they justified bringing the case to the grand jury, stating, "At the time of the indictment, all available evidence satisfied us that the complainant was reliable. But evidence gathered in our post-indictment investigation severely undermined her reliability as a witness in this case."[13]

Given the seriousness of the offense, the notoriety of the defendant, and the potential evidentiary problems with these types of cases, it certainly should have warranted a longer investigation period to explore the facts. In fact, it only took two and a half weeks until the June 7 letter from Diallo's attorney alerted the district attorney's office that the complainant had not been truthful. In a June 28 interview with her lawyer, three prosecutors, and an investigator, she also admitted lying to the grand jury. On June 30, the prosecutor disclosed the false statements and other potentially exculpatory evidence to the court, starting the unraveling process.

Why then the rush for an indictment? In the Recommendation for Dismissal, the prosecutors note, "Pursuant to CPL §180.80, the People were required within 144 hours to present evidence to a grand jury and obtain an indictment in order to avoid the defendant's release from custody."[14] In the normal course of prosecuting felony cases, investigating the strength of the evidence—including the reliability of witnesses—should take top priority before accusatory instruments are prepared. This case is a perfect example of the wisdom of this approach.

By opting to keep the defendant in custody based on an indictment, the clock was set and the results not unexpected. One cannot blame the grand jury. They were presented with the evidence prepared by the police and the prosecutor; DSK refused to testify as was his right; and what else was the grand jury to do? Right, it indicted.

The alternative to a quick indictment was having the prosecutor agree to bail so both sides could gain time to investigate the case. Most importantly, the prosecutor would have time to continue the investigations and not lose face in the process.

In the end, one has to inquire about the role of the district attorney in the progress of this case. There is little escape from drawing a conclusion that he was the primary decision maker, and lots of evidence that points the finger at him.

As leader, he is responsible for setting the policies and priorities for the office and for ensuring that the decisions made by others are consistent with them. When chief prosecutors are first elected to the position, the community seldom knows how the prosecutor will define and use the discretionary power accorded to the position.

Cyrus Vance Jr. was in his first term as Manhattan's district attorney, following in the footsteps of the legendary Robert Morgenthau, who retired after 34 years as district attorney. Vance was well connected politically through his father, who was secretary of state for Jimmy Carter, and schooled in the diplomacy of power and success. After graduating from Georgetown Law School (1982) he became an assistant district attorney in the prestigious Manhattan district attorney's office until 1988. There he rose quickly through the ranks, gaining experience in prosecuting complex felony cases, including conducting grand jury investigations and prosecuting organized crime, political corruption, international art theft, and white-collar crimes. His experience tagged him as an up-and-coming young candidate for higher office where his skills as a good and valuable assistant prosecutor could be extended.

In 1988 he moved to Seattle, Washington, motivated by a desire to escape his father's shadow.[15] There he co-founded a law firm specializing in litigation, real estate, technology law, and business. He also taught law as an adjunct instructor at the University of Seattle Law School. In 2004 he returned to New York as a principal in a private law firm where he remained until his decision to run for district attorney.

His public credentials were further enhanced by his active involvement in sentencing reform policy, serving appointments to the governor's sentencing commission, and a number of other commissions involving ethics, judicial appointments, appellate review decisions, and so on; all activities leading finally to his candidacy for district attorney in 2008 and assumption of office in 2010.

Not surprisingly, like most first-term prosecutors, his record as the New York County (Manhattan) district attorney has been inconsistent. He is given credit for supporting community-based justice and making it a priority to reduce case backlog in the criminal court. Also, like most newly elected prosecutors, he reorganized parts of the office he inherited by establishing a number of new units and programs that reflected his previous experiences and current priorities. Some of these included a conviction integrity program to review allegations of wrongful convictions, a cold case unit, a hate crimes unit, a special victims bureau, and a violent criminal enterprises unit.

His conviction record has been both notable and sometimes disappointing.[16] When newly elected prosecutors take office, their first term is generally tumultuous as the new "boss" imposes change. It is not uncommon in the larger offices to see staff loyalty divided between the "old" and the "new," especially when the "old" has had close to a generational life span with one district attorney. It is also not uncommon for a first-term prosecutor to second-guess his staff's procedures, sometimes with negative results. It does not help his private or public image that this case with all its attendant publicity ended up with the court dismissing all charges.

The media has raised the question about how his handling of this case will affect his political power. His supporters[17] claim that he followed the rules and that under pressure of the time constraints imposed by the law and the court, he had no choice but to act as he did. In fact, they praise his professionalism and honesty, citing his quick response and courage to drop all charges once the investigation destroyed the credibility of the witness. They praise the trial policy of the office, which calls for prosecution only if there is a belief that the office could prove beyond a reasonable doubt that the defendant is guilty. As additional support they contrast his timely dismissal of the charges once they became known with abuses by other prosecutors who "deliberately ignore evidence that may prove a defendant innocent."[18]

On the other hand, his antagonists condemn him for micro-managing and interfering with accepted procedures, for making decisions for political gain, not supporting victim's rights, being insensitive to women's rights, and letting the defendant's reputation, social status, and power influence the handling of the case. Other professionals in the system believe that he may have caved in to the rush because of its intense media attention and the likelihood of a big win for the office. There is probably much to be said for both sides.

However, reform activists can applaud this case and use its many twists to argue for reforms to the bail system with its rigid time constraints on release, ensuring the privacy of the suspect and victim until the evidence supports prosecution, and providing sufficient time to investigate serious cases while still controlling unnecessary delay.

Conclusion

For a case with such a short life span, the lessons learned far exceed the time it consumed. District Attorney Vance has probably learned a lesson about being cautious with the power that comes with his job. This does not necessarily mean that he will become fearful or indecisive. There is little in his background to point to this, and there is much in his statement acknowledging a policy of taking cases to trial only if they can be proven beyond a reasonable doubt as a justification for dismissal. To his credit, he did not publicly lay blame on others or try to excuse his actions, but rather accepted responsibility for an "unforeseen" turn of events. Still, abandoning well-known principles for reviewing cases thoroughly, and carefully assessing the quality of evidence before charging a case, places the prosecutor in peril.

Unlike other prosecutors who for one reason or another could not admit mistakes, this case provides a hopeful aspect. This prosecutor has a chance to grow in his job.

CHAPTER SEVEN

The Duke Lacrosse Players: Prosecutorial Misconduct

In the DSK case discussed in the last chapter, it was clear that charges were filed in a case where it was not clear that a crime had been committed, the defendant was an unlikely criminal, and there were no corroborating witnesses to back up the victim, who was clearly unreliable. In the end, the prosecutor had to admit there was no case and dismiss charges that probably should not have been filed. That was the correct disposition, just occurring too late.

The prosecution of members of the Duke University lacrosse team for rape is another example of a case that should not have been filed, but with much more pain and suffering as the defendants and their families twisted in the wind while being smeared by the university and its faculty.

While all this was happening, a newly elected prosecutor, although he had many years as an assistant prosecutor, was failing to follow the tenets of the profession and to discharge his sworn duties as an officer of the court. Unlike the prosecutor in the DSK case, he could not come to terms with his poorly documented charging decision. That inability to reverse course and end the pain and suffering he created led to a path that would cost him dearly. Here are the details.

The Facts

On March 13, 2006, the Duke University lacrosse team hired two women as exotic dancers for their team party. The dancers were the only outsiders among the 47 lacrosse players. The strippers (or exotic dancers) were black; 46 of the 47 players were white. Sometime between 11:30 p.m. and 12:53 a.m. one of the women, a 27-year-old dancer named Crystal Gail Mangum, who was also a college student at historically black North Carolina Central University, claimed that she had been sexually assaulted and beaten by three white men around midnight at the off-campus party.

The dancers, who had not met each other before that night, arrived together at 11:30 p.m. According to police reports, Mangum was intoxicated at that time. A short time later they left the house fearing for their safety after the players allegedly made some racial remarks. Mangum told police that the two were coaxed back into the house with an apology, at which point they were separated. That's when Mangum said she was dragged into a bathroom and sexually assaulted, beaten, and choked for a half-hour.

The second dancer, Kim Roberts, 31, also a student at North Carolina Central University, called the police at 12:53 a.m. from outside the house, complaining that she had been called racial slurs by white men gathered outside the house. This was partially corroborated by a taxi driver who had been called by Reade Seligmann (a lacrosse player who was to become one of the defendants). The cab driver reported that he picked up Seligmann at about 12:19 a.m. and saw a woman leaving the party in anger. He overheard someone say that she was just a stripper and was going to call the police. The two women left the party and drove to a grocery store where the security guard called 911 at 1:30 a.m. to report a woman in the parking lot who was drunk, mean, and would not get out of the other lady's car. The police responded in about five minutes and reported that Mangum was unconscious, stating, "She's just a passed out drunk."

Upon questioning by the police, Mangum was barely coherent, but when she said she had been raped, the police transported her to the hospital for an examination. The description of the woman's medical exam does not mention her being drunk. It states only that the woman's injuries and behavior were consistent with having been raped, sexually assaulted, and having suffered a traumatic experience. Roberts, the second dancer, said that Mangum never gave her any reason to believe that she had been attacked.

In an April interview with the Associated Press, Roberts said she initially doubted the accuser's story but had changed her mind. "I was not in the bathroom when it happened, so I can't say a rape occurred—and I never will." But she added, "In all honesty, I think they're guilty." Defense attorneys said that they believe Roberts changed her story to gain favorable treatment in a separate criminal case.[1]

In the week following the arrests, the district attorney, Michael Nifong, by his own admission, told the media that he planned to prosecute the case himself, and by his own account gave more than 50 interviews and spent 40 hours responding to media requests for information.[2]

Ten days after the party, Nifong's chief assistant obtained a court order requiring 46 members of the team to submit to DNA testing and other identification procedures including a photo lineup. The 47th member of the team was excused because he was black and the accuser said her attacker was white.

On March 28 the findings of the DNA tests conducted by the State Bureau of Investigation (SBI) stated that there was no rape kit evidence of semen, blood, or saliva. In spite of this Nifong vowed to press ahead with the case. He argued that in 75 to 80 percent of all sexual assault cases, there is no DNA evidence. In those cases prosecutors had to proceed "the good old-fashioned way. Witnesses got on the stand and told what happened to them."[3]

On March 31, 2006, Nifong sat with the two primary Durham Police Department detectives on the case. The accuser was having trouble identifying her attackers. According to notes taken by Sergeant Mark Gottlieb, Nifong suggested that the officers have the accuser look at pictures of 46 team members to see whether she remembered seeing them at the party. This type of lineup violated police department guidelines that called for at least five nonsuspects for every suspect. The guidelines also called for an independent administrator to conduct the lineup, not an investigator in the case. No one in the police department objected.[4]

On April 4 Mangum identified the three defendants as the men who raped her. The following day Nifong filed a motion in court asking the judge to order a private lab to conduct additional DNA tests. He claimed that the DNA tests performed by the SBI failed to reveal the presence of semen on swabs from the rape kit or the victim's underwear.

On April 17, 2006, a grand jury indicted lacrosse team members Reade Seligmann and Collin Finnerty on charges of rape, kidnapping, and sexual assault.

In North Carolina, the prosecutor is not allowed in the grand jury room. He or she may prepare papers or opinions for the grand jurors, but the prosecutor's presence in the room is not permitted. Law enforcement officers typically present the case. The officers claimed that they were not informed about the results of the DNA testing at the time of the indictment and, therefore, did not report them to the grand jury. Later a member of the grand jury claimed that if they had known that the DNA tests were inconclusive, they would not have voted to indict.

During this two-month period between March and April, Nifong was campaigning in a contested contest for the Democratic nomination. He admitted later that the campaign interfered with his attention to the case.[5] He won the election on May 2, 2006, which essentially ensured his victory in November since the Republicans had not put up a candidate.

Sometime before May 12 the results from the private lab (DNA Security) became available. Nifong met with its director, Brian Meehan, in an
undocumented meeting to discuss the findings. Director Meehan later
stated in court that he and the district attorney agreed to omit the finding
that the DNA tests showed the semen of other unidentified men on the
accuser. Although this information would be vital to the defense, it was
omitted on the grounds that it would "invade the privacy of the lacrosse
players" and was "too explosive."[6] It was this meeting and the subsequent
report dated May 12, 2006, that was to bring about Nifong's downfall by
year's end.

On May 15, 2006, one day after he graduated from Duke, the third
defendant, David Evans, was indicted on the same charges as Reade and
Seligmann.

Communication between Nifong and the private attorneys for the accused
was nonexistent since he refused to meet with them or discuss their evidence. Just after Seligmann was indicted on April 17, his attorneys tried to
show Nifong phone records, sworn statements, and photographs that would
prove that the player had an alibi. Nifong refused to see them. They claimed
that he had an assistant relay his reason: "I saw you on TV proclaiming your
client's innocence, so what is there to talk about?"[7]

Because of his earlier public pretrial statements to the press, Nifong
opened the door for defense counsel to make their case publicly also. Once
one side talks to the press, ethics rules say the other side can make statements that "a reasonable lawyer" would believe to protect a client from bad
publicity. As a result, the voice of the lawyers for the defense gained added
strength and reached a wider audience than expected.

Defense counsel continually protested to the court that Nifong had
not turned over all the evidence as mandated by North Carolina's recent
discovery legislation. The court in response questioned Nifong about the
status of the evidence and whether it had been given to defense counsel.
Relations between the prosecutor and defense counsel continued to dete-
riorate. For example, on May 18, the court ordered Nifong and defense
attorney Kirk Osborn, who were arguing over the evidentiary relevance
of the accuser's cell phone conversations and its admissibility, to work out
a solution so that the material exchanged could be downloaded and provided to the judge for his private review.

On June 23, defense counsel claimed that the evidence given to them
cast more doubt on the case in addition to the accuser's ever-changing
testimony. They were unwavering in their claims that they were not receiving all the evidence while Nifong continued to pursue the case and ignore
their protests.

Meanwhile Nifong's position was becoming more unacceptable and untenable to his colleagues. In late summer and early September, the North Carolina Conference of District Attorneys made preparations to offer Nifong a menu of assistance ranging from advice to the transfer of the case to another prosecutor's office. Its offers went unanswered.

In court hearings in September and October, Nifong stated to the court that he had turned over all DNA evidence and test results to the defense and that he had not interviewed the accuser; and he declared the investigation was largely ended.

On October 27, Nifong continued to insist that all discovery and DNA test results had been forwarded to defense counsel. Based on Nifong's assurances, the judge signed an order that stated, "Mr. Nifong indicated that he did not discuss the facts of the case with Dr. Meehan and that Dr. Meehan said nothing during these meetings beyond what was encompassed in the final report of DNA Security, dated May 12, 2006."[8]

As summer turned into fall, publicity about the case did not diminish; instead, its effects spread in an ever-widening circle. The coach of the lacrosse team resigned under pressure from the university.[9] Eighty-eight faculty members signed a student newspaper advertisement that decried a campus culture of racism and sexism.

Despite the uproar and publicity, on November 7 Nifong was elected district attorney for a four-year term. In December his house came crashing down.

The coup d'état occurred on December 15, when the director of DNA Security, Brian Meehan, testified in court that he and Nifong had agreed the previous spring to omit from the May 12 report results that would be favorable to the defendants—namely, that the tests found DNA from at least four unidentified individuals on vaginal and rectal swabs from the accuser's body and underwear. They did not match anyone on the lacrosse team. He stated that he and Nifong agreed to leave out that information from the report because the case was so "explosive." Meehan admitted that in doing so, he violated the protocols of his own lab.

Nifong told the judge on December 15, "The first I heard of this particular situation was when I was served with this particular motion"[10] on Wednesday, two days earlier.

On December 22, Nifong dismissed the rape charges against the players. According to the dismissal form, the accuser could not be certain she had been raped. This action was taken as a result of interviews by Nifong's chief investigator who did not find her testimony credible. This left the state with prosecutions for kidnapping and sexual assault. Defense counsel claimed that with no DNA evidence linking the suspects, mistakes in the way the photo lineup was conducted, and the accuser's changing story, the DA should drop all charges. Nifong refused.

On December 28 the North Carolina Bar Association filed ethics charges against Nifong accusing him of violating ethics rules by making misleading and inflammatory public statements, of violating a prohibition against making comments that would increase the likelihood of heightening public condemnation of the accused, and engaging in "conduct involving dishonesty, fraud, deceit or misrepresentation."[11]

On December 29, in a seldom-used procedure, the North Carolina Conference of District Attorneys called for Nifong to recuse himself from the case.[12]

On January 12, 2007, Nifong was sworn in as district attorney in a private ceremony. Eleven days later he sent a letter to the state attorney general (AG), Roy Cooper, asking his office to take over the case. Under state law and the North Carolina Department of Justice guidelines, the state AG's office takes over cases in which a prosecutor has a conflict of interest, such as a district attorney with a bar complaint pending against him.

His request was granted, and all files were transferred to the AG's office and assigned to the special prosecutions unit. There a team of special prosecutors appointed by the attorney general reviewed them.

On April 11, 2007, almost 13 months after the incident, "the Attorney General and his prosecutors determined that the three individuals were innocent of the criminal charges and dismissed the cases April 11, 2007."[13]

Analysis

Once more, the way charges are filed has a major impact on the way the case is disposed. Clearly the two presentations made to the grand jury in this case were central to the return of bills of indictment. The exculpatory evidence provided by SBI, which was available at the time, was not shown to the grand jury. That left only the uncorroborated statements of the victim and the poorly conducted lineup to determine probable cause for the three defendants.

The second DNA test results, which ruled out all the lacrosse players for rape, were available prior to May 15 when Evans was indicted, but that hard evidence was not presented either. That also could have countered the previous indictment. The police clearly would not have known about the second DNA test results, otherwise they would have shown them to the grand jury.

It is hard to fathom why Nifong did not dismiss all charges at that stage. Only by not disclosing those results could he continue to prosecute the case. He also chose not to interview the victim, who would have clear credibility problems in a trial. Most other prosecutors would have cut their losses and dropped the charges. However, Nifong had little room to maneuver after he made that fatal decision to withhold evidence favorable to the defense and lied to the judge. It would take seven long months before the defendants and their families would be free of the nightmare, which was easily avoidable.

A lifelong resident of North Carolina, Nifong started his career as an unpaid assistant in the district attorney's office in Durham in 1978. He was given a permanent position in 1979 and, over the next two decades, worked his way up to Superior Court, trying more than 300 felony jury trials (nearly a quarter of which involved homicides).[14] According to those who worked with him, he was tough, smart, always prepared, supremely arrogant about his trial skills, and intolerant of mistakes made by other attorneys.

In April 2005, after his boss, District Attorney James Hardin, was appointed to the bench as a Superior Court judge, Governor Mike Easley appointed Nifong district attorney to complete Hardin's term. No one envisioned the possibility of this experienced prosecutor overstepping his responsibilities and getting himself in a heap of trouble.

In 2006, Nifong filed for election as district attorney. The primary was to be held in May 2006, just as publicity about the Duke lacrosse team rape case began to intensify. He won the primary, and in November 2006 won the general election with 49 percent of the vote. But he lost the support of the governor who, in a speech at New York University on January 22, 2007, admitted that he "almost un-appointed him when he decided to run." His reason was that Nifong had broken his promise not to run for the office to which he was being appointed.[15]

At the pinnacle of his career, Nifong was top dog, an elected district attorney in his own right with a four-year term in front of him. Or so he thought until the Duke lacrosse case upended him.

While the criminal case was slowly moving toward dismissal, the ethics charges filed against Nifong were resolved more rapidly. The time from the filing of the first complaint on December 28, 2006, until his disbarment in June 2007 took less than seven months.

The major complaints as summarized by the grievance commission and responded to by Nifong included the following:[16]

1. He violated state statutes by withholding DNA evidence favorable to the accused until the judge ordered him to hand it over.

Defense attorneys suggested that any evidence of sexual activity on the accuser's part might have resulted from encounters before the party, not an attack by team members. They claimed that the district attorney had intentionally excluded test results favorable to the defense and then lied about it to the judge. Nifong responded that this information was available in his discovery. He stated that he did not have to point it out or summarize it for defense counsel because "the statute does not require the report to be in any particular format."

2. He was not candid with the court about the existence and nature of the exculpatory evidence produced by the DNA tests.

"At no time did I represent to the Court that I 'did not know that the DNA lab had determined that DNA taken from the complaining witness' body came from unidentified male donors who the lab had determined were not members of the Duke lacrosse team."

The complaint said that when the DNA testing failed, Nifong told a reporter that the players might have used condoms even though he had received a report from the emergency room nurse in which the accuser said her attackers did not use condoms.

3. He created pretrial prejudice by giving numerous interviews to the media.

The bar's rules limit what lawyers can say to the media. Lawyers cannot say things likely to prejudice a case, especially a criminal case. The rules caution lawyers to be careful when discussing the character or credibility of a suspect, a person's failure or refusal to make a statement, or any opinion about a suspect's guilt or innocence. And the rules say prosecutors must refrain from comments that would heighten public condemnation of the accused.

The bar association's charges cited 40 quotations and eight paraphrased statements to newspaper and television reporters, saying they contained "improper commentary about the character, credibility and reputation of the accused." Among them, Nifong called the lacrosse players "a bunch of hooligans." He declared, "I am convinced there was a rape, yes, sir." He told ESPN, "One would wonder why one needs an attorney if one was not charged and had not done anything wrong."

Nifong was unable to overcome the complaints lodged against him. The North Carolina Bar Association imposed its severest sanction in June 2007 by disbarring him. He had no choice but to resign as district attorney. In the meantime, he was still facing a criminal contempt charge brought by the judge in the case, W. Osmond Smith III, which accused him of lying to the court about DNA evidence favorable to the three Duke lacrosse players. For that charge, the court found Nifong guilty and sentenced him to one day in jail.[17]

Conclusion

The problems with this case started when the prosecutor assumed the investigative function, which is normally and traditionally conducted by law enforcement. Absent their chief of police, who was on leave caring for his sick mother, Nifong ordered the Durham Police Department detectives involved with the case to submit their reports to him, thus becoming the de facto director of the law enforcement activities in this case.

This was not a decision for him to make, and the Durham Police Department failed to object to or reverse it. Prosecutors should be the recipient of police investigations and reports about the facts of an offense; they should not undertake this task themselves because their primary objective is to prove the guilt of a defendant. Their responsibility is to review the evidence gathered by others, then decide whether to go forward with a criminal case or not.

Because the Durham Police Department did not maintain its independence in the investigation, they were partially responsible for Nifong's mishandling of this case and its outcomes. The system of checks and balances was disturbed by their failure to follow protocols and to vest the district attorney with their powers.

Couple Nifong's decision to direct law enforcement activities with the fact that he was an appointed district attorney fighting a hotly contested primary election for his first elective office, and it was not surprising, as he later admitted, that he was not able to give the case the attention it merited. Mistakes and misjudgments were unavoidable.

Combine these circumstances with a powerful ego expanded by 27 years of being a successful prosecuting attorney, a naïveté about the differences between the jobs of chief prosecutor and trial attorney, and the political demands on elected officials, and the odds were that this combination would create a mess.

So why did this situation occur? Was it because the district attorney thought that professional and ethical standards did not apply to him, or believed that his role as prosecutor was to convict defendants rather than seek justice? Was it because he saw this as a golden opportunity to win a contested primary election coming up in just two months? Or was it because as a newly appointed district attorney he was not used to operating as a politician in the intense glare of national and international media attention?

The reasons for his ill-timed statements and actions may never be known, but it is clear that this was not merely a simple mistake. In April, one month before his primary election, he said, "I'm not going to allow Durham's view in the minds of the world to be a bunch of lacrosse players at Duke raping a black girl from Durham."[18] On April 17, 2006, "I no longer get to go anywhere in my community without people knowing who I am."[19] He fully recognized, according to his campaign manager, that the television coverage was giving him "a million dollars of free advertisements."[20]

On November 7, 2006, Mike Nifong was elected to his first full term of office. So why, when his future was assured for the next four years, didn't he dismiss the charges based on the DNA evidence that he had, the lack of a credible accuser who kept changing her testimony, and the other supportable evidence that the defense had that supported the innocence of the defendants? He would have lost nothing by seeking a dismissal based on insufficient evidence. Perhaps, in the long run, his ego would not allow it.

There are three other factors that have to be recognized as defining the course of this case. The first and primary one was the fact that all the defendants were represented by high-priced and experienced defense counsel, paid by their respective families and friends. One can only guess what might have happened with court-appointed attorneys or public defenders who typically don't have the time and access to the resources available to these privately retained specialists. In one sense, they served as the first line of checks on the system.

The second influential factor was the media. Much of the detail in this chapter is based on newspaper reports, many in headlines. Without their interest and publicity, the public's knowledge of possible misconduct probably would not have existed. In this case, they can be commended for their education of the public in addition to increasing sales.

Finally, the ramifications of this case did not create a few victims; rather, it spread its destructive impact over Duke University as an institution, some of its personnel and faculty, the city of Durham, the Durham Police Department, and others. With legal bills estimated at more than $3 million, it is not unreasonable that the families of the accused would look to civil suits to recover expenses.[21]

The interaction of these two forces, one knowing and using the law and professional ethics to resist injustice and the other keeping the public's attention on the responsibilities of the participants in the system, give support for this little-discussed concept of checks and balances.

CHAPTER EIGHT

JonBenet Ramsey: The Case That Never Was

The two previous chapters were examples of cases that probably should not have been charged. In contrast, this chapter is about a "case" that never was charged even though a six-year-old girl lay dead in her house.[1] It is yet another view of the prosecutor's discretion.

JonBenet Ramsey was murdered in her home sometime during Christmas night, 1996. The plight of this little six-year-old girl captured the media's attention because photos showed her participating in beauty pageants at this young age. Not surprisingly, her mother, Patsy, was a former Miss West Virginia beauty queen who was married to a multimillionaire businessman, John Ramsey. In 1991, the family, including a nine-year-old son, Burke, and JonBenet, moved from Atlanta, Georgia, to Boulder, Colorado, when John's business, Media Access, required his relocation.

During the next five years, the Ramseys forged friendships in the Boulder community through their social and charitable works in addition to business connections, although to many of Boulder's elite social class, they were still "outsiders" lacking family roots and community heritage.

The Facts as Known

On this Christmas night, John and Patsy Ramsey, Burke, and JonBenet drove home from a neighbor's party. The details vary but basically, before retiring, John helped his son Burke put together a toy or read to him while Patsy gave JonBenet some pineapple.[2] While the rest of the family went to bed around 10 p.m., Patsy stayed up to prepare for the family's early departure to Michigan the following day. Sometime about 1 a.m. JonBenet woke after wetting her bed, and Patsy might have helped her change out of her wet pajamas.

About 5:30 a.m. Patsy awoke. Going down the back staircase to the kitchen, Patsy found a two-and-a-half page handwritten note on the staircase stating that JonBenet had been kidnapped by a "small foreign faction" and demanding $118,000 or she would be executed. After determining that JonBenet was missing, a frantic Patsy called the Boulder Police Department (BPD) at 5:52 a.m. to report the kidnapping.[3]

Shortly thereafter, about 5:55 a.m., the Ramseys asked two couples, their closest friends, and the family's minister to come to the house and be with them. They arrived between 6:10 a.m. and 7 a.m. Fleet White and John Fernie drove Burke to the Whites' house where his family and friends looked after him.

At 6:00 a.m., the Boulder police arrived. They conducted a cursory, external search of the house that was mostly unproductive. One officer found footprints in the snow in the yard but no sign of a forced entry. Mostly they waited for a ransom call that never came and a search warrant to permit a more comprehensive search.

In the meantime, the police officers notified their sergeant of the kidnapping. He called in two detectives and also notified the sheriff's department, the FBI, the deputy district attorney (the district attorney was on vacation), and the Boulder public information officer (PIO) of the kidnapping. He also called his detective division commander (also on vacation) who gave him a list of things to do.

Detectives Linda Arndt and Fred Patterson arrived at 8:10 a.m. The sergeant briefed them about the exterior search, and then they and several officers spoke with the Ramseys. Patsy changed her story and several of her statements were inconsistent. John stated that he had checked all the doors before retiring but he later denied this. The Ramseys also provided them with a list of possible suspects who had access to the keys to the house.

To comfort the Ramseys, the police called victim advocates who arrived with coffee and bagels for the family. Later, they wiped the kitchen counters clean with spray cleaner.

At 10:30 a.m. JonBenet's room was finally sealed with yellow tape. Detective Patterson left to interview Burke at the Whites' home. Around noon, the victim advocates left for lunch, leaving only Detective Arndt to control seven adults who moved around the house despite her request for them to remain in one area. The detective paged the sergeant for an update and to request more police at the scene. Her call went unanswered.

About 1 p.m. the detective asked John Ramsey, Fleet White, and John Fernie to search the house and make note of anything missing, changed, or different. Ramsey immediately headed for the basement, noting to White on the way down that he had broken a window there in the summer and had not yet fixed it. At the end of the basement corridor was a door with a white wooden latch on the outside. He opened the door. It was dark because the light switches were inside the room. Turning them on, they found JonBenet. She had been strangled, bludgeoned, and showed signs of sexual molestation.

Her body was wrapped papoose-style in a white blanket and was stiff from rigor mortis. John pulled duct tape off her mouth, picked her up, and carried her upstairs. He placed her body on the foyer floor. Later, Arndt moved the body into the living room, placed it in front of the Christmas tree and covered it with a nearby coverlet.

By 1:25 Arndt's supervisors and other officers were at the scene. The Ramseys gave handwriting samples on two tablets of white lined paper. Later the lab identified that the tablet marked as Patsy's had what appeared to be a practice ransom note or the start of another ransom note in the middle of the tablet written by a black felt tip pen. The paper matched the ransom note and the pen matched the pens in the kitchen.

John Ramsey was overheard making arrangements with his pilot to ready a flight for their return to Atlanta. Sergeant Mason told him, "You can't go."

At 2:15 p.m. a detective arrived with a form for John's signature permitting the search of the house. Sergeant Mason was told that based on Commander Eller's orders, the Ramseys were to be treated as victims, not suspects. When the Ramseys emerged from the house, John signed the form, a sobbing Patsy climbed into a car that drove away, and John got into a van. All the family and friends went to the Fernies' residence. No one was taken to police headquarters for interrogation.

About 4 p.m. officials from the district attorney's office began arriving, including the chief trial deputy, Pete Hofstrom, and three other assistants. The district attorney, Alex Hunter, was on vacation in Hawaii. By 8 p.m. the first search warrant was issued to allow the search of the house and the removal of the body. For the rest of the night and through the following days until January 4, 1997, police officers searched the house. By 11:44 p.m., the house was empty. Detective Arndt was the last person to leave. Earlier that evening John Ramsey picked up other family members at the Denver airport. A three-person team of private investigators and attorneys representing the Ramseys interviewed the Whites. Detectives visited the Fernie house for 40 minutes to schedule formal interviews with the Ramseys. John Ramsey would not talk to them alone on the advice of his attorney, and Patsy was "too medicated to talk to anyone."

The 10-day search of the house, which was "not a pristine crime scene" according to the technicians, yielded little additional information. On the bathroom counter was a balled-up child's red turtleneck shirt. Dust, film, and debris covering the windowsill of the broken window in the basement were undisturbed. Part of the murder weapon used to garrote JonBenet was a broken paintbrush belonging to Patsy. No one had thought to collect the clothes worn by either John Ramsey or the detective, both of whom had been in direct contact with the body.

By the day after the murder, December 27, the Ramseys had hired a team of private investigators and attorneys to represent the family.[4] This was the beginning of Alice's strange trip in Wonderland. The typical progression of a murder case starts with the arrest of suspects, case review and charging by the prosecutor, indictment by a grand jury and/or a bill of information, arraignment in court, pretrial motions, and finally either a guilty plea or a trial. In Wonderland, this did not happen. A criminal case never existed, no suspects were ever arrested, and no charges were ever brought forward for prosecution.

Analysis

One cannot begin to understand how this noncase happened without starting with the environment within which it occurred. Boulder, Colorado, with a population of about 90,000, is a college town dominated by the University of Colorado at Boulder. Its residents are predominately literate, liberal, and nonconfrontational. People do things "the Boulder way," which is based on a philosophy of "live and let live" and an acceptance of the premise that people are not inherently bad. They mostly just make mistakes.

The middle and upper classes in Boulder and its environs form a tightly knit social stratum. For the most part, they know each other, their families and family history, and rally around each other in hard times. In contrast to the mobility of the student population, these residents give Boulder and its activities constancy and focus. Those interested in politics and the law have ties that start at the governor's office, flow down to county and city officials, and ultimately to the criminal justice system. In other words, the legal community has lots of ties with the political community.

Boulder's easygoing environment allowed Alex Hunter, the Boulder district attorney, to win his first election in 1972 running on a platform to decriminalize marijuana. He was also elected six more times with little or no opposition. His long tenure of 28 years as the district attorney had solidified his political power, reaching to the highest state government levels. It also brought stability to the prosecutor's office, which in turn fine-tuned its belief that most defendants should be given an opportunity to rehabilitate themselves before the gavel excluded them from society.[5]

Although this was an easy position to maintain in a predominately liberal college town, it did little to establish good relations with the Boulder Police Department, which considered the office weak and ineffectual because it embraced plea bargaining, conducted few trials, and opted for rehabilitative sentences rather than punishment. As a result, the office gained a reputation among many officers of being soft on crime, lazy, or incompetent, depending on to whom you listened.[6]

To the citizens of Boulder, Hunter defined his office in ways that the community agreed with and came to expect. Only the term limits imposed by the state on locally elected prosecutors in 1995 were powerful enough to bring his long tenure in office to an end.

Police chiefs, in contrast, usually do not enjoy long tenures in office. By the time they rise through the ranks to that position, retirement is not far away. Nevertheless, they are appointed by the same city or county officials who share views similar to those held by the elected DA and the values of the community that elected him or her. The Boulder chief of police was no different.

It is this environment that created a case that was never closed and probably never will be, and marginalized a local criminal justice system without anyone being able to stop it. There are few hard facts available about this case. Something happened in the middle of the night to JonBenet Ramsey that left her dead in her own home. Other than that, the facts speak more to what happened after the crime than to the circumstances of the crime itself.

It is within these events that one can find clues to the reasons why this "case" ended without resolution. The reasons cluster broadly around four areas: the weak evidentiary strength of the case; deteriorating police-prosecutor relationships; the prosecutor's policies, priorities, procedures, and actions; and media influence.

Some physical evidence pointed to suspects in this case, but it was not conclusive. There was a kidnap note left on the back staircase that laboratory analysis determined was written on a pad of paper kept in the kitchen with a pen that matched those also kept in the kitchen. Handwriting analysis ruled out John Ramsey but was inconclusive about Patsy. Experts were available to testify but could not agree.

The crime scene was so compromised that other evidence was similarly weak. John Ramsey found the body in the wine cellar in the basement, a room that had been looked into earlier by his friend John Fernie, who testified that he saw nothing there although he did not go into the room to turn on the lights.

The body was in rigor mortis when John ripped off the duct tape covering her mouth and carried it upstairs. One arm was upright; a garrote was loosely tied around her neck and tightened with a broken paintbrush belonging to Patsy.

The autopsy found that the cause of death was by blunt force trauma to the head causing a subdural hematoma that would have been fatal but was aided by asphyxiation. Signs of vaginal penetration were inconclusive. The weapon causing the blunt force trauma was not identified. DNA testing of the two hairs found in the pubic area could not be matched to anyone tested in the suspect pool or in any other databases tested.

The initial investigation by the police cleared all suspects with the exception of John and Patsy and possibly some unknown intruder. There also was no established procedure in the prosecutor's office to designate on-call assistants to respond to serious crimes, protect the evidence, and advise what should be collected.

Since the initial complaint was kidnapping, it was not unreasonable that seven individuals—two family members, four friends, and a minister—were in and out of the house from 7 a.m. until 1 p.m. when JonBenet's body was discovered in the wine cellar. When John Ramsey found his daughter, ripped the duct tape off her mouth, and carried her body upstairs into the foyer, he contaminated a crime scene. Other ordinary protections like bagging the clothes of those who were in contact with the body and the crime scene, sealing off areas for investigation, and maintaining pristine conditions simply were not taken.

Finally, since the Ramseys were designated as victims rather than witnesses by the police and with the acquiescence of the prosecutors, the detectives were unable to interrogate them and clear up any inconsistencies in their stories, some of which had already been noted from the early-morning questioning. Testimonial evidence from the principals in the case was not collected until 18 months after the crime and then under less than desirable circumstances.

Contributing to the evidentiary problems were deteriorating working relations between the police and prosecutor. Good relations are based on mutual trust and common goals. Open communication between the two agencies promotes trust and respect for each other's separate but distinct roles. Police investigations, hopefully, produce suspects. Prosecutors review police work for the sufficiency of the evidence and its ability to meet probable cause standards.[7] Their discretionary authority lets them decide whether to accept or reject a case for prosecution or send it back to the police for additional information.

This much-simplified definition of intake and screening requires coordinated operating procedures, policy agreement on expected results, and respect for each other's distinctly different responsibilities. From the beginning, the relationship between the two offices was bifurcated and conflicted.

Even though District Attorney Alex Hunter and Chief John Koby were friends who functioned comfortably in the laissez-faire environment of Boulder, the police officers and detectives were not necessarily in agreement with their "live and let live" policies. The prosecutor's soft approach to handling defendants conflicted with the police department's more traditional, hardline approach to law enforcement.

Criticism and complaints flowed both ways. The police accused the prosecutor of giving preferential treatment to the Ramseys, sharing information they uncovered in their investigations with the Ramseys' team, and leaking other sensitive information to the press and media. As the investigation developed, they criticized the prosecutor's lack of cooperation in approving warrants to obtain additional information. They accused the prosecutor's office of limiting their ability to interrogate witnesses, refusing to convene a grand jury, and other actions that impeded moving the case forward to a disposition. In the end, the line police officers even leveled criticism against their chief when he did not take action on their complaints.

The prosecutor responded by criticizing the police for not securing the crime scene, not establishing a command center for the kidnappers independent of the crime scene, and for requesting search warrants that did not add to the quality or meet the needs of the investigation.

At the working level, personality clashes were more obvious. Even though the deputy district attorney (DDA), Peter Hofstrom, claimed expertise in violent crimes, having 23 murder trials under his belt, he also had the reputation of being the best negotiator of guilty pleas in the office. In the eyes of the police, his attempts to direct their investigations were not justified. The clashes and accusations—exacerbated by leaked evidence by both agencies—increased, and any mutual trust, if it ever existed, decayed rapidly.

In an attempt to negotiate a truce between the two offices, Chief Koby and District Attorney Hunter agreed to form a "war room" where detectives, investigators, and assistant district attorneys (ADA) assigned to the case could meet and exchange information with the caveat that nothing written left the war room and nothing discussed there would be discussed anywhere else. The leaks continued. Some were traced to war room members; others were untraceable. The war room became one more ineffectual tool in the investigation.

The relationship between police and prosecutor was finally resolved through media intervention, although not without creating a fatal blow. At first blush, one would not have thought the murder of a little six-year-old girl would ever become such an international, high-profile media event. But the photos of JonBenet participating in beauty pageants were hard to resist as the media tugged at the heartstrings of public sympathy and outrage. Once the tabloids like *Vanity Fair* and *Globe* dug into the story, they found ready gossip, leaks, and even pieces of reality available from every source, police, prosecutor, the Ramseys' team, people who knew people, and imagination.

The rush for information was so intense that Jeff Shapiro, a researcher for the tabloid *Globe*, first became a confidant of Alex Hunter, meeting with him daily either in person or by phone; and later, a confidential informant for the police. As such he contributed to the destruction of police and prosecutor relations by taping conversations with Hunter for Koby to hear. They were so critical of Koby personally and his department that they ended forever any chance for cooperation. Adding to the conflict between police and prosecutor were the actions and treatment of the Ramseys by the prosecutor. John Ramsey's millions and his prominence in Boulder's business and social community allowed him to establish early damage control to protect his family. By the evening of December 27 he was well represented by the best counsel available to protect the family from being designated as suspects.

The team he created to privately investigate factors and issues that they deemed relevant to solving the case was at various times composed of five attorneys, an investigator, and at least three consultants—including John Douglas, a retired profiler for the FBI; and two to three public relations experts.[8] They never wavered from their assumption that the murderer was an intruder.

The attorneys, furthermore, were some of the best in town and were no strangers to the prosecutor's office. Many had had business with Alex Hunter's office either at the time or in the past. Most of them were familiar with Hunter; all had succeeded within the "Boulder environment." The members of the team immediately sought to run their own investigation with the help of the district attorney's office.

Charging is the prosecutor's prerogative. With few exceptions, only the prosecutor can file charges with the court, asserting that there is reason to believe that a defendant committed the offense charged. Most criminal cases entering the judicial system are either the result of an arrest or an indictment by a grand jury. In the former, the police are the initiators; in the latter, the prosecutor initiates action. Until charges are filed, a suspect does not have legal standing in the courts and therefore cannot avail him- or herself of the court's protection of his or her rights.

The charging policy endorsed by Alex Hunter for Boulder County was first described and named "defendant rehabilitation" in Jacoby's book *The American Prosecutor*, published in the 1980s. It was, therefore, surprising to find it described by Schiller in his book in almost the same basic terms 16 years later in 1996.[9]

The intent of a defendant rehabilitation charging policy is to screen cases submitted for charging in light of their circumstances, emphasizing the defendant's history and actions. The objective is to determine the most appropriate disposition for the defendant and his or her rehabilitation, if possible, and place charges accordingly. To implement this policy, extensive communication with defense counsel is required with negotiated guilty pleas usually being the final disposition.

Hunter added an unusual twist to this policy. He instituted a procedure called precharging negotiations. While a case was being reviewed at intake by a screening assistant and before a charging decision was made, defense counsel could ask to speak to the charging ADA and negotiate a charge that was agreeable to both sides as reasonable and appropriate for a guilty plea.[10]

The benefit of this individualized approach to case screening allowed the office to tailor "a punishment to fit the crime." It gave prosecutors flexibility in charging, letting them take into consideration the characteristics and actions of the offender. The need for this type of flexibility, ultimately, sowed the seeds for programs known now as alternatives to prosecution, like community service, diversion, treatment programs, and deferred prosecution.

However, it created a conflict for the few cases that did go to trial. Hunter stated that before charges were filed, the office had to have sufficient evidence to prove guilt on the charges beyond a reasonable doubt. His beyond reasonable doubt charging standard was incompatible with the probable cause standard typically used by law enforcement, and it provided more fertile ground for the growing conflict between the two agencies.

It was not surprising that Hunter's response was to open the door to the team representing the Ramseys and their interests. However, such an action was inexcusable to the police. To them it showed Hunter's bias toward the Ramseys in an unprecedented fashion.

The office provided the Ramseys' counsel with copies of police reports, notes, and the results of laboratory tests and analysis. Normally, this information is not distributed until after charges have been filed against a defendant or after arraignment under terms of discovery. To make it available to attorneys representing potential suspects is very unusual.

Allowing counsel for an undesignated "suspect" to have free access to the prosecutor's office, to move freely about it, and to be present at meetings and briefings with police is even more questionable. What was not in question was the fact that the Ramseys would not talk to police directly but only through their attorneys to the prosecutor's staff, who acted as middlemen in this communications mess.

The team's close relationship with the district attorney's office and its refusal to cooperate with the police investigators only exacerbated the conflict between the police and prosecutor. The rift widened as the investigation wore on until it culminated with the police handing the case over to the prosecutor 18 months later, on June 24, 1998.

It is well known that prosecutors have different attitudes about the benefits of seeking outside assistance in criminal cases. Unless the assistance sought is highly technical or specialized and not normally available at the local level, it is viewed reluctantly as an indicator of incompetence. Pride goes a long way in maintaining the status quo in many offices. Here, the delay had negative effects on every part of the system, especially since relations between the police and prosecutor were so difficult.

Even though FBI agents were present at the station house because it was initially reported as a kidnapping, and they offered their assistance, as did the sheriff and other police agencies, it was not accepted until too late.

To counteract the legal talent in the prosecutor's office and on the Ramseys' team, the BPD finally accepted the pro bono offers of assistance from three prominent attorneys[11] experienced in investigations and criminal law. All three admitted to knowing and working with some of the Ramseys' attorneys and/or attorneys in the prosecutor's office, but they vowed "to represent only the Boulder Police Department and our interests,"[12] which they stated was to find the killer of a little girl.

In 1998, as the stalemate continued, the Boulder Police Department and the district attorney's office received an invitation from the FBI's Child Abduction and Serial Killer Unit (CASKU) to make a presentation of the case to some of the nation's foremost pathologists, behavioral science specialists, CASKU team members, hair and fiber experts, and other veteran teams and agents.

After two days of presentation by police, prosecutors, and representatives of the Ramseys' team and questioning by CASKU members, the results of their professional analysis were presented to the Boulder group. In brief, the team members believed that the crime was not the act of an intruder; rather, it resembled a staged event by someone who had never "intended to kill this child."[13]

The FBI profilers also questioned a number of evidence collection issues: Why hadn't phone records been gathered? Why had the Ramseys lawyered up so fast? Why, when Patsy had volunteered to take polygraphs, had the opportunity to do so not been given to her? The FBI encouraged the district attorney's representatives to convene a grand jury immediately and assist the police department's investigation.[14]

In response to all their questions, the DA's DDA, Peter Hofstrom, privately ventured a goal; if experts could determine prior vaginal trauma and an expert could identify the author of the ransom note, the investigation would reach a "turning point" for prosecution. Both of these areas were still inconclusive after numerous laboratory tests and analyses.

In the end, no progress was made. Finally on June 24, 1998, the Boulder Police Department handed the case over to the district attorney's office, thereby ending the investigation of the murder by the police.

A grand jury was finally convened three years after the murder and the prosecutor was responsible for the delay.[15] Police have the responsibility for arresting suspects if they believe they have probable cause to do so. But they didn't. Theoretically, the prosecutor is not required to take any action until an arrest has been made. If a prosecutor is uncomfortable with the charges and the evidence provided by the police, a grand jury can be impaneled. Even if the grand jury returns an indictment, the prosecutor still doesn't have to file the case if he or she feels that the charges are not supported by the evidence. That is exactly what happened when the grand jury was impaneled and charged the Ramseys with child neglect rather than homicide of any variety. The lack of the prosecutor's signature on the indictment is a de facto rejection of the charges as currently constituted.

Conclusion

The impact of the prosecutor's intake and screening operations and his charging policy were key factors in defining the nonoutcome of this noncase. Both critics and supporters have raised a number of interesting and sometimes controversial questions about the factors that created this unsatisfactory result.

Did the sloppy police work at the scene of the crime predetermine its failure? It is possible, but probably not. Many crime scenes have been corrupted or even destroyed, but justice has been done. Think about fires that consume houses leaving only the remains of bodies, cases where bodies have never been found, or even if they were, had been moved from some unknown location where the fatal act had occurred. These are problems, but they are often surmountable.

Did the lack of cooperation between the police and the prosecutor produce the impasse in solving the case? Not necessarily. Relationships between these two agencies exist in a variety of forms all over the United

States. In some jurisdictions, the prosecutor believes his or her duty is to prosecute everyone whom the police arrest. In other words, the prosecutor abdicates his or her prosecutorial responsibility to screen cases.

Did the early "lawyering" of the Ramseys protect them from being named suspects? It may have, to some extent. It was certainly helpful as a form of support to the Ramseys that their interests were being protected. It may have swayed public opinion away from the Ramseys as suspects by widening the issue to include other conceivable suspects such as an unknown intruder. But in the long run it was not the Ramseys' team and its early knowledge of the investigative details that helped them, but rather the prosecutor who enabled their protective activities.

Did the failure to empanel a grand jury early contribute to the case being an unsolved crime? Since the police made no arrest, the grand jury was the only other accusatory route that was available to bring criminal charges. If a grand jury had been impaneled, the Ramseys still did not have to testify, nor could any defendant be forced to testify under comparable conditions.

Why did the prosecutor not exercise one of the choices available? He could ask the police to make arrests and bring the evidence for his review and charging. He could convene a grand jury to investigate the case, or he could evaluate the evidence available and either accept or reject the case or ask for further investigation. His insistence on finding all possible suspects before bringing charges, his reluctance to support law enforcement requests for warrants to investigate potential suspects whose reputations might be damaged, and his requirement that the case be trial sufficient were effective barriers to making arrests, even though he could change these conditions.

This result is hardly a satisfactory end. Many prosecutors are faced with decisions not to prosecute serious cases that are weak from an evidentiary basis. Prosecuting cases to make a point when the case is highly unlikely to end in a conviction is seldom the right course. However, the value of JonBenet's noncase should be as a wake-up call for prosecutors, the police, the local justice system, and the Boulder community to reexamine their own actions that led to a "case" that never was.

CHAPTER NINE

Casey Anthony: Truth and Consequences

The acquittal of Casey Anthony three years after the reported disappearance of her child, Caylee, for offenses that could have resulted in a death sentence raises serious questions about whether the decisions made as the case moved to trial could have produced a more reasonable or appropriate disposition than they did. In hindsight, these questions are pertinent if they can identify factors that need serious and informed consideration before charges are placed or changed during the course of a case's progress to disposition.

This is not an easy task in this case because of the paucity of verifiable information and the almost overwhelming prevalence of untruths, questionable truths, and unspoken truths. Under these circumstances, finding the reasons why some decisions were made requires more conjecture than normal. Despite this, it is still possible to evaluate results against the standards of whether reasonable and appropriate outcomes were produced.

The Facts

The last time two-year-old Caylee was seen alive was on June 16, 2008, when she left her grandparents' house with her mother at 12:50 p.m., according to Casey's father, George Anthony. A June 15 videotape shows Caylee visiting an assisted-living residence with her grandmother, Cindy Anthony. Based on a later analysis of Casey's cell phone activity, the estimated time of Caylee's death was placed around June 16 to 18.[1]

Thirty-one days later, on July 15, 2008, Caylee was reported missing by her grandmother, Cindy Anthony, after Casey finally admitted that she had not seen her daughter for weeks. It took only one day for the detectives and investigators in the Orange County (Florida) Sheriff's Department to discover that Casey Anthony had been lying not only about the disappearance of her daughter but also, among other things, her employment history and a "nanny," Zenaida Fernandez-Gonzalez, who supposedly kidnapped Caylee.[2]

On July 16, 2008, Casey was arrested and charged with child neglect, making false statements, and obstructing an investigation. Over the next three months, while Casey was in and out of jail on two unrelated sets of charges involving check fraud, police investigators conducted intensive checks on the ever-changing stories Casey offered. They finally came to the conclusion that they were almost all lies.

The forensic evidence accumulated over August and September pointed to the conclusion that Caylee was most likely dead and Casey was to blame. Accordingly, the state attorney for the Ninth Judicial Circuit of Florida, Lawson Lamar, asked for a grand jury indictment on October 14, 2008. The grand jury returned an indictment the same day, charging Casey with first-degree murder, aggravated child abuse, aggravated manslaughter of a child, and four counts of providing false information to the police. Because the felony charges qualified as capital crimes, which could be eligible for a death sentence, she was held without bond.

For the next two months, an intensive search was made for Caylee. Her skeletal remains were finally recovered on December 11, 2008, one-quarter mile from the Anthony home. Other than DNA identification and a finding that Caylee's body had been, at some time, in the trunk of Casey's car, which her mother, Cindy Anthony, described to the 911 dispatcher as smelling "like there's been a dead body in the damn car," initially there was no evidence to conclusively support a cause of death.[3]

On December 19, 2008, the medical examiner, Dr. Jan Garavaglia, ruled it a homicide based on three red flags: the presence of duct tape found near the head of the skeleton, the location of the body bundled in a blanket and put in a trash bag with the other remains, and the fact that 100 percent of all accidental deaths are reported as such. However, there was not enough evidence to specify the cause of death, which Dr. Garavaglia ruled as undetermined.[4]

During 2009 Casey sat in jail as her defense team focused on mostly pretrial maneuverings. The defense, headed by Jose Baez, filed motions to dismiss evidence. On April 14, the prosecutor, Lawson Lamar, changed his previously stated position and filed a motion of intent to seek the imposition of the death penalty. Judge Stan Strickland denied a defense request to remove the death penalty. This ruling effectively prevented any pretrial release for Casey.

The year of 2010 was more active as the pretrial stage was moving to closure. In January 2010 Casey pleaded guilty to 13 fraudulent check charges and made full restitution. The judge sentenced her to time served. In April, after defense motions accused him of having inappropriate conversations about the case, Judge Strickland stepped down. Judge Belvin Perry Jr. was appointed to take over the case. In the meantime, in August and the following months, Cindy and George took their proclamations of Casey's innocence to the *Today Show* and other media outlets.

Finally, three years after Casey Anthony's initial jailing, the court ended the pretrial process with rulings on defense motions to exclude various pieces of evidence.

On May 20, 2011, after 11 days of jury selection, a jury of five men and seven women, plus three men and two women as alternate jurors was sworn. Under Florida's discovery laws, the court is open to television and the press has access to the hearings. For the next six weeks, a new soap opera emerged, garnering high ratings from TV viewers.

The state's case was that Casey used chloroform and duct tape to suffocate Caylee so she could return to her former, responsibility-free life. The defense countered by arguing that Caylee's death was due to accidental drowning in the Anthonys' swimming pool, that Casey panicked, and her father, George, helped her cover it up.

The trial itself relied extensively on the prosecutor presenting scientific evidence to establish that a homicide had been committed, and that Casey's car at one time held the body of Caylee in its trunk. The defense's role was to rebut each of the prosecutor's expert witnesses and cast doubt on the reliability of the forensic evidence, in addition to pursuing an accidental death scenario.

In the end, neither side was able to overcome the jury's standard of proof beyond reasonable doubt with regard to the alleged murder. As a result, on July 5, 2011, verdicts of not guilty for the three felony charges and guilty for the four misdemeanor counts of providing false information to a law enforcement officer were rendered.

Analysis

The mixed reactions produced by the verdict reflect how unexpected or inexplicable the outcome was to the public. Even today, the public cannot agree on the question of whether Casey killed her daughter. Some say "maybe," others that she didn't mean to, and still others, that she did and lied about everything. The existence of this type of controversy can only be explained by an unrealistic prosecution whose priorities were not adhered to in a manner consistent with the standards of justice.

The priority of a case for prosecution is the major element in deciding the charges to be placed and to obtain reasonable and appropriate dispositions. It is primarily determined by three elements of the case: the seriousness of the offense, the evidentiary strength of the case, and the nature and actions of the offender.

The seriousness of the offense played a major role in this case. First there was the question of whether a crime was even committed. Initially, before Caylee's remains were discovered, it was not known whether she was alive, dead, or incapacitated, only that she could not be found. At age two, it was likely that she had been either kidnapped or killed. Without real proof of her status and with Casey claiming Caylee was with her nanny, the prosecution's initial charge of child neglect was reasonable; murder was not.

On October 14, 2008, four months after Caylee's disappearance and before Caylee's remains were found, the prosecutor assumed she was dead. He concluded that there was enough evidence to charge her mother with first-degree murder and related charges, and called a grand jury to indict her on felony murder charges.

When the remains were discovered in December 2008, the medical examiner (ME) ruled that death was a homicide from undetermined causes. This finding was consistent with the prosecutor's already pending charges. However, the downside to the ME's ruling was that it left the door wide open for any number of versions about what happened to cause Caylee's death. Any proffered theory about the circumstances leading to it could not be ruled out. At this point the defense sowed the seeds of doubt and created numerous scenarios of what might have happened. The confusion that ensued and gripped the TV nation focused on questions about what really happened and what is the proof?

Why the prosecutor decided to make this a top-priority case is unknown. There is no doubt that this was a serious offense. It involved the murder of a toddler allegedly committed by a mother who was seemingly unconcerned about her daughter's disappearance. The seriousness of this offense would receive top priority under most conceivable circumstances.

The strength of the evidence is another story. The standards used to measure the strength of the evidence in criminal cases change as the case progresses toward trial. In the accusatory stage, evidence is weighed by its reasonableness; namely, is there sufficient evidence for a reasonable person to believe that a crime was committed and the defendant probably did it? If the answer is yes, the case moves forward to its pretrial stages during which most guilty pleas are negotiated, bringing the case to a swift end. If this does not happen, then cases move to trial where the standards of proof change from sufficient to conclusive.

To illustrate the distinction between sufficient and conclusive standards of proof, look back to the DSK case, which was ultimately dismissed because while there was sufficient evidence to prove that a sexual encounter occurred between the victim and the defendant, there was no conclusive evidence to prove that it was an assault. DSK's claim that it was consensual could not be overcome since there were no witnesses to the incident or other corroborating evidence. This case rested on the credibility of the testimony offered by the two principals, and DSK's prevailed over that of an admittedly illegal immigrant whose motives for pressing charges were questionable at best.

The evidentiary strength of the Casey Anthony case was weakened by the testimony of the defendant, who changed stories without explanation; the undetermined cause of death; the absence of corroborating testimony about any mistreatment by Casey of her child; and her unknown role, if any, in the homicide. Based on this evidence, one could conclude she was involved but not how.

Earlier research on decision making analyzed the influence of 28 factors relating to evidentiary strength on prosecutors' assignments of priority.[5] These factors were divided into four categories: the inherent complexity of the case for prosecution; constitutional issues arising from illegal searches and seizures, failure to give Miranda rights, and so on; the testimonial strength of witnesses and whether it is corroborated; and the circumstances of the arrest including evidence found, guns or weapons involved, and whether the defendant admitted, confessed, or denied involvement.

Further research on decision making also suggested that the factors influencing the prosecutor's assessment of evidentiary strength could be classified into two categories: those that supported the case and increased its priority for prosecution, and those that limited the strength of the evidence.[6] Corroboration by two or more witnesses (especially police witnesses) and the presence of a gun significantly increase the strength of the evidence. Limiting evidentiary strength are factors that indicate constitutional problems with the case (such as no Miranda rights given) or an intimate relationship between the victim and the defendant.[7]

The priority of this case was weakened by the nature of the defendant, who changed stories without explanation; the undetermined cause of death; the absence of corroborating testimony about any mistreatment by Casey of her child; and her unknown role, if any, in the murder. The evidentiary strength of Casey Anthony's case was based on circumstantial evidence from which one could conclude she was involved, but it was deficient in proving her role and lacked any testimony to the contrary.

Casey was never a sympathetic defendant who aroused feelings of pity or garnered public support. Anger was a more predictable response when everyone learned that she did not report her child missing for 31 days and then only because her mother was so angry with her that she called 911 to report their car stolen and mentioned that Caylee was missing.

As a 22-year-old single mother (she claimed her alleged husband was dead), a high school dropout and mostly unemployed, Casey lived a life independent of her child that few in our society could relate to. Her parents became the primary caregivers until Casey moved out of their house, taking Caylee with her.

Unlike most mothers of missing toddlers, she never voiced any concern to her family or friends about the fact that Caylee was missing, instead saying that she was with her "nanny." Even Detective Yuri Melich, lead investigator for the case, made special note in his report that "at no time during any of the above interviews did Casey show any obvious emotion as to the loss of her child. She did not cry or even give any indication that she was legitimately worried about her child's safety."[8]

This unusual response by a mother of a missing two-year-old widened the investigative net cast by the detectives in the Orange County sheriff's office. It concluded that "over the course of this investigation . . . there is no evidence that Casey did anything to look for her missing child." The result was the initial arrest for child neglect on July 16, 2008, that the state attorney's office supported by filing felony charges of child neglect on August 5, 2008.

Not only was Casey not overly concerned about her missing daughter, but the intense investigation also found that Casey was a compulsive and habitual liar and an unremorseful thief who had a record for forging checks and committing other "economic crimes." Almost all who knew her and were questioned by the detectives confirmed this. As the report stated, "All claimed she is a habitual liar and has been known to steal from friends in the past." Perhaps the best insight into her compulsive lying was given by her uncle, Rick Plesca, brother of Cindy, who summed it up this way: "If she sees something or hears something, she will spin it into her own little world to make it work for her, whatever kind of lie it is."[9]

The combination of a very serious offense committed against a toddler by a mother who was unconcerned about her welfare, and who was known by all her friends as a compulsive liar and "a pro at cashing bad checks," coupled with the smell of decomposition in the trunk of her car, a finding of a hair from Caylee in the trunk, and the "alert" signaled by a trained K-9 dog at the trunk of Casey's car weighed heavily in the prosecutor's decision to charge murder as the investigation continued.

The potential, and later confirmed, harm to a defenseless child by an irresponsible mother may have outweighed the fact that as a young single mother with a short, criminal history of only nonviolent property crimes, Casey did not rate being labeled a high-priority offender. Based on her background and actions compared to other defendants with long criminal records and prior convictions, it would be more consistent for the prosecutor to seek less punitive sanctions than the death penalty, not the other way around.

Prosecutors may vary the importance of one element in the priority for prosecution over the other two. Sometimes the seriousness of the offense outweighs the strength of the evidence; in other instances, the defendant's actions might be so reprehensible that they demand top-priority attention even though the offense did not produce serious injury. Universally, the combination of these factors provides prosecutors with a rational (and measurable) means for assessing the importance of cases for prosecution and designing trial tactics to obtain expected (or desired) results.

Decisions about the priority for prosecution are important to management because they guide the amount of resources that the office assigns to cases and how the case will be handled. High-priority cases with the potential for lengthy incarcerations are more likely to be tried by juries, which are expensive and time-consuming for everyone: the court, defense counsel, and prosecutor. They may be settled by a negotiated plea but only if the result does not conflict with their priority.

The Casey Anthony case was given top priority as indicated not only by the seriousness of the charges but also, later, by the decision to seek the death penalty. Its outcome, acquittal, was hardly consistent with the prosecution's expectations of incarceration and/or death.

Lawson Lamar was the state attorney for Orange-Osceola Counties from 1988 until 2014. He was defeated by Jeff Ashton, his trial assistant, who made his name as one of the prosecutors trying the Casey Anthony murder trial. Lamar was a native Floridian who earned his law degree from the University of Florida College of Law. He was a U.S. Airborne Intelligence officer in Vietnam and worked his way up in the Orange County State Attorney Office to chief assistant state attorney. He then served two terms as Orange County sheriff before being elected state attorney.

As prosecutor, Lamar watched his office grow in size and complexity, reflecting the population growth in his jurisdiction. He was skilled in organizing and establishing new programs in the office. Among these were the first Metropolitan Bureau of Investigation, which operated a strike force against organized crime, and an expansion of the school resource officer program designed to reduce truancy in elementary schools to include all middle and high schools.

As an experienced prosecutor Lamar could probably be best described as a professional administrator. His policies and interests were influential in broadening the scope and quality of prosecution services in his office. By identifying problem areas and developing programs or plans, he was able to provide adequate resources for his trial assistants and effectively manage the costs associated with case delay due to poor management.

With his experience and administrative skills, the question yet unanswered is how he could ignore the three basic components that define a case's priority. The seriousness of the offense is indisputable. The strength of the evidence was inconclusive. The role of the defendant in the crime could not be accurately defined. She certainly was involved, but absent a cause of death, any number of theories could be offered as reasonable alternatives. Coupled with a less than credible defendant and little if anything to tie her to the death except circumstantial evidence, the overall case appears more weak than strong.

In summary, to answer the question about why the highest priority was assigned to this case, it appears that here the priority was based more on outrage at the offense than assumptions that the evidence was irrefutable in identifying Casey as the killer.

This conclusion brings forth the question, was the case overcharged? Initially the charge of child neglect filed by the prosecutor on August 5, 2008, seemed headed for an almost slam-dunk conviction. Jeff Ashton, forensic trial attorney in the Anthony case and author of the book *Imperfect Justice*, which documented the trial, addressed the reasons why on October 14, two months before Caylee's remains were discovered.[10] It was then that the state attorney's office indicted Casey on three felonies: murder, aggravated manslaughter, and aggravated child abuse in addition to four misdemeanor offenses.

Ashton indicated that the decision to ask the grand jury to indict Casey was made by Lawson Lamar at the trial team's urging because Casey was presently out on bail pending the existing child neglect charge. Also, they did not want to argue "a conviction on child abuse when we all believed the child in question had been dead thirty-one days, not just missing."[11]

He also cited two other problems entering into their consideration to increase the seriousness of the charges. One dealt with Florida's "speedy trial" rule; the other, the U.S. Constitution's prohibition of double jeopardy.

Florida's speedy trial rule states that a person must be charged and tried within 180 days from the arrest, which for Casey was in July. Additionally, the rule also states that the timeline applies to any related crimes as well. To Ashton the definition of related crimes was unclear. He said, "If we choose the wrong course, then some appellate court years from now could decide we were wrong and Casey might walk, even if we found Caylee's body and she was convicted of murder."[12]

The definition of double jeopardy was similarly unclear. It revolved around the question of whether child abuse and murder would be considered the same offense. If they chose to convict her of child abuse, and then they found Caylee's body, they might "be forever prohibited from prosecuting her for murder."[13] The power of these arguments on Lamar's decision to impose more serious charges is unknown.

As Lamar stated in an interview with the *Orlando Sentinel* after the trial, "Any time that you've got a case where you believe the defendant—morally, ethically—you believe the defendant is guilty, you should go for it. It belongs before a jury. . . . The fact that it was charged as a first degree does not mean that jury had only first degree as a choice." Lamar said he consulted with other prosecutors who agreed that the death penalty was called for because of expert testimony "that the tape was over little Caylee's mouth and nose."[14]

The only potential murder weapon that the investigators could find at the time was the chloroform, which, even if it only accidentally caused Caylee's death, still constituted felony murder. "The bottom line. We believed she'd killed her daughter, and we couldn't wait for a body to be found. We had to go with what we had."[15]

Lamar decided to seek a grand jury indictment on the charge of first-degree murder. The grand jury, on October 14, 2008, handed up an indictment for three capital offense felony charges including the murder charge and four misdemeanor charges for lying to law enforcement.

Absent strong evidence, the initial decision not to pursue the death penalty was understandable. Its reinstatement six months later during the trial on April 14, 2009, based on new evidence, indicated that Lamar considered this case as extraordinarily serious and its evidence strong enough to support a death penalty.

Without being privy to Lamar's considerations, Ashton describes his reasoning behind the second decision to reinstate the death penalty provisions as based on the two considerations: Florida law, which requires certain additional factors before the death penalty can be imposed, and the responsibility of the jury alone to consider the death penalty as an option based on their individual interpretations of the facts.[16]

In Florida, death penalty cases must find the following aggravating circumstances: the type of victim (young, old, infirm, police officer, government official); the motive (financial gain, eliminate a witness, disrupt the functioning of government); how the crime was committed (premeditated or planned, torture or cruelty, conscious suffering by victim); and the defendant's criminal record (ever in prison, on probation, history and convictions for violent offenses). If the aggravating circumstances are not present, the death penalty can never be applied.

Additionally, only the jury can make the choice for a sentence of death. Therefore, the important factor for prosecutors was to decide what facts should be presented to the jury. If the jury believed that Caylee was unconscious when she died by suffocation, then two aggravating factors would be present, premeditation and physical pain and fear. If she were conscious, then torture would replace the premeditation as an aggravating factor. In other words, the prosecution was analyzing and developing its case in such a manner as to prove not only guilt but also the presence of aggravating circumstances.

Plea negotiation is the preferred route to disposition rather than a jury trial. However, the prosecutor's offer has to be acceptable to the defense, and it typically results in a reduction in charges or length of sentence. Increasing the seriousness of the charges from child neglect to capital felonies, with an expectation of life imprisonment, would give the defendant an incentive to negotiate a plea to lesser charges. When this did not occur, the office moved to go forward with an even harsher threat, a death penalty. The effectiveness of this strategy was questionable since, from the outset, Casey had rejected all previous offers of immunity.

The second reason for increasing the seriousness of the charges is that the office truly believed its evidence was so conclusive that a guilty verdict was likely even if it included the death penalty. This is not an unusual scenario if an office becomes cemented in their beliefs about what happened and how the evidence proves it. Having to play devil's advocate, considering other possible explanations and proving their validity, is not an option assistant prosecutors are likely to entertain during trial. It requires a Plan B or even C if it looks as if the defense will prevail, and the flexibility to respond quickly, even in the middle of trial.

Without evidence to the contrary, it appears that both Lamar, as decision maker, and Ashton, as one of the prosecutors, truly believed that the death penalty was appropriate and that the jury should have the opportunity to consider it.

However, this added another task to the prosecution. They had to convince the jury that they had proved their case beyond a reasonable doubt. The burden of proving guilt beyond reasonable doubt is a relatively new standard for criminal cases. It was only in 1970 that the Supreme Court held in *In re Winship*, 397 U.S. 358 (1970), that proof beyond a reasonable doubt is a due process constitutional requirement in criminal cases.[17]

Yet what is "proof beyond reasonable doubt"? It is a Supreme Court ruling that did not include a definition. As a result, its definition is left more to the jurors' subjective evaluations with some judicial guidance. But even judicial guidance depends on the interpretations of individual judges who also lack a definition of the term. As the United States Courts stated in their discussion, "The standard of proof in a criminal trial is 'beyond a reasonable doubt,' which means the evidence must be so strong that there is no reasonable doubt that the defendant committed the crime."[18]

The burden is on the state to prove its case beyond a reasonable doubt and additionally, in this case, to argue for the death penalty as an appropriate sanction. The defense does not have to respond at all, but clearly if there are credible alternative theories to offer, it can present them without having to prove them.

In the end, proof beyond reasonable doubt is a subjective evaluation by the jurors. A working definition was offered by the Florida State Attorneys as an amendment to jury instructions in criminal cases. It states in part:

> The defendant is not required to present evidence or prove anything. Proof beyond a reasonable doubt is proof that leaves you with a firm and stable conclusion that the defendant is guilty. Proof beyond a reasonable doubt does not mean proof beyond all possible doubt. Doubts based on speculation or imagination are not reasonable doubts. . . . To overcome the defendant's presumption of innocence the state has the burden of proving that the crime was committed and the defendant committed the crime. It is to the evidence introduced in this trial, and to it alone that you are to look for truth. . . . A reasonable doubt may arise from a careful and impartial consideration of all the evidence, or from the lack of evidence. If after carefully considering, comparing and weighing all the evidence there is not a firm and stable conclusion that the defendant is guilty then there is a reasonable doubt. If you have a reasonable doubt you should find the defendant not guilty. If you have no reasonable doubt you should find the defendant guilty.[19]

This was the issue facing the jurors. Competing with the prosecution's theory that there was a murder by Casey so she could return to her former life free from burdensome duties like child rearing was the defense theory that it was an accidental death covered up by Daddy so Casey could avoid a child neglect charge. With lots of forensic and circumstantial evidence but no "smoking gun" to tie Casey to the actual murder or evidence to indicate how it was carried out by Casey, the jurors unanimously agreed that they couldn't convict on murder charges. However, they also unanimously agreed that Casey was a liar and, whether premeditatedly or not, obstructed justice.

Conclusion

The medical examiner justified calling Caylee's death a homicide because she saw three red flags. Parts of Caylee's body were found with a blanket inside a trash bag, including a skull that contained duct tape residue over what used to be her mouth and nostrils. The child was not reported missing by the parent for 31 days, and 100 percent of accidental deaths are reported as accidents.

If the prosecutors had looked for comparable red flags in their case, they would have flagged a young defendant with a minor record of property crimes, most notably fraud and theft, who was a confirmed and unrepentant liar, whose testimony was not credible, and whose witnesses could be similarly tainted. They would have found a case with no cause of death or conclusive evidence linking the defendant to a murder, but possibly with enough evidence to convict on lesser charges involving at least negligence. They also could have concluded that the defendant and defense counsel were not interested in negotiating pleas, having previously rejected prior offers of immunity.[20]

The fact that the jury did not convict the defendant on the felony charges but only on four misdemeanor charges of filing false information to law enforcement lends support to the assumption that the system of criminal justice is basically rational, and that juries are not necessarily prone to making irrational decisions.

The interesting aspect of this case lies with the jurors, whose discussions will never be made public. Ashton believes that they did not work hard enough to come to logical and stable conclusions; that they wanted the case presented to them all tied up in a neat package. This argument may indeed have merit. However, it does not explain why the jury did not explore lesser included offenses, an opportunity that Ashton claims was offered time and time again.[21]

Although the evidence was iron-clad for the misdemeanor guilty findings, it does not shed much light on the felony not guilty verdicts. Perhaps a jury seeking to impose some accountability on Casey used the only remaining misdemeanor charges as the vehicle. If this were the case, and there is some evidence to support this based on postverdict interviews with some of the jurors, then we can question whether the charging decisions were too harsh and punitive.[22]

In other words, did the prosecutor place charges that were reasonable and appropriate? Were there other offenses that could have been charged, which might have allowed the jury to reach a guilty verdict? This case and its evidence involved lies, theft, obstruction, and most importantly child neglect.

Child neglect is a very serious felony under Florida law.[23] It is defined in part as "[a] caregiver's failure to make a reasonable effort to protect a child from abuse, neglect, or exploitation by another person." Depending on the level of charge, it may result in punishments not exceeding 15 to 30 years.[24]

There is a difference between "aggravated child abuse," which was included in the indictment, and "child neglect," which was originally filed and later dismissed.[25] Aggravated child abuse is defined as "knowingly or willfully abuses a child and in doing so causes great bodily harm, permanent disability or permanent disfigurement to the child."[26] Child neglect, in contrast, does not require proving that the defendant killed the child or abused her to such a degree that it ended in death. Aggravated child abuse assumes that Casey murdered or conspired to murder her daughter, a claim the jury did not buy.

Tailoring a case around a different set of charges excluding murder might have produced a more favorable outcome for the prosecution that included imprisonment, and simplified the trial by making plea negotiations more attractive to defense counsel while giving the prosecutor wiggle room to produce an acceptable disposition.

If there is a lesson to be learned from this case, it is to keep it simple and realistic, to initiate charges based on what is possible or provable. Trial strategies like plea negotiation require flexibility and a Plan B if they are not productive. This means that the three basic dimensions, the seriousness of the offense, the strength of the evidence, and the actions and history of the defendant, should be assessed not in light of what is desired but what is reasonable and appropriate. There is an old country saying that applies here: "Keep It Simple, Stupid." It may not give some people their 15 minutes of media fame, but it does help achieve the end result, obtaining justice.

The outcomes of Casey Anthony's murder trial and that of O. J. Simpson's were similar. Both inflamed the passions of everyone, both supporters and antagonists. Reaction ranged from incredulity to outrage to violent death threats, and infrequently, to support and compassion. Yet, unlike O. J.'s acquittal, which overturned a mountain of evidence, Casey Anthony's acquittal was won by the failure of any evidence to lead to the simple truth—that she and only she killed her child.

CHAPTER TEN

Orenthal James Simpson: The Murder Trial of a Victim?

From the very beginning, the case looked like a slam-dunk for the prosecution. On June 12, 1994, Nicole Brown Simpson, 35, O. J.'s former wife, and her friend Ronald Goldman, 26, were found murdered outside Brown's condominium in Brentwood, an affluent subdivision of Santa Monica in Los Angeles County. Almost 14 months later, on October 3, 1995, Simpson was found not guilty of the two murders, a verdict seen live on TV by more than half the U.S. population.

Under most circumstances, this case would not have reached the level of notoriety that it did even though it involved a once famous football star and a nationally televised "slow" chase down Los Angeles freeways. But events in Southern California involving the rich and famous seem to take strange twists and turns, attracting more media attention than if they occurred elsewhere. The O. J. Simpson case not only reached a pinnacle of public attention but the not guilty verdict also ensured its lasting infamy.

Trying to simplify the reasons why this criminal trial failed to convict is not an easy task when it was the longest ever held in California, costing more than $20 million to fight and defend, and producing an estimated 50,000 pages of trial transcript from 150 witnesses.

While the public remained transfixed on the daily televised court proceedings, producing a nation of "virtual" jurors, the real business of the court to administer swift, sure, and certain justice proceeded slowly, very slowly.

Involved in this seemingly endless process were law enforcement agencies, criminalists who collected the evidence at the scene, and laboratories that analyzed blood samples, DNA, and the like. The "Dream Team," a bevy of famous and infamous lawyers hired to defend O. J. Simpson, reduced to rubble the forensic evidence, which was the mainstay of the prosecution's case. Instant "stars" were made daily, each having 15 minutes of fame with the media and their "talking heads."

Even the judge, Lance Ito, the son of Japanese American parents, did not escape the media glare. Prosecutors declared him to be "an ex-prosecutor judge." These judges are so eager to appear unbiased that they tend to bend over backward to rule favorably for defense counsel.[1] Ito ordered the jury sequestered for 10 months, allowed televised court proceedings, and did little to keep the lawyers under control or speed up trial proceedings.

The prosecution and defense strategies were so diametrically opposed that one produced a trial about racial discrimination, police corruption, and white man's justice, and the other, to use the prosecutor's words, a "mountain of evidence" against a murderer. The end result was that proving the guilt or innocence of the alleged killer of two people became incidental to the jury's attitudes about racial discrimination and black injustice.

Examining the course of this case from a prosecution perspective highlights a long list of factors that affected the ability of prosecution to function successfully and some that were important in jury trials. They include not just the quality of the evidence gathered by the police and the credibility of the witnesses, but also the prosecution's trial strategies and responses to the unexpected. The flexibility and creativity of the defense were similarly important along with the characteristics of the jury itself. Almost everyone has an opinion about the correctness of the verdict. For the prosecutor, it was a disposition that probably should not have happened.

The Facts

The prosecutor's slam-dunk case was relatively straightforward and simple. The mountain of evidence proved motive and opportunity, and directly linked O. J. Simpson to the murder of his ex-wife, Nicole Brown, and her friend Ron Goldman. Nicole Brown, a German-born beauty, was Simpson's second wife. They were married in 1985 when she was 26 and he 38. Seven years and two children later (Sydney Brooke Simpson, 1985, and Justin Ryan Simpson, 1988), they divorced in 1992.

It was not a happy marriage from the outset as documented by police reports of several instances of domestic violence. By the time of the murder trials in 1995, the Los Angeles prosecution had compiled a list of O. J.'s abusive behavior involving incidents of physical and mental mistreatment.

O. J. Simpson, born in 1947, grew up on the streets of San Francisco. At 13 he was a gang member and at 15 was in custody in the Youth Guidance Center. He first played football in Galileo High School in San Francisco, then at the City College of San Francisco from 1965 to 1966, where he was named to the Junior College All-American team as a running back. Earning an athletic scholarship to the University of Southern California (USC), 1967–1968, he became an All-American during his varsity seasons, collecting the Heisman Trophy in 1968 among many other honors. He became famous as a professional football player primarily for the Buffalo Bills, 1969–1977, and then in 1978 for the San Francisco 49ers until he retired in 1980.[2]

On the night of the murder, around 10:15 p.m., Nicole Simpson came out of her house to meet Ron Goldman, a 26-year-old friend and waiter at the nearby restaurant where she had dined earlier that evening with her children and mother. Her mother had dropped her glasses outside the restaurant and Ron, who lived nearby, was bringing them to Nicole. It was to be the final act of many kindnesses for which he had acquired a reputation.

Shortly before 11 p.m. Nicole's white Akita signaled the brutal murders by wandering the street, barking and running back and forth.[3] The dog followed a neighbor home where its blood-matted fur reinforced the fear that something was terribly wrong. Two neighbors took the dog for a walk in hopes of calming it down. Dragged by the dog to Nicole's house, they saw the shape of a body at the foot of some steps.

About midnight, the first LAPD patrol car arrived at the scene. The officers discovered Nicole's body at the foot of her stairs, her throat sliced so savagely that her head was almost decapitated. Ron Goldman lay just off the walkway, dead from multiple stab wounds. The crime scene was drenched with the blood.

The officers called for backup and within minutes the crime scene was secured. Paramedics confirmed that the victims were dead. Police officers entered the house, awakened the sleeping children and arranged for them to be taken to the police station.

About 2 a.m. Homicide Detective Supervisor Ron Phillips accompanied by Detective Mark Fuhrman arrived to make a visual inspection of the scene. Twenty minutes later Fuhrman's partner, Brad Roberts, arrived. The sign-in sheet set up by the patrol officers showed that Roberts was the eighteenth police officer on the scene by this time.

By 4 a.m. the investigation had been transferred to the Homicide Special Section (HSS) of the Robbery/Homicide Division. Detectives Tom Lange and Phil Vanatter were appointed lead investigators. Following LAPD protocols, detectives Phillips and Vanatter walked through the crime scene without physically touching anything. The two men never got closer than six feet to the two crumpled bodies.[4]

They observed bloody footprints leading away from the bodies toward the back of the house; a trail of drops of blood followed the same course. Also noted at the scene were a set of keys, a dark blue knit cap, a beeper, a blood-spattered white envelope, and a bloodstained left-hand leather glove only a few inches from Nicole Brown's body.

Detectives Phillips, Fuhrman, Lange, and Vanatter were told by Commander Bushey, chief of the LAPD West Bureau, to contact O. J. Simpson in person to make arrangements with him to collect his children. Fuhrman knew where Simpson lived and went with Lange and Vanatter to his house.

Simpson, who lived two miles from Nicole's house, had no alibi for the time of the murder.[5] He had returned home earlier in the evening with a friend, Kato Kaelin, who lived in a small guesthouse on Simpson's property. Simpson had hired a limousine driver to take him to the airport at 10:45 p.m. for a red-eye flight to Chicago where he was scheduled to play in a golf tournament. The driver testified that Simpson was not at home when he arrived a little early (about 10:30) and had not answered repeated cell phone calls to the house. About 10:53 p.m. he saw a black male enter the house.[6] Only then did Simpson answer the driver's calls, stating he would be out shortly.

There was substantial physical evidence linking Simpson to the crime. He had purchased a knife similar in size and shape to the murder weapon. He dropped his bloody gloves, one at the crime scene, and the other at his home. He wore expensive and uncommon shoes that were the same size and shape of the bloody footprints leading away from the crime scene. His blood was everywhere, some of it mixed in with that of the victims. It was in his house, on his clothing, and in his Ford Bronco. DNA tests indicated the presence of his blood along with that of the two victims on his gloves, his socks, and on and in his car.

Unaware of Simpson's departure flight to Chicago, Detectives Mark Fuhrman, Tom Lange, and a private security guard tried to arouse somebody at the Simpson house but repeated phone calls went unanswered. After Lange noticed blood spots on the Bronco parked outside, they thought that this might be another crime scene. Fuhrman climbed the five-foot stone wall and unlocked the gate from the inside. Finding the main house empty, the group made their way to the three bungalows on the property, awakening Kato Kaelin in one and Arnelle Simpson, O. J.'s daughter from his first marriage, in another.

It was during this time that the infamous glove was discovered by Fuhrman. He reported his find to Detectives Lange and Vanatter, who went with him to view the bloodstained leather glove that appeared to be the right-hand match to the one still lying at Nicole's house.

After being notified of the murders, Simpson returned from Chicago, collected his young children, nine-year-old Sydney and six-year-old Justin, and was taken into custody. Fearing that he was about to be arrested, he slipped out of the house and led the police and the nation in a televised slow chase in his white Bronco. He had in his possession his passport, a gun, a disguise, $8,750 in cash, and what was later to be called a suicide note that was never presented as evidence. After finally returning home, he was arrested.[7]

Simpson hired a team of attorneys who came to be known as the Dream Team. As reported by Alan Dershowitz, it included "a trial team with experience in forensics (Barry Scheck, Peter Neufeld, Robert Blasier) and in examining police witnesses (Johnnie Cochran, F. Lee Bailey, Robert Shapiro)"[8] and Patrick James McKenna, a private detective who discovered the existence of the "racist" tape recordings between Mark Fuhrman and a former journalist, Laura Hart McKinley. When Judge Ito allowed the jury to hear the tapes, a murder trial ended and another against racism and white justice began.

Scheck and Neufeld were pioneers in genetic fingerprinting, which linked science with psychology, victims with their abusers, and produced concepts like the "battered woman's syndrome" that came to be useful defense arguments. Their unrelenting attacks on the professionalism of the criminalists who collected the blood samples and evidence did much to add to the jury's confusion about the quality of the evidence.

Add this to the racism charges and the defense strategy was simple. Their client was innocent. He had been framed by lying police officers, notably Fuhrman, and supported by incompetent law enforcement officials and technicians. They, in turn, were aided and abetted by prosecutors who were seeking to win at any cost. Simpson was painted as yet another black victim of a white judicial system. He was on trial because he was a black man, being framed and set up by a white man's legal system. The defense refrain was "If it doesn't fit, acquit."[9]

Much has been written in hindsight about the reasons why this case was lost. They range from personal opinions about the experience of participants to hard evidence of potentially irrelevant information being treated as fact. The stardom granted by the press and media to all including the judge, police, prosecutors, and defense counsel created an even more toxic trial environment. Only in Hollywood!

Analysis

Here the focus, however, is narrower. It looks at decisions made by the participants in the criminal justice system and special features of its environment that probably contributed to an unexpected outcome. Primary among these were the DA's choice of venue, which determined the composition of the jury; his initial prosecution strategy or absence thereof; reliance on the physical "mountain of evidence" to prove the state's case; and the lack of supervision and management of the trial team as it was forced to change prosecution tactics in response to defense charges of discrimination. The road to destruction rested on the effects of these decisions.

The decision to change the venue of the case to Los Angeles obviously was based on a variety of considerations, some that were sensible and practical, others that were of questionable benefit, and some based on erroneous information. The net result, however, was that instead of a jury composed of Simpson's peers in Santa Monica, it was composed of citizens who least represented the society in which he moved with ease and acceptance. The final decision by District Attorney Gil Garcetti to file the case in downtown Los Angeles and try it there rather than in Santa Monica where the murders occurred was a gamble he took and lost.

Normally, Los Angeles County files cases in the Superior Court district in which the crime occurred, which would have been Santa Monica. By choosing to file the case in downtown Los Angeles, Garcetti had to weigh a number of considerations before making his final decision, and then be prepared to justify his choices to the public and press.

The primary benefit to prosecution was that filing downtown would allow Garcetti to get an indictment from a grand jury instead of a preliminary hearing. Prior to 1994 California rarely used grand jury indictments as its accusatory mode. Almost all felony cases proceeded by preliminary hearing to find probable cause. Unlike many other states, California did not allow hearsay evidence in its preliminary hearings. As a result, "prelims" became "mini-trials" that could last days or even months. The hearing showed the defense the strength of the state's case and suggested possible prosecution trial strategies. Grand jury indictments, in contrast, could be obtained quickly through proceedings that are secret and not open to defense counsel. If Garcetti wanted an indictment, he would have to file the case in downtown Los Angeles, not in Santa Monica, because Los Angeles only had one grand jury and it was only located downtown.

Before Garcetti decided to file the case in downtown Los Angeles (L.A.), he had to consider a number of other factors. Primary was the composition of the jury. He believed erroneously that a grand jury indictment in L.A. would preclude the trial from being held in Santa Monica where the jury would be predominately white and wealthier. Santa Monica's population was 79 percent white and 7 percent black with a higher socioeconomic status than the predominately Hispanic (59 percent) and black (31 percent) populations that would be reflected in a Los Angeles jury.[10]

In his book *Outrage*, Vincent Bugliosi, a former assistant district attorney who successfully prosecuted the Manson family murder case, claimed that Garcetti was aware of the political problems associated with trying Simpson before a predominately white jury and that he justified his decision by claiming that jurors would be selected countywide, and, therefore, the jury pools would be similar in either location.[11]

Another benefit in choosing L.A. as the venue for the trial was that it offered an opportunity to avoid a major backlash from nonwhites in Los Angeles that might result if a white jury in Santa Monica found Simpson guilty. Garcetti was especially sensitive to this issue because of the racial violence that ignited L.A. in 1992 after a jury found four white officers not guilty of the Rodney King beatings. It seemed reasonable to assume that an L.A. jury's verdict would have more credence with the black community than any verdict from a Santa Monica jury.

The prosecutor's decision not to seek the death penalty also affected the character of the jury because California death penalty cases had to have a death-qualified jury, which excludes anyone opposed to the death penalty. Some controversial studies have indicated that death-qualified juries disproportionately excluded blacks and females, and that they were more likely to convict.[12]

Bugliosi believed that the trial prosecutors themselves were not really concerned about jury issues. They did not even take the advice of their own jury consultants who urged them to use their peremptory challenges to exclude black and female jurors. In fact, when the DA's focus groups showed that black women, who traditionally were more tolerant of domestic abuse than men, disliked ADA Marcia Clark, the district attorney did not seek a male replacement.[13]

Garcetti may have believed that a guilty verdict by a downtown jury would have more credibility with the black community. It is also possible that he thought the case was so airtight that it could be tried anywhere. In deciding upon L.A. as the venue, he set the stage for a disastrous result.

The result was an initial jury composed of eight African Americans, two of mixed descent, one Hispanic, and one white. The alternates consisted of seven African Americans, one Hispanic, and four whites. By the end of the trial only six of the original jury would still be serving. The actual jury that deliberated the charges was composed of one black male, eight black females, two white females, and one Hispanic male.

Evidence takes two forms, testimonial and forensic. This investigation and the subsequent trial relied almost exclusively on forensic evidence, thereby producing a weaker, more one-dimensional prosecution. The book authored by Mark Fuhrman,[14] initially the lead homicide detective in the case, documented and often corroborated the investigation and the evidence collected. It is clear that mistakes were made by both police and criminalists in collecting and preserving evidence.

During the course of their investigation, the criminalists destroyed evidence and were careless in following the protocols for collecting and preserving evidence. The result was the loss of additional potentially crucial physical evidence.[15]

For example, the detectives never insisted that the criminalist who collected the blood samples collect *all* of them. Rather, they allowed him to collect a sample. As the blood and other evidence decayed with exposure to the elements, later collections and analysis were similarly tainted. Defense counsel did not let this fact go unnoticed by the jury when it was presented.

From the Dream Team's perspective, the two primary issues being tested were the police department's actions and the prosecutors' reliance on physical evidence collected by the criminalists at the scene. These formed the basis for defense charges that Fuhrman was a confirmed racist who planted the bloody glove at Simpson's house. Unfortunately, they were not the primary focus of the prosecution, which had other issues to consider.

The prosecutorial decisions made from the start had effects that created a series of unanticipated consequences. First, the defense succeeded in having the grand jury indictment dismissed on the grounds that "its members had heard excerpts from the tapes of the 911 call Nicole made in 1993."[16] Without any challenge from the district attorney's office, the court ruled in favor of the defense, and the preliminary hearing the prosecutor so wanted to avoid was conducted anyway.

The lengthy preliminary hearing allowed the defense to plant the seeds of evidence tampering and racial bias. In an article in the *New Yorker* Jeffrey Toobin suggested "that the LAPD detective (Fuhrman) who testified in the preliminary hearing about discovering the glove at Simpson's estate had, in fact, planted it there."[17] The article also referred to the detective's past behavior and racist views.

To the lead detectives, these suggestions were refutable. Fuhrman had been the 17th police officer to log in at the crime scene, almost two hours after the arrival of the patrol officers. Not one of the other officers had seen or reported more than the one glove found near the bodies.[18] However, neither the police nor prosecutors immediately rebutted the details, adding more credence to charges of police lying and planting false evidence.

By the time the trial began, the racial issue had been adopted as the basis for the defense trial strategy. This was due, in large part, to voice tape recordings acquired by the defense in which Fuhrman made racist remarks to a journalist. More significantly though, it was given the green light by Judge Ito, who despite prosecutor Chris Darden's eloquent appeal at an early pretrial hearing on January 23, 1995, not to allow defense counsel to introduce the race issue, ruled "I will allow cross examination on that issue."[19]

Darden's prediction was to come true when he implored Judge Ito, "There is a mountain of evidence pointing to this man's guilt, but when you mention that word ["nigger"] to this jury or any African-American, it blinds people. It will blind the jury . . . to the truth . . . it will impair their ability to be fair and impartial. . . . Mr. Cochran wants to play the ace of spades and play the race card . . . but you shouldn't allow him to play that card."[20]

One can't downplay the impact of the allegation that Mark Fuhrman was a racist on the outcome of this trial. Yet not only did the prosecution put him on the stand as a witness, thereby opening him to defense cross-examination, but he was left "twisting in the wind." The prosecutors never rebutted the allegations even though, because he was a veteran police officer, a large pool of testimonial evidence was available that could have been presented to offset them.[21] Whether the failure to do so rested with the police chief or the prosecutor is hard to determine since neither agency tried to counter this "stain" on the LAPD's reputation.

The Trial

Despite knowing in advance of trial that racism would be part of the defense, the prosecutors did not change their trial strategy of emphasizing physical evidence as proof beyond a reasonable doubt. As a result, they simply lost control of their case. Forced into a position of reacting to defense claims of lying, racism, and cover-ups, they forgot to keep reminding the jury that the evidence pointed only to Simpson as the murderer, not some unknown person, and that there was no other reasonable alternative theory.

For 99 days the prosecution put forward 72 witnesses. "Much of the 'mountain of evidence' seemed to lose its credibility, either because the prosecution did a less than stellar job in preparing and presenting it, or because Simpson's lawyers were smart enough to interpret it in such a way"[22] that it introduced more reasonable doubt to the jurors.

Under normal circumstances, prosecutors develop a trial strategy for each case, which involves outlining the overall theme of the prosecution, usually presented in the opening statement to the jury; the order of presenting evidence and which prosecutor would present which aspects;

testimony to support it; anticipating defense attacks and having witnesses or evidence available to rebut them; organizing impeachment evidence to reduce the credibility of defense witnesses; and an overall plan of attack for cross-examining the defendant.

A major obstacle to producing a comprehensive strategy in this case was identified by Bugliosi when he noted that Garcetti had assigned an "unprecedented twenty-five prosecutors to the case, thirteen full-time and twelve part-time," which resulted in a "disjointed, almost amorphous prosecution, with no one prosecutor establishing rapport and credibility with the jury."[23]

Comprehensive trial strategies require skilled case managers to plan and coordinate the timing and order of the trial and anticipate changes in defense strategies.[24] Such a comprehensive trial strategy was basically nonexistent when the case started. The costs of no manager at the helm were illustrated by three fatal mistakes: the decision to call Mark Fuhrman to the stand, the decision to ask Simpson to try on the bloody glove in front of the jury, and the decision not to introduce specific pieces of circumstantial or testimonial evidence.

In fairness to the prosecution, Judge Ito excluded some of their attempts to introduce these types of evidence. For example, he did not allow into evidence the testimony of the correctional guard who overheard Simpson yell into his phone in a conversation with Rosie Grier at the jail that he didn't mean to do it, and that he was sorry, and Grier's response that he had to come clean.[25]

Although physical evidence was the heart of this case, testimonial evidence has the ability to interpret it and produce conclusions that guilt is beyond a reasonable doubt. Looking at what the prosecution chose not to introduce as evidence, clues are found as to what the prosecutors viewed as strong evidence and, more importantly, what they believed was sufficient for the jury to hear as proof of guilt. The prosecutors were wrong.

Some of the evidence that the jury never heard offers supplemental information about why Simpson was guilty. Simpson's statement to Detectives Vanatter and Lange was not offered into evidence. The reason for this was also never explained to the jury even though they knew of its existence. Nor was the suicide note that Simpson wrote prior to his arrest offered. Both documents, according to Bugliosi, clearly implicated him in the murders and "reek[ed] with guilt."[26]

There was no discussion about the evidence retrieved from the white Bronco's "slow chase" indicating that Simpson was going to flee: the false beard and mustache, $8,750 in cash, a passport, and the gun. Even the inconsistent and contradictory statements made by Simpson to the detectives immediately after his return from Chicago were suppressed.

Testimony by witnesses who saw Simpson near the murder scene was not presented. Details about the knife purchased by Simpson hinting at premeditation were not introduced when the prosecutors learned that the *National Enquirer* had paid store employees $12,500 for telling their story about the sale to Simpson. Omitted also were statements made by Nicole Brown Simpson to a variety of persons that she knew O. J. would kill her if he caught her with another man.

Whether the inclusion of these and similar facts would have changed the verdict is impossible to predict. But their omission and the prosecution's reliance on physical evidence reflect the weakness of the prosecutor's trial strategy. Even though some testimonial evidence could be viewed as weaker than physical evidence, its importance in trial situations is commonplace because its cumulative effect is to satisfy the need for proving guilt beyond a reasonable doubt.

As it was, the jury based their decision on forensic evidence, which defense claimed was "planted" or contaminated. Without additional information to help interpret events or provide an explanatory background, it is little wonder that it took the jurors less than five hours to reach a verdict about a trial that had consumed more than nine months.

Bugliosi explains the verdict as a result of the public's (and jurors') reliance on "the best that money can buy" as the standard for excellence and more importantly, credibility. Although he personally believes that Simpson's defense counsel were incompetent, he also believes that all participants—including the police, prosecutors, and Judge Ito—were awed by the celebrity status of O. J. and held a trusting belief in his innocence.

Bugliosi believes that the incompetence of the "talking heads" who daily reported on TV and radio about the excellent points made by the Dream Team left the prosecution in "rubble" with a case full of holes and falling apart.[27] He also lays the blame on "the terrible jury that heard it and the incredible incompetence of the prosecutors, not because of anything special at all done by the main lawyers for the defense."[28]

Notwithstanding the influence of some or all of these factors on the outcome, the defense trial strategy worked. Johnnie Cochran, in his closing argument to the jury, summed it up when he urged the jury to take a stand against "a lying, genocidal racist cop," a police department that had covered up for him, and prosecutors who were seeking to win at any cost. The result was not a trial about the guilt or innocence of a defendant accused of two murders, but rather a trial about a black victim in a white legal system.

When cases break down, a single agency or entity can rarely be blamed. The O. J. Simpson case confirms this in splendid detail. There were certainly problems in the investigation and collection of evidence, with the defense's "credible" theory of racism and cover-ups in a white man's justice system, and in the damaging decisions made by Judge Ito that allowed the race issue to be introduced as relevant to a case involving a double murder. His decision to sequester the jury for 99 days to protect them from the publicity surrounding the trial was counterproductive to their health and ability to view the case objectively. By ruling that the trial could be televised, the judge built an avenue that gave instant credibility and 15 minutes of fame to "expert" talking heads in addition to an enduring soap opera for the viewing public.

Not much blame can be assigned to defense counsel in this case. Once they were allowed to play the race card, other alternative strategies became secondary in importance. Alan Dershowitz, who was a consultant to the Dream Team, described the results that ensued: "I believe that the prosecution put on a case it knew to be partially false, in order to prove what it honestly believed to be the true guilt of the defendant. . . . In the end, the jurors concluded that the defense had put on a more honest case than the prosecution."[29]

Conclusion

Despite the cumulative effect of all these mishaps, the largest share of the blame belongs to the prosecution's unrealistic belief that the physical evidence would eventually overcome all other deficiencies or questions, and that the jury would see through the defense's tactics and convict a murderer. Although the prosecutor erred in his decisions to try the case in downtown Los Angeles, to assign a female as lead prosecutor against the advice of jury consultants and experts, and to rely on forensic evidence to the near exclusion of available testimonial evidence, the real problem was that the trial team and its leaders were unable to anticipate and respond to the defense's counterattacks and charges, especially those of racism and cover-ups.

The conclusion reached by Bugliosi and others was that the prosecutor simply did not have a comprehensive prosecution plan in place at the start of the trial, supported by experienced attorneys who could keep the prosecutor's case on track for the jury and at least one step ahead of the defense by anticipating and rebutting their claims and witnesses.

This was the prosecutors' case to lose and so they did. Instead of prosecuting the only suspect in this crime for killing two innocent people, they defended themselves against charges of racism and did themselves in. In one sense, the prosecutors became the defendants in a case where the defendant became the victim. That left no one to be tried.

All of this makes for interesting conversation. However, it sidesteps the question of whether the inappropriate use of prosecutorial discretion resulted in this undesirable-outcome case. Even though many of the discretionary decisions yielded negative results, they were probably not sufficient to produce this disposition. The prosecutors reviewed and evaluated the case at intake and filed murder charges based on more than sufficient evidence that the crime had been committed and O. J. Simpson was the killer. Although the prosecutor eventually decided not to file death penalty charges, the expectation that the sentence would be life without parole was appropriate and reasonable given the reputation of the defendant and his very limited, juvenile criminal record.

The DA's decision to indict rather than take the case through a preliminary hearing was also reasonable given the mini-trial nature of California's prelims and the high media attention to the case. Whether this decision was politically or racially motivated by District Attorney Garcetti is not known, but it is clear that he was not fully informed about the procedures associated with grand jury indictments and may even have considered factors that led to wrong conclusions, like the composition of the jury and its venue. The decision to use an indictment as the accusatory instrument was reasonable because of its efficiency and secrecy, both traits benefiting the prosecution. On that basis, the discretion that was embedded in these decisions cannot be faulted.

Finally, the discretionary decisions about plea negotiations or dismissals were not in play simply because the defendant refused to consider them or the evidence was overwhelming. In sum, each of these decision points alone or *in toto* cannot be cited as the root cause of the result.

So where does the finger point? To a typically underrated function of prosecution called *management*. Prosecution management is the responsibility of the elected official, and none other. The DA is responsible for establishing the policies under which the office will work, ranging from a policy emphasizing community priorities and restorative justice to one that believes in preventive detention and incarceration as a means of reducing crime. Some policies may combine features from a number of other policies.

The chief prosecutor's policies are administered by an organization and implemented through programs and procedures established by it that allow people in the office to make decisions that are consistent with policy. This produces reliable and uniform decision making needed to ensure that cases are prosecuted equitably, and that reasonable and appropriate dispositions are obtained with the least use of resources in the shortest time. The responsibility for managing an office rests solely with the prosecutor and his chiefs. They did not do this, and justice did not prevail.

The problem with this case stemmed from failures in case management, which includes developing a trial plan and strategy, and having experienced leadership and proper resources to obtain a just disposition. At the operational level of trials, good management is crucial. Trial teams don't necessarily require more attorneys; they require skilled leadership for planning, coordinating, and organizing the various stages of the work involved.

Coordination among many units, detectives, analysts, criminalists, witnesses both expert and civilian, and legal researchers is essential for a meaningful and understandable prosecution. The trial team organization has to have experience in several functional areas including planning, coordination, scheduling, and administration. It develops practices and procedures that ensure the smooth flow of information to the jury in a timely manner. The fact that this case was deficient in these management tools was obvious. Its result is not surprising.

At the policymaking level, Garcetti and his deputies were responsible for ensuring that the case was properly managed. They did not do so. Merely adding 25 or so attorneys to a trial team does not improve case management; it only adds confusion to the process. It appears that the very highest levels of management were totally unaware of their responsibility for policy direction, administration, and management. As the district attorney, Garcetti or his top deputies were responsible for making sure that serious problems were addressed as soon as they appeared.

The breakdown should have been obvious to Garcetti, who reportedly watched the trial proceedings daily or had deputies who did. The support and assistance that should have been sent to the beleaguered trial team wasn't sent, and for this Garcetti should be held accountable. Preparing for trials of this magnitude and media interest requires skilled planning and coordination. None was visible, and the presentations of evidence confirmed this, leading in part to criticism about the competence of the trial team. The analogy to a sports team is obvious; without a coach, few games are won.

Being the elected leader of the largest prosecutor's office in the United States[30] does not exempt the chief prosecutor from his responsibility to run a good office. It only makes it a little more complex. There are multinational corporations in the private sector that successfully manage and operate even more complex organizations. Having top-notch leadership and management with strong organizational skills available to all branch offices and at all levels of management is critical to ensuring prosecutorial equity and justice. Choosing to devalue the management requirements for this trial was the prosecutor's inappropriate choice and one for which he should be held accountable.

Perhaps the quality of management is yet another discretionary decision belonging to the prosecutor against which prosecutorial performance can be evaluated. A prosecutor's choice to devalue the importance of management increases the likelihood that the checks and balances needed to maintain an adversarial system of justice would be disrupted. This happened here.

Afterword

For those who are interested in O. J.'s actions after his acquittal, we have included a brief update. The Goldman and Brown families filed a civil suit for compensatory and punitive damages in 1996. On February 4, 1997, after a four-month trial and six days of deliberation in the Santa Monica courthouse, the jury of one black, one Asian, one Hispanic, and nine whites returned a verdict finding him guilty of the murders "based on the preponderance of the evidence." In a civil case, Simpson could not invoke the Fifth Amendment and was forced to testify.

The jury awarded the families $33.5 million in compensatory and punitive damages. As expected, very little was collected. Simpson was heavily in debt because of his murder trial, but he escaped experiencing poverty because his $4 million pension fund from his football years could not be attached. He moved to Florida and lived off his pension fund's more than $20,000 monthly income until 2007.

On September 13, 2007, a group of men led by Simpson broke into a hotel room in Las Vegas and stole sports memorabilia at gunpoint from a dealer. Simpson was arrested three days later. On October 3, 2008, he was found guilty of all 12 charges and sentenced to 33 years in prison. He will be eligible for parole in 2017 when he turns 70. He is currently serving his sentence for felony kidnapping, armed robbery, and other charges in medium-security Lovelock Correctional Center in Nevada.

CHAPTER ELEVEN

Professionalism and Innovation

The previous chapters served as examples of how different sets of forces can influence prosecutors' decisions and produce ineffective results. At a glance they appear to be calling for some sort of reform or adjustment to the prosecutor's discretionary powers. This is an unfortunate conclusion because discretion is essential for keeping our system of justice flexible. It allows us to tailor a punishment to fit a crime, a criminal, victims, and society. By focusing on notorious cases, we can identify the factors in the criminal justice system that influence the prosecutors' decisions and show their ability to combine or coalesce to produce unanticipated results. We can also demonstrate how the effects of factors external to prosecution may impact outcomes and create a sense of unfairness.

Fortunately, these cases do not represent the overwhelming majority of adjudications in our justice system, nor do they call for system-wide reform. Despite their results they show the need for flexibility in applying the law, but they fail to reach the goal of obtaining reasonable and appropriate dispositions in the quickest time with the least use of resources. The vast majority of successful prosecutions are not widely publicized. Their identity rarely reaches beyond the jurisdiction of the prosecutor's office or the state. Many of them garner only a whiff of notoriety.

In this chapter we will examine the successful facets of prosecution by describing three cases: one representing a prosecution of a double murder, one already familiar to you that demonstrates the ability of prosecutors to learn from their mistakes and change their policies and priorities, and one that began as a small venture but successfully expanded into nationwide acceptance of what is known as "community prosecution."

Our concluding section attempts to explore the future of prosecution and the criminal justice system as it responds to innovative societal and technological changes.

Neo-Nazi Murders in North Carolina

This attention-getting title does little to describe the monotony of successful prosecutions even when horrendous crimes have been committed. Fort Bragg is a major U.S. Army installation located in Cumberland, Hoke, Harnett, and Moore counties, North Carolina, near Fayetteville. With a resident population of about 30,000, it is noted for its Special Operations Forces and as home to the 82nd Airborne Division, which distinguished itself in World War II. Fayetteville is the county seat of Cumberland County, which has a population of about 200,000. In 1995 Cumberland County was represented by an experienced district attorney, Edward W. Grannis Jr.

The Timeline[1]

On the night of December 7, 1995, three white soldiers from Fort Bragg's 82nd Airborne Division, Private James N. Burmeister II, age 20, Private Malcolm Wright, 21, and Army Specialist Randy Lee Meadows, 21, were enjoying a night off the base eating and drinking. The conversation turned to their neo-Nazi interests and their beliefs in the antiblack movement. Private Malcolm Wright's spider web tattoo under his eye became part of the conversation when he told the others that in some skinhead groups it indicated that the wearer had killed a black person. Burmeister was duly impressed and indicated that he had a 9-millimeter Ruger pistol with him and thought that he could earn his tattoo that night.

After dinner, the trio drove around, drinking beer and looking for trouble. They ended up in a predominantly black, working-class neighborhood. In a dimly lit area they spotted a black couple, Michael James, 36, and Jackie Burden, 27. Burmeister and Wright got out of the car, telling Meadows to wait for them, but after he heard gunshots being fired, Meadows left the car and went in search of them.

When the police arrived, they found both victims dead. Each had been shot in the head and Jackie Burden in the back. Meadows did not flee. Instead he approached the police and led them to a trailer and the suspects. There they awakened the sleeping Burmeister and Wright. A search of the trailer yielded a gun, white supremacy literature, a bomb-making manual, pamphlets on Adolf Hitler and Nazi Germany, and magazines for survivalists and paramilitary groups.

The police arrested the three soldiers and a probable cause hearing was set for December 19, 1995. Burmeister and Wright were each arraigned on two counts of first-degree murder and conspiracy in the deaths of Jackie

Burden and Michael James. During the summer of 1996 all three soldiers were discharged from the army.

Two separate jury trials were held. The first to be tried was Burmeister, who on February 27, 1997, after two weeks of testimony, was convicted on all charges by a mostly white jury that deliberated more than 10 hours over three days. Because District Attorney Grannis added a death penalty charge to Burmeister's and Wright's charges, the juries heard additional evidence during the sentencing hearing. The prosecutor did not present any additional evidence. The jury deadlocked on March 6, 1995, with a vote of 11–1 in favor of execution. Burmeister is presently serving two consecutive life sentences at the Central Prison in Raleigh, North Carolina.

Malcolm Wright's trial was moved to New Hanover County Superior Court in Wilmington, 100 miles from the crime scene, because of the pretrial publicity in Fayetteville stemming from Burmeister's conviction. On May 3, 1997, Wright was convicted by a jury of 11 whites and 1 black of two counts of first-degree murder and one count of conspiracy to commit first-degree murder. It took the jury less than one day to convict Wright of the charges. They also did not impose the death penalty. In addition to the two consecutive life sentences, the judge added 12 to 15 more years to Wright's sentence for conspiracy.

Randy Lee Meadows was the prosecutor's star witness against Burmeister and Wright. He pleaded guilty to the lesser charges of conspiracy and accessory in exchange for his testimony and was sentenced in the fall of 1997 to time already served in jail.[2]

The strength of the evidence was the major factor leading to the convictions of all three persons arrested. The strongest was the testimonial evidence provided by Meadows and the testimony of Burmeister's former girlfriend, Kelly Cook Kelly, who described when Burmeister became involved in skinhead activities such as displaying the Nazi flag and listening to white power anthems and lyrics about killing blacks and Jews. Forensic evidence was similarly strong. The gun used by Burmeister, although clean for fingerprints, was identified by the North Carolina Bureau of Investigation as the weapon that killed the victims. The evidence collected from a search of the trailer where Burmeister and Wright were sleeping added to the conclusion that these murderers could be called neo-Nazis and white supremacists.

From the prosecutor's point of view, the fact that Meadows, who was with the others prior to the shooting, returned to the scene and told the police what had happened was critical. Gaining his testimony in return for a reduced sentence, that is, a plea bargain, illustrates how this tool is used in a very productive way. Without Meadows's testimony the conviction of the others would have been very much in doubt.

The defense had little to counter with. Burmeister's lawyer called a pharmacologist who testified that Burmeister was so drunk on that night that he could not have pulled the trigger. He also suggested that Wright was the one who pulled the trigger.

Although the death penalty was sought for both defendants, neither jury could unanimously agree.

The Result

There was little more a prosecutor could ask to achieve in the prosecution of such a serious crime. The crimes were heinous; the evidence was strong both from a testimonial and a forensic perspective. A guilty verdict was almost certain, but a death sentence was not. Even though the murders were motivated by racist and antiblack sentiments, the failed unanimous agreement by both juries to impose the death penalty illustrates the power of the jurors to judge cases in accordance with social values in addition to the law. The prosecutors did not present any additional evidence at the sentencing hearings.

It may be that another factor came into play—namely, the characteristics of the defendants: young, in the army, and with no serious criminal histories, only antisocial beliefs. A history of violent crimes or criminal histories might have influenced the jurors as they decided the defendants' life or death penalties.

Oddly enough it was the military's reaction that was most far reaching. At that time, the military permitted membership in racist white supremacy groups and other groups that violated a person's civil rights, but banned active participation. They launched a worldwide investigation of local practices under this policy but found little evidence of participation. Twenty-two soldiers were discharged, including the three defendants. However, the investigation produced stronger policies against racism in the troops.

District Attorney Grannis summed up the prosecutions when he stated, "I feel we had a very successful prosecution" and added that both defendants "have been branded racists and will be treated accordingly."

Experience Counts

In the beginning of 2010, it looked as if Cyrus Vance Jr., Manhattan's newly elected, first-term district attorney, might lose his job after his office filed charges too hastily against Dominique Strauss-Kahn (DSK), alleging rape of a hotel cleaning woman.[3] Vance's decisions reflected those of many newly elected or appointed chief prosecutors who have not yet gained the judgment and expertise of the existing assistant prosecutors presently staffing the office. But Vance fared better than his North Carolina counterpart, Mike Nifong, who stubbornly refused to change his prosecution of the Duke University lacrosse team rape case.

In a *New York Times Magazine* article, Chip Brown conducted an extensive interview with Vance, who was one year into his second four-year term.[4] The article enumerates the changed policies and new programs undertaken by the district attorney since the start of his first term in 2010 and his eventual dismissal of the charges filed against DSK. It was a remarkable turnaround for a new district attorney heading an office employing about 535 assistants.

To his credit, Vance used his experience to rethink his role as district attorney. This led him to choose a different goal, that of driving the crime rate lower by what he called "intelligence-driven prosecution." It involved changing the traditional prosecution focus from the facts of the 105,000-plus cases handled yearly to a focus on the offenders involved in those cases. Vance reasoned that information about offenders was equal to, if not more important, than the evidentiary strength of a case. With this new focus, he could give priority to removing serious violent offenders from society and thereby reduce the number of violent crimes.

Implementing this strategy was not an easy task. It required selling the concept and coordinating changes with numerous law enforcement agencies and their disparate computer systems. To structure the workload and develop procedures, he created a Crime Strategies Unit (CSU) and divided Manhattan's 22 police precincts into five areas to which he assigned a senior assistant and a crime analyst. Much like the career criminal and repeat offender programs of the early 1980s with their goal of incapacitation, the database started with police in each area submitting information about their 25 worst offenders.

After extensive systems work the CSU had a searchable database and operating procedures known as the Arrest Alert System. This system monitored the arrests of violent offenders in the database for any violation. It identified "hits" and notified police and prosecutors of pending actions.

The "refocused" Vance has not disavowed his traditional hardline prosecutorial policy of incapacitation; rather, the DA added another dimension, linking crime prevention to public safety. His priorities focused on dismantling gangs and reducing violent crimes. His successful coordination with the New York Police Department and its resultant increases in arrests has increased his popularity with the electorate and improved his chances for a third elected term.

Still, Vance is not without critics. Some worry about a "too close" coordination with police. They want more independence between the two agencies. To the extent that prosecutors can become "closet cops," this might interfere with their independent role as prosecutors sworn to decide whether the evidence supports prosecution and with what charges. However, it can also be argued that communication and coordination between the police and prosecutors are essential ingredients for the successful operations of criminal justice systems. It appears that Vance has retained the independent discretionary power to place charges, incapacitate serious offenders, and protect the safety of the public.

By designating violent recidivists as top priority for prosecution attention and by developing systems to coordinate information-sharing among the stakeholders (police, prosecutors, probation, and corrections), Cyrus Vance Jr. has started on the long, difficult journey of testing the powers of a prosecutor's influence, especially with regard to reducing violent crime. In time the focus may shift from crime reduction to community safety. At that point, Vance enters a new world of community involvement that may force changes in the use of discretion. The important fact now is that Vance's career to date demonstrates that experience is a great teacher. However, the student must be willing and ready to learn. Ultimately, the chief prosecutor is also the chief law enforcement officer in the jurisdiction, and making the community safer is an achievable goal.

Loitering, Vagrancy, Petty Theft: Success and More

These crimes aren't newsworthy; in fact, they are rarely even counted. Increases in petty thefts over a given time period are rarely monitored. There is no systematic way to even count arrests for a poorly defined charge of vagrancy, and loitering is another murky area. Although misdemeanors and ordinance violations comprise the highest volume of work in the courts, their assembly-line processing consumes the least amount of time and resources in the criminal justice system.

Yet in Ferguson, Missouri; Staten Island, New York; Baltimore, Maryland; and other communities, the propensity for police violence has reopened long-standing complaints of police discrimination against people of color, the poor or homeless, and others dependent on public assistance and low-paying jobs to survive.

This was not an overwhelming problem in Multnomah County (Portland), Oregon, in 1990 when its district attorney, Michael D. Schrunk, instituted a new program originally called the "District-based Prosecution Project" and later referred to as the "Neighborhood DA Program."

But these problems existed in many areas of the city that clearly needed improvements in their quality of life. Some areas were affected by gangs or drug dealers who had turned playgrounds into drug-dealing hot spots. There were complaints from the downtown retail center that aggressive panhandlers were driving customers away from sidewalk cafes attached to upscale restaurants. A neighborhood or business district might be experiencing a variety of real problems that the surrounding areas or the city as a whole were not.[5]

The aim of Schrunk's new venture was to reduce or eliminate these low-priority maintenance and order crimes using existing resources in the community, especially its citizens and other stakeholders. Schrunk recognized that these problems could not be reduced or eliminated using the traditional tools in the criminal justice system. But Schrunk also reasoned that if citizens were committed to using their energy to solve these problems and to maintain the solution afterward, the demise of quality of life crimes in a neighborhood could be enhanced by using a mix of criminal and civil laws, ordinances, and regulations.

The first opportunity for Schrunk to "operationalize" the program arrived when he was approached by the business community of Lloyd District, which was located in a strip mall across a busy street from a motel. The business community could not cope with the crimes emanating from the "gulch." This small gulch was located at the rear of the motel and ran parallel to the street. It was populated by a large homeless and transient community, which had built shacks and shacks on top of shacks, until the area's transient population, trash, and litter gave it the appearance of a slum in a developing nation. No water, sewage, power, or other amenities for living—just trash and shacks.

The effect of this "residential" community on the business community was devastating. Customers were turning away because the vagrants and homeless were using the motel's swimming pool and Jacuzzi as a toilet, bathtub, or even, if necessary, a laundry. During the day, they congregated in or in front of the stores, panhandling, annoying or disturbing the customers, and stealing from the merchants, many of whom had hired private security guards.

Despite frequent complaints to the police and some arrests, little improvement occurred. In desperation, the businesses approached District Attorney Schrunk asking for relief. They offered to pay for the costs of hiring an assistant district attorney (ADA) if he or she would focus exclusively on their problems by prosecuting violations to the fullest extent.

Schrunk realized that this unique offer could be construed as a form of private prosecution by his critics,[6] but more importantly he realized that without the city's and business community's commitment to help, this effort would also fail. The community had to commit to share in the work required. On this basis, Schrunk negotiated a one-year contract with the Lloyd District Community and hired a "Neighborhood DA" to identify the problems, recommend solutions, facilitate actions and programs, and use the prestige and power of the prosecutor's office to produce and maintain success. But Schrunk also warned them that if the criminal caseload of the office increased, the Neighborhood DA would be recalled to help. On the other hand, if the effort was successful, he would hire a second Neighborhood DA from his budget to expand the program.

Fortunately, the appointed Neighborhood DA, Wayne Pearson, was a skillful planner and coordinator. He brought together the citizens and the business community's personnel to persuade local government officials to "post" the gulch with no trespassing notices stating that camping in the gulch was illegal and that violators would be prosecuted. Designated citizens patrolled the gulch daily with the Neighborhood DA, replacing torn-down signs and identifying persons refusing to leave so violations could be issued. Finally a date was set notifying those that remained that the gulch would be cleared, and that all property found would be designated as "lost" and stored at a public storage facility some distance from the gulch.

On that day, a phalanx of trash trucks and tractors convened in the gulch and cleared it to the ground. Wearing the yellow uniform of the trash collectors was the Neighborhood DA, Pearson, and a bevy of citizens. One year later, with continuing citizen and business support, the gulch was still clean and unoccupied.

Thus started the expansion of Schrunk's improved Neighborhood DA Program in Portland. His second Neighborhood DA was hired, then a third, a fourth, until nine were on board. As their numbers grew, the county was able to tailor law enforcement and prosecution responses to a variety of community situations that needed relief. Community courts were created to support the needs of specific areas, and the progressive actions of the criminal justice system introduced even more flexibility into an essentially rigid and often bureaucratic system.

Schrunk's approach to solving crime problems was not unique. Across the country in Brooklyn, New York, in 2000, District Attorney Charles (Joe) Hynes was working with the courts to open the first community court in Red Hook, an enormous public housing area. The court was designed to meet the needs of the residents, offering services in the areas of employment, landlord-tenant affairs, and criminal cases.[7] Both of these first endeavors in the field of community prosecution and community courts served as the foundation for more successful and safe outcomes.

As Michael Schrunk noted in an interview with the Center for Court Innovation, "You need to work things in a holistic manner. If you start with the quality of life crimes but also take care of the serious crimes, things are going to work out. So when crimes spike or there are different crimes in different areas, you can deploy resources where needed."

Conclusion

Prosecutors come in all different sizes and colors and have different career objectives when they enter the profession. Some are there for a career, while others are in it for experience or political advancement. Two of the three prosecutors discussed here, Grannis and Schrunk, are long-term professionals and have been reelected to office many times. In general, that means the office has been successful in delivering the quantity and quality of justice desired by their constituents. Vance was reelected to his second term in 2013. The voters will determine the length of his career. As a prosecutor pursues a career by winning multiple elections, the primary objective changes from prosecuting individual cases to managing the office and providing leadership to younger prosecutors in the office. For some, a significant leadership role in the community will evolve.

Ed Grannis, now retired, needed to make sure that justice was done to safeguard all the citizens in Cumberland County. Even the idea that a crime of this type could occur in his town was taken personally. The system worked, including the police work, the prompt meeting of the grand jury that indicted the criminals, and eventually the trial court and the jurors announcing the guilty verdicts. That is the way the criminal justice system is supposed to work.

Cyrus Vance Jr. had a baptism by fire when the DSK case was dropped in his lap. The case was a hot potato with racial implications, political overtones, and a VIP accused and jailed. Information is the lifeblood of an investigation and the initial information was sketchy. Given the characteristics of the case and the quality of the initial police work, charges were premature, resulting in unnecessary and unwanted publicity. By his second term, Vance had learned the true value of information in focusing on what would make safer neighborhoods.

Mike Schrunk stretched the boundaries of prosecution even further. The Neighborhood DA program was an exercise in innovation and leadership. Sensitivity to local problems in his jurisdiction allowed him to expand the power of the prosecutor to resolve community needs that were not being successfully addressed by the conventional criminal justice system. It served as a welcome extension of the "broken windows" strategy of law enforcement, which also requires active participation by the local prosecutor. Being the chief law enforcement officer of Multnomah County, Oregon, Schrunk saw this as his responsibility to attack and expand beyond the conventional, and he acted.

Prosecutors across this country are facing ever-changing challenges that require professional and innovative responses. These three prosecutors are excellent examples of how the prosecutor can provide solutions to complex criminal justice environments.

CHAPTER TWELVE

Lessons Learned

John Adams, the second president of the United States, once remarked that the United States was now a nation of laws and not of men. This observation is quite accurate since new laws are created almost daily at the federal, state, and local levels of government. Many of those laws involve civil and even criminal penalties. In the early years of the country there were few federal laws with criminal penalties. But today there are roughly 4,000 such laws. Most concern areas like banking, the environment, and almost any act that crosses state boundaries.

State laws deal with the vast majority of the common criminal acts discussed in this book. Of course, there are 50 states and each will have somewhat similar criminal statutes, but the statutes may have varying definitions and different penalties. In some cases, the particular laws are not in agreement about the same criminal act. The use of marijuana is the latest case where states differ among themselves and with the federal government. For example, a resident of Colorado driving through some southern states headed for Florida while carrying a personal stash of pot could be in jeopardy. Another common difference in statutes between states concerns handguns and handgun licenses.

Local laws add another layer to the picture. Counties and municipalities have numerous ordinances dealing with areas that concern the community within the political boundaries of the entity. Ordinances that are issued to control the behavior of visitors or tourists are common, and many of those people come from jurisdictions with a different local legal environment. Some of these may even have criminal penalties.

In some situations a case may move between these layers. A crime occurring in a municipality may be adjudicated in the county or district attorney's jurisdiction. Similarly, a district attorney may have the U.S. attorney handle a state case. These are situations where there are separate laws available, and one law may provide a more reasonable and appropriate disposition in the view of the prosecutors involved.

These factors make comparisons across states of the dispositions of what seem to be similar cases and defendants very difficult and probably meaningless. More importantly, variation even exists within a state for the many reasons addressed in this book. It would not be unusual for dispositions in a college town to be different from those in an industrial or mining town in the same state operating under the same laws. Similarly, large urban cities with a plethora of street crime and small rural jurisdictions will see the same criminal event differently. In a small town a person accosting a citizen on the street and discreetly showing a handgun or knife would be charged with armed robbery. A major city prosecutor would likely see that as "aggressive panhandling." A lot depends on the environment where the criminal event takes place. The locally elected prosecutor will reflect those attitudes.

While two cases may be similar in seriousness and the defendants may have equivalent criminal histories, there may be a world of difference in the evidence available to prove that a crime was committed and that the person charged did commit the crime. Generally, the quality of the evidence gathered is largely the purview of the local police department. The prosecutor has to make a judgment as to the adequacy of the evidence when deciding whether to accept the case or reject it and, if accepted, what charges to file.

The prosecutors' discretionary powers allow them to make these decisions, which reflect a variety of factors with the quality of evidence allowing the first cut. If the evidence is insufficient to meet the statute's requirements, it is rejected. If it is sufficient, then the other factors, seriousness of the offense and criminal history, are assessed. The problems with accepting cases that have deficiencies in evidence and investigation were well demonstrated in the DSK and the Duke lacrosse players' cases. The final dispositions of dismissal were correct but left substantial wreckage on the scene for the participants.

On the other hand, the problems with gathering evidence in both the JonBenet Ramsey and O. J. Simpson cases probably doomed them from the start. The first case never started, leaving a very unsatisfactory conclusion, and the second ended in acquittal because reasonable doubt was raised by the defense team.

The key point is that much depends on the training and ability of the police to conduct proper investigations and to clearly report the findings to the prosecutor. If the prosecutor is continually concerned with the quality of police work, it may be important to strengthen police-prosecution relations at the highest policymaking levels. Dismissals and acquittals are rarely reasonable and appropriate dispositions. Plea negotiations are not only the primary route to disposition but they are also usually more efficient and productive to the entire criminal justice system.

The chief prosecutors' primary function is not to be engaged in trials. Their primary function is to be the leader of an organization that follows policies and procedures uniformly and consistently. They also have to be effective administrators, controlling the volume of cases accepted in addition to their times to disposition. In this role, they establish supportive working relationships with the other participants in the criminal justice system. Finally, they are policymakers for criminal justice in their communities. By being sensitive to their communities' concerns and problems, they can work jointly with citizens to reduce crime and improve public safety. To the extent that prosecutors exhibit these talents, they reflect the ideals of prosecutorial excellence.

Translating these lofty expectations into operations in an office requires more practical rules or standards to guide assistant prosecutors in their work. It means making good decisions early in the adjudication process, not accepting cases that are deficient in evidence, being aware of cases where prosecution may not be in the public interest, and filing charges that will be sustainable in court. In addition, it asks assistants to be prepared to dismiss weak cases as early as possible, identify the 3 percent of the caseload that are likely to be litigated and set them aside for the trial teams, and negotiate guilty pleas for the remaining majority that are reasonable and appropriate as early in the process as possible. Cases do not get better with the passage of time.

With the achievement of a reasonable and appropriate disposition, the prosecutor usually has an opportunity to influence the sentence, assuming it is not prohibited by state statute or that the presiding judge has no interest in receiving such a recommendation. This may be the last chance for the prosecutor to have an impact.

Early in case adjudication, the prosecutor makes a charging decision. If the state has structured sentencing or sentencing guidelines, the prosecutor has a chance to align the charges with the desired sentence in the guidelines. That is the best point to influence the sentence if the defendant is convicted. The differences in sentencing guidelines between states and how the prosecutor uses the charging decision to provide for an acceptable sentence, from the prosecutor's point of view, is another reason that similar defendants that have committed similar crimes can receive different sentences if convicted.

Finally, the discretion that prosecutors exercise is a function of the statutes in each state. The way that crimes are defined and the evidence that is required are set in the statutes as well. How the prosecutors and judges operate in the world of structured sentencing is also defined by individual state laws. Prosecutors and judges do not necessarily agree with laws passed by legislatures and lobby to change the statutes when necessary. Structured sentencing and mandatory minimums were opposed when they were passed. The unintended consequences of such legislation are still with us.

John Adams may have overstated his remark that the United States was a nation of laws and not of men. It was not until the 1830s and the Jacksonian era that the power of many local functionaries was converted to the power of elected officials. In criminal justice this was exemplified by elected judges and elected prosecutors in many, but not all, states.

The creation of an independent prosecutor and the courts' decisions supporting the prosecutor's discretionary powers built the foundation for our 21st-century prosecutors. As the gatekeepers of the criminal justice system, prosecutors provide the grist for conversations about their role, their decisions, and the quality of justice that communities are provided. An informed public is essential to ensuring that the gatekeepers are providing reasonable and appropriate dispositions with the least use of public resources based on clearly stated policies and priorities.

Notes

Chapter 1

1. We recognize that many prosecutors have civil and appellate duties that also embody discretionary power, but in this book we are focusing on discretion in criminal cases.

2. There have been legal exceptions to the unreviewable aspects of these decisions, but they are rare and relate to exceptional circumstances. For the overwhelming majority of prosecutions, these decisions are unreviewable. See Frank W. Miller, *Prosecution: The Decision to Charge a Suspect with a Crime* (Boston: Little, Brown, 1969) for a summary of case law relating to these issues and specific case references.

3. In this book the term *dismiss* is used interchangeably with *nolle prosequi*.

4. Joan E. Jacoby, Leonard R. Mellon, Edward C. Ratledge, and Stanley Turner, *Prosecutorial Decisionmaking: A National Study* (Washington, D.C.: U.S. Department of Justice, National Institute of Justice, 1982). The results of this nationwide research, using the standard case set, confirmed that these factors were used in decision making and that they explained almost all of the differences among prosecutor offices nationwide.

5. Joan E. Jacoby, L. E. Mellon, and W. F. Smith, *Policy and Prosecution* (Washington, D.C.: National Institute of Justice, U.S. Department of Justice, 1982), 73. Estimates of the median for felony declination rates are between 14 to 27 percent. The range is from a low of 2 percent to a high of 80 percent. This wide range is a direct result of the prosecutor's charging policy and the quality of policing.

6. Some states have attempted to limit the power of the prosecutor to dismiss or *nolle* cases after bind-over or indictment by inference (Michigan) or by statute (Wisconsin). However, trial judges rarely decline to accept the prosecutor's reasons for discontinuing prosecution. See Miller, *Prosecution*, 307–321.

7. If the lower (misdemeanor) court is not a court of record, then misdemeanor convictions can be appealed to the felony court for a new trial. These cases usually are designated as misdemeanor appeals or called *trials de novo*.

8. *ABA Standards for Criminal Justice: Prosecution Function and Defense Function,* 3rd ed. (Washington, D.C.: American Bar Association, 1993).

9. Jacoby, Mellon, Ratledge, and Turner, *Prosecutorial Decisionmaking,* 37.

10. It is not unusual, however, for a plea to a reduced charge to be offered in hopes of gaining some partial success if the strength of the evidence is weak.

11. See Joan E. Jacoby, *The American Prosecutor: A Search for Identity* (Lexington, MA: Lexington Books, 1980) and Jacoby, Mellon, and Smith, *Policy and Prosecution,* for more detailed descriptions of these policies.

12. This law has had dubious results including overcrowded prisons and injustices resulting from its inflexibility. This legislation is so restrictive that it can easily become a modern-day version of Victor Hugo's *Les Miserables* and Jean Valjean's theft of a loaf of bread.

13. As of June 2003, 22 states and the District of Columbia are listed as contacts for the National Association of Sentencing Commissions indicating their use.

14. In some states, traffic cases and moving violations are processed administratively, outside the criminal justice system.

15. In some states, the grand jury also has the power to hand up indictments based on its investigations and without the consent of the prosecutor. These are known as grand jury originals.

16. Joshua Rozenberg, *The Case for the Crown: The Inside Story of the Director of Public Prosecutions* (Wellingborough, Northamptonshire, England: Equation, 1987).

17. Thomas W. Church Jr., Alan Carlons, Jo-Lynne Q. Lee, and Teresa Tan, *Justice Delayed: The Pace of Litigation in Urban Trial Courts* (Williamsburg, VA: National Center for State Courts, 1978).

18. Leslie T. Wilkins, *Consumerist Criminology* (London: Heinemann Educational Books, and Totowa, NJ: Barnes & Noble Books, 1984). Wilkins made the distinction between crimes and "ought to be crimes." The latter are those events that a community fears regardless of their legal status. For example, it may not violate any law if young boys hang around a playground or school yard, but it may cause concern to the parents of other children.

19. Joan E. Jacoby, "Pushing the Envelope—Leadership in Prosecution," *Justice System Journal* 17 (1995): 291–307.

20. Albert J. Reiss Jr., "Discretionary Justice," in *Handbook of Criminology,* ed. Daniel Glaser (Chicago: Rand McNally, 1974), 689.

Chapter 2

1. Joan E. Jacoby was the director of the Office of Crime Analysis at the time.

2. Joan E. Jacoby, P. S. Gilchrist III, and E. C. Ratledge, *Prosecutor's Guide to Police-Prosecutor Relations* (Washington, D.C.: Jefferson Institute for Justice Studies, 1999), 7.

3. Ibid.

4. An active sentence means jail or prison time is part of the sentence.

5. Ibid.

6. Interview with Buchanan County (St. Joseph), Missouri, prosecutor Dwight Scroggins, 2000. For related information on misdemeanor processing see Joan E. Jacoby, Peter S. Gilchrist III, and Edward C. Ratledge, *Prosecutor's Guide to Misdemeanor Case Management* (Washington, D.C: Jefferson Institute for Justice Studies and Missouri Office of Prosecution Services, 2001), contract number 01-J7-03-17, http://www.jijs.org/publications/prospubs/Misdemeanor.pdf.

7. This occurred in the late 1960s and early 1970s in the U.S. Attorney's Office for the District of Columbia. Charles Work was the USAO prosecutor when the PROMIS system was under development.

8. This is not to criticize prosecutors for having investigators. They have a legitimate and valuable role in prosecutors' offices. In medium- to large-sized offices, they are essential for trial preparation and victim-witness activities. Antagonistic relationships simply add another reason for their employment.

9. Interview with Missouri prosecutor Dwight Scroggins.

10. Interview with District Attorney Peter S. Gilchrist III, 1999, describing the Memorandum of Understanding (MOU) that he and the Charlotte police chief signed. For related information see Jacoby, Gilchrist III, and Ratledge, *Prosecutor's Guide to Police-Prosecutor Relations*, 21, http://www.jijs.org/publications/prospubs/Police-Pros.pdf.

11. Joan E. Jacoby, Carl B. Hammond, Edward C. Ratledge, and Stephen Ward, "Evaluation of Illinois' Multi-Jurisdictional Drug Prosecution Programs and Local Drug Prosecutor Support Programs," *Illinois Criminal Justice Information Authority*, 1999, http://www.icjia.state.il.us/public/pdf/researchreports/EvalMjdrug.pdf.

12. Interview with Montgomery County, Maryland, state's attorney Andrew Sonner, 1996. For additional information see Joan E. Jacoby, Heike P. Gramckow, and Edward C. Ratledge, *The Impact of Community Policing on the Criminal Justice System* (Washington, D.C.: Jefferson Institute for Justice Studies, 1995), 58–69, http://www.jijs.org/publications/prospubs/Commpol.pdf.

13. Jacoby, Gramckow, and Ratledge, *Impact of Community Policing on the Criminal Justice System*.

14. J. E. Jacoby, H. P. Gramckow, and E. C. Ratledge, *Asset Forfeiture Programs: Impact, Issues, and Implications* (Washington, D.C.: Jefferson Institute for Justice Studies, 1992), 36.

15. J. M. Bryson and B. C. Crosby, *Leadership for the Common Good: Tackling Public Problems in a Shared-Power World* (San Francisco: Jossey-Bass, 1992).

16. Joan E. Jacoby, "Pushing the Envelope—Leadership in Prosecution," *Justice System Journal* 17 (1995): 291–308.

17. B. R. Barber, "Neither Leaders nor Followers: Citizenship under Strong Democracy," in *Essays in Honor of James MacGregor Burns*, ed. M. R. Benchloss and T. E. Cronin (New York: Prentice Hall, 1989), 125.

18. Jacoby, "Pushing the Envelope," 296–299.

19. W. Bennis and B. Nanus, *Leaders: The Strategies for Taking Charge* (New York: Harper & Row, 1985).

20. Jacoby, "Pushing the Envelope," 300.

21. Quoted in ibid., 302.

22. Barber, "Neither Leaders nor Followers," 125.

Chapter 3

1. Joan E. Jacoby, *The American Prosecutor: A Search for Identity* (Lexington, MA: Lexington Books, D. C. Heath, 1980), 28–30.

2. Joan E. Jacoby, Leonard R. Mellon, Edward C. Ratledge, and Stanley H. Turner, *Prosecutorial Decisionmaking: A National Study* (Washington, D.C.: U.S. Department of Justice, National Institute of Justice, 1982), 82–87.

3. Joan E. Jacoby, Leonard R. Mellon, and Walter F. Smith, *Policy and Prosecution* (Washington, D.C.: U.S. Department of Justice, National Institute of Justice, 1982), 27.

4. Other techniques are for teams of assistants to be assigned to intake, or charges approved by the chief deputy or head of intake before filing or dismissal.

5. See National Institute of Justice reports on types of drug courts, performance measurement, program evaluations, and available resources, http://www.nij.gov /topics/courts/drug-courts/Pages/welcome.aspx.

6. Brian A. Reeves, "Felony Defendants in Large Urban Counties, 2009—Statistical Tables" (U.S. Department of Justice, Bureau of Justice Statistics, State Court Processing Statistics, NCJ243777, 2013), 24.

7. Thorsten Sellin and Marvin E. Wolfgang, *The Measurement of Delinquency* (New York: John Wiley & Sons, 1964). This book represents the beginning of changes in identifying the forces that influence charging discretion.

8. Robin L. Lubitz and Thomas W. Ross, "Sentencing Guidelines: Reflections on the Future," *Sentencing & Corrections, Issues for the 21st Century* (Washington, D.C.: U.S. Department of Justice, National Institute of Justice, Research in Brief, 10, 2001), https://www.ncjrs.gov/pdffiles1/nij/186480.pdf.

9. We are excluding the criminal history files maintained by law enforcement agencies since they only describe a history of cases disposed, not open pending cases.

10. This recently has become a contentious issue in the protests about law enforcement relationships in low-income, minority communities. They claim that their arrests for minor or nonexistent crimes have been made in large part to increase the city's revenues through fines imposed on people who are already too poor to afford them.

Chapter 4

1. This may only be a temporary disposition because if the defendant does not follow the conditions of the program, the prosecutor gets another chance to decide whether to prosecute.

2. C. Flango and B. Ostrum, *Examining the Work of State Courts, 2003, Criminal* (Williamsburg, VA: National Center for State Courts, 2003), 44.

3. J. E. Jacoby, L. R. Mellon, and W. R. Smith, *Policy and Prosecution* (Washington, D.C.: U.S. Department of Justice, National Institute of Justice, 1982) 63.

4. Flango and Ostrum, *Examining the Work of State Courts*, 44.

5. Joan E. Jacoby and Edward C. Ratledge, *Cold Case Assessment Program: Findings and Recommendations* (Raleigh, NC: North Carolina Conference of District Attorneys, 2005).

6. In a study conducted by the Jefferson Institute for Justice Studies, sheriffs, judges, prosecutors and defense counsel were asked to specify a minimum acceptable sanction for a sample of simulated cases. There was considerable overlap among all parties with the sheriff's department generally recording more severe sanctions than all the others. Analysis of the responses indicated that minimum and maximum ranges could be established using the quartile distribution of the severity of the sanction selected. The majority tended to state sanctions that grouped within a small range.

7. Interestingly, the distributions showed that law enforcement personnel tended to select the most severe sanctions in the range more often than the prosecutors, defense counsel, or judges.

8. Fred C. Zacharias, "Justice in Plea Bargaining," *William and Mary Law Review* 39 (1998): 1136, 1137, fig. 1.

9. The "three strikes and you're out" legislation in California has overcrowded prisons with three-time losers even though it does not contain the entire universe of three-timers, nor does it deter offenders after their second conviction.

10. Theresa White Cairns and John A. Kruse, "Alaska's Ban on Plea Bargaining Reevaluated," *Judicature* 75 (1992): 310–311.

11. Muhammad was one of the two defendants convicted of the sniper killings in the Washington, D.C., metropolitan area. See Tom Jackman, "Prosecutors Sharpen Call for Removal of Sniper Judge in Fairfax," *Washington Post*, September 19, 2004, C6.

12. Of course, while we are talking about easy ways to clear the daily calendar, we cannot ignore the simplest one, which is the defendant's failure to appear. One only has to look at the file for warrants issued but not served to understand the magnitude of this problem. Unfortunately, this statistic is not readily available because its publication would undermine the credibility and effectiveness of the criminal justice system and the court if defendants become aware of how easy it is to walk away from adjudication.

13. Joan E. Jacoby, Charles R. Link, and Edward C. Ratledge, *Some Costs of Continuances: A Multi-Jurisdictional Study* (Washington, D.C.: Jefferson Institute for Justice Studies, 1986), 25.

14. This is a coded way for defense counsel to inform the judge that he or she has not yet been paid.

15. Dr. Stanley H. Turner, Professor of Sociology, Temple University, Philadelphia, Pennsylvania.

16. In jury trials, however, jurors may not be privy to all the information that the judge has received since the judge rules on whether it is admissible or not.

17. A Canadian study of U.S. practices found that "less than 18 percent of victims or families attend sentencing, only 15 percent submit written statements, and only 9 percent present oral statements where permitted." Valerie Finn-DeLuca, "Victim Impact Statements," *Criminal Law Bulletin* 30, no. 5 (1994): 403–428.

18. For a more complete discussion of the issues see Robin L. Lubitz and Thomas W. Ross, "Sentencing Guidelines: Reflections on the Future," *Sentencing & Corrections: Issues for the 21st Century* (Washington, D.C.: U.S. Department of Justice, National Institute of Justice, Research in Brief, June 2001), no. 10.

19. Joan E. Jacoby, "Expedited Drug Case Management Programs: Some Lessons in Case Management Reform," *Justice System Journal* 17, no. 1 (1994): 27.

20. For a wide-ranging discussion see "Victim Impact Statements," *John Howard Society of Alberta* (1997): 5, www.johnhoward.ab.ca/PUB/C53.htm.

21. A. Abramovsky, "Victim Impact Statements: Adversely Impacting upon Judicial Fairness," *St. John's Journal of Legal Commentary* (1992): 21–22.

22. Ellen C. Lemley and Gregory D. Russell, "Implementing Restorative Justice by Groping Along: A Case Study in Program Evolutionary Implementation," *Justice System Journal* 23, (2002): 157–190.

Chapter 5

1. Jeff Turrentine, "The N-word," *Indyweek* (March 6, 2002), http://www.indyweek.com/indyweek/the-n-word/Content?oid=1185947. This article discusses Randall Kennedy's book *Nigger: The Strange Career of Jim Crow* (New York: Vintage Books, 2002). See also Benjamin Niolet, "DA's Footing in Lacrosse Case Unclear," *News & Observer,* December 22, 2006.

2. Steve Weinberg, *Harmful Error: Investigating America's Local Prosecutors* (Washington, D.C.: Center for Public Integrity, Summer 2003).

3. Ibid.

Chapter 6

1. "Dominique Strauss-Kahn," *Times Topics,* August 4, 2011, http://www.NewYorkTimes.com/timestopics/people/dominiquestrausskahn.

2. The indictment charged the defendant with two counts of criminal sexual act in the first degree, one count of attempted rape in the first degree, one count of sexual abuse in the first degree, one count of unlawful imprisonment in the second degree, one count of forcible touching, and one count of sexual abuse in the third degree.

3. Nate Rawlings, "Latest Twist in the DSK Case: A Civil Suit, and Sordid New Details," *Time,* August 9, 2011, http://content.time.com/time/nation/article/0,8599,2087648,00.html.

4. "Recommendation for Dismissal," Supreme Court of State of New York, County of New York: Part 51. People of the State of New York against Dominique Strauss-Kahn. Indictment No. 02526/2011, August 22, 2011.

5. "Inquisitorial Systems." *West's Encyclopedia of American Law* (Minneapolis/St. Paul, MN: West, 1998).

6. "Recommendation for Dismissal," 8.

7. John P. Bellassi, "A Short History of the Pretrial Diversion of Adult Defendants from Traditional Criminal Justice Processing. Part One: The Early Years," National Association of Pretrial Service Agencies, https://www.rinabook.com /new-read/161096/a-short-history-of-the-pretrial-diversion.html.

8. "History of Pretrial Services Programs," Pretrial Justice Institute, http://www .pretrial.org/PretrialServices/HistoryOfPretrialRelease/Pages/default.aspx.

9. The bail set included "$1 million in cash plus a $5 million bond. The conditions of bail included surrender of the defendant's passport, his home confinement in New York County, and electronic monitoring at his expense." "Recommendation for Dismissal," 5.

10. "Criminal Justice Procedures," Suffolk County, New York District Attorney's Office, http://www.suffolkcountyny.gov/da/CriminalJusticeProcedures.aspx; New York Criminal Procedure—Article 195, §195.40 Waiver of Indictment; Filing of Superior Court Information, April 24, 2010.

11. Alan Feuer, John Eligon, and William K. Rashbaum, "Strauss-Kahn Case Adds to Doubts on Prosecutor," *New York Times*, July 2, 2011, reported that "Early on, Mr. Vance took the case away from the sex crimes unit and gave it to other experienced assistant district attorneys," http:www.nytimes.com/2011/07/03/nyregion /collapsing-strauss-kahn-case-adds-to-doubts-on-manhattan-prosecutor. It should be noted, however, that the "beyond reasonable doubt" standard is applied by a jury or judge at trial. It is not a standard that prosecutors should use for charging. Instead they should use, among others, a trial sufficiency standard that assumes there is sufficient evidence that the charge can be sustained at trial.

12. "Recommendation for Dismissal," 2.

13. Ibid., 2.

14. Ibid., 5.

15. John Eligon, "In Campaign for Top Prosecutor, Candidate Finds Own Path," *New York Times*, NY/Region, August 30, 2009, http://www.nytimes.com /2009/08/31/nyregion/31vance.html?r, print version published December 12, 2009.

16. Feuer, Eligon, and Rashbaum, "Strauss-Kahn Case Adds to Doubts on Prosecutor."

17. Scott Turow, "Reasonable Doubt and the Strauss-Kahn Case," *New York Times*, August 27, 2011, www.nytimes.com/2011/08/28/opinion/sunday/cyrus-vance -jrs-high-marks-in-the-strauss-kahn-case.html; Robert Mintz, "Did US Justice Fail in the DSK Case?" *Guardian.co.uk*, July 6, 2011, www.guardian.co.uk/comment isfree/cifamerica/2011/jul/06; Joe Nocera, "The D.A. Did the Right Thing," May 7, 2011, *New York Times*, www.nytimes.com/2011/0705/opinion/05nocera.html; Bennett L. Gershman and Joel Cohen, "DSK and Bail: But Aren't the French Right?" May 24, 2011, *HuffPost Politics*, www.huffingtonpost.com/bennett-l-gersham/dsk -and-bail-but-arent-the-french-right.

18. It should be noted, however, that much of what is praised is required by legislation, professional ethics, and standards imposed by the American Bar Association (ABA).

Chapter 7

1. She was arrested March 22 on a probation violation stemming from a 2001 conviction for embezzling $25,000 from a Durham employer.

2. It was during this period that his pretrial statements provided the basis for complaints to the bar association later in the year.

3. Joseph Neff, "Nifong Ignores Clues from DNA Tests," *News & Observer*, April 16, 2007, http://www.newsobserver.com/100/v-print/story/564692.html.

4. The role of the Durham Police Department is currently under investigation by the city commissioners and is named in a civil lawsuit brought by the defendants.

5. Anne Blythe, "Nifong Has No Recall of Session," *News & Observer*, March 3, 2007, http://www.newsobserver.com/141/v-print/story/548876.html.

6. Peter Whoriskey and Sylvia Adcock, "Prosecutors Drop Duke Rape Counts," *Washington Post,* December 23, 2006, A1.

7. Benjamin Niolet and Michael Biesecker, "DA: I Haven't Heard Accuser's Account." *News & Observer,* October 28, 2006.

8. Ibid. See also a more recent book, William D. Cohan, *The Price of Silence: The Duke Lacrosse Scandal, The Power of the Elite and the Corruption of Our Great Universities* (New York: Scribner, 2014). Also see book review by Nick Anderson, "The Price of Silence: The Duke Lacrosse Scandal by William D. Cohan," *Washington Post*, April 18, 2014.

9. He subsequently settled his complaint against the university for undisclosed terms.

10. J. Neff, B. Niolet, and A. Blythe, "Lab Chief: Nifong Said Don't Report All DNA Data," *News & Observer*, December 16, 2006.

11. State of North Carolina, Wake County, Before the Preliminary Hearing Commission of the North Carolina State Bar 06 DHC 35. North Carolina State Bar, Plaintiff v. Michael B. Nifong, Attorney, Defendant. Amended Complaint, Filed DHC, January 24, 2007.

12. This was another blow to Nifong but it was not unexpected. A small group of the most influential district attorneys in North Carolina had previously tried to reason with him during the summer and fall, but he refused to meet with them or discuss the case. Finally, they collared him at the conference's December meeting and "had an intervention." The following Tuesday he announced that he was dropping the rape charges. But it was too late.

13. "Durham County Superior Court case file Nos. 06 CRS 4332-4336, 5582-5583. Summary of Conclusions," North Carolina Attorney General's Office, North Carolina Department of Justice. Undated.

14. "District Attorney Michael B. Nifong: About Your District Attorney," www.ncdistrictattorney.org/mikenifong/your_district_attorney.html.

15. Benjamin Niolet and Joseph Neff, "Easley: Nifong Broke His Word," *News & Observer*, February 3, 2007, http://www.newsobserver.com/1185/story /539319.html.

16. The following summarizes the "Point by Point Response to the Three Allegations Contained in the Substance of the Grievance." Michael B. Nifong, Letter to Ms. Katherine E. Jean, Counsel, North Carolina State Bar, Grievance Committee, December 29, 2006.

17. Julia Lewis, "Nifong Guilty of Criminal Contempt; Sentenced to 1 Day in Jail." WRAL.com 2011 and Associated Press, http://www.wral.com%2Fnews%2F local%2Fstory%2F1763323.

18. "Complaints against Mike Nifong," *News & Observer*, December 3, 2006, www.newsobserver.com/1185/v-print/story/517202.html.

19. Benjamin Niolet, Jim Nesbitt, and Joseph Neff, "Two Indicted in Duke Lacrosse Case," *News & Observer*, April 18, 2006, http://www.newsobserver.com /news/crime_safety/duke_lacrosse/v-print/story/429.html.

20. Joseph Neff, "Quest to Convict Hid a Lack of Evidence," *News & Observer*, April 14, 2007, http://www.newsobservor.com/1537/v-print/story/564100.html.

21. Anne Blythe, "With Criminal Case Over, Watch for Civil Action," *News & Observer*, April 12, 2007, http://www.newsobserver.com/141/v-print/story /563042.html. See also Stuart Taylor Jr. and K. C. Johnson, *Until Proven Innocent: Political Correctness and the Shameful Injustices of the Duke Lacrosse Rape Case* (New York: St. Martin's Press, 2007).

Chapter 8

1. For the police perspective, see Steve Thomas with Don Davis, *JonBenet: Inside the Ramsey Murder Investigation* (New York: St. Martin's Press, 2000). A more balanced perspective is presented in Lawrence Schiller, *Perfect Murder, Perfect Town* (New York: Harper Paperbacks, 1999). Some details were excerpted from J. J. Maloney and J. Patrick O'Connor, "The Murder of JonBenet Ramsey," Crime-magazine.comjonbenet.htm; and Marilyn Bardsley and Patrick Bellamy, "Murder of JonBenet Ramsey: An Investigative Analysis," www.crimemagazine, http:// www.crimelibrary.com.

2. Accounts differ. John also stated that he carried a sleeping JonBenet up to her bed and put her in it without her waking.

3. Later, an enhanced version of the taped call identified Burke's voice in the background, contradicting previous statements that he was not awake at the time.

4. Thomas and Davis, *JonBenet*, 42.

5. Joan E. Jacoby, *The American Prosecutor: A Search for Identity* (Lexington, MA: Lexington Books, D. C. Heath, 1980), 255–270.

6. Thomas and Davis, *JonBenet*, 114–116. Police could not understand or agree with case dispositions obtained by the office. Thomas and Davis cited the fact that the DA had never sent a killer to death row; in one year 13 rape cases were

filed but there were no trials, and half of the suspects didn't spend a day in jail; out of 60 cases of sexual assault on children, only one offender went to prison; of 23 murder cases filed between 1992 and 1996, none went to trial. All were plea bargained.

7. Thomas and Davis, *JonBenet*, 197. *The Colorado Peace Officers Handbook* defines probable cause for an arrest exists "[w]hen you have sufficient reliable information that under the totality of the circumstances, there is a fair probability that the suspect has committed . . . a crime."

8. Schiller, *Perfect Murder*, 757–764.

9. Ibid., 269–286.

10. Ibid., 271.

11. The attorneys were Rich Baer, Dan Hoffman, and Bob Miller.

12. Thomas and Davis, *JonBenet*, 226–227.

13. Ibid., 243.

14. Ibid., 244.

15. Only recently (2013) did the *Denver Post* disclose information contained in the grand jury indictment of John and Patsy Ramsey that was issued in 1999 but was not signed by DA Alex Hunter. The indictment remained sealed until the court unsealed it. The indictment accused John and Patsy Ramsey of two counts each of child abuse resulting in death in connection with the first-degree murder of their daughter. The indictment alleged that the parents permitted JonBenet to be placed in a dangerous situation that led to her death and accused them of helping whoever killed the girl. Kirk Mitchell and John Ingold, "JonBenét Ramsey Grand Jury Indictment Accused Parents of Child Abuse Resulting in Death," *Denver Post,* October 25, 2013, http://www.denverpost.com/breakingnews/ci_24385866/jonbenet-ramsey-indictment.

Chapter 9

1. An analysis of Casey's cell phone records showed pings recorded near the site where the remains were found. See Detective Yuri Melich, Orange County Sheriff's Office, Investigative Report, Case Number 07-074777, July 15, 2008, to November 2008, 43.

2. Ibid., 14.

3. Ibid., 35.

4. Kyle Hightower, "Prosecutors Focus on Duct Tape in Casey Anthony Trial," Associated Press, *Daytona Beach News-Journal*, June 11, 2011, http://www.news-journalonline.com/news/florida/2011/06/11/prosecutors-focus-on-duct-tape-in-casey-anthony-trial.html.

5. Joan E. Jacoby, Leonard R. Mellon, Edward C. Ratledge, and Stanley Turner, *Prosecutorial Decisionmaking: A National Study* (Washington, D.C.: U.S. Department of Justice, National Institute of Justice, 1982), 35.

6. Leonard R. Mellon, "A Concept for Measuring the Legal Evidentiary Strength of Criminal Cases." Paper presented to the American Society of Criminology, Bureau of Social Science Research, Washington, D.C., 1979.

7. Jacoby, Mellon, Ratledge, and Turner, *Prosecutorial Decisionmaking*, 37.

8. Melich, Investigative Report, 15.

9. Ibid., 41.

10. Jeff Ashton with Lisa Pulitzer, *Imperfect Justice: Prosecuting Casey Anthony* (New York: HarperCollins, 2011).

11. Ibid., 126.

12. Ibid., 127.

13. Ibid.

14. Hal Boedeker, "Casey Anthony: Lawson Lamar Defends Seeking Death Penalty," *Orlando Sentinel*, June 24, 2012, http://articles.orlandosentinel.com/2012 -06-24/entertainment/os-casey-anthony-lawson-lamar-20120624_1_legal-analyst -bill-sheaffer-casey-anthony-anthony-prosecution.

15. Ashton and Pulitzer, *Imperfect Justice*, 128.

16. Ibid., 169–174.

17. Ray Moses, *Jury Argument in Criminal Cases* (Houston, TX: Center for Criminal Justice Advocacy, 2001), 5.

18. "Federal Courts: Understanding the Federal Courts, How Courts Work, Criminal Cases," U.S. Courts, Administrative Office of the Courts, http://www.uscourts.gov /federalcourts/understandingthefederalcourts/howcourtswork/CriminalCases.aspx.

19. In the Supreme Court of Florida No. SC09-906. In re: Amendments to Florida Standard Jury Instructions in Criminal Cases—2.03. Comments of the Twenty State Attorneys Together through the Florida Prosecuting Attorney Association. Filed July 10, 2000.

20. Even at the 11th hour when defense attorney Mason Cheny approached the prosecution about a negotiated plea and reached agreement with them, Casey Anthony refused to discuss or accept it. Ashton and Pulitzer, *Imperfect Justice*, 293.

21. Ibid., 316–317.

22. "Casey Anthony Juror: We Were Sick to Our Stomachs at the Verdict." *New York News*, July 6, 2011, http://www.newsday.com/news/new-york/casey -anthony-juror-we-were-sick-to-our-stomachs-1.3009201.

23. Florida statute Title XLVI, Chapter 827.03, Abuse, Aggravated Abuse, and Neglect of a Child; Penalties.

24. Florida statute Title XLVI, Chapter 775.082, Definitions; General Penalties; Registration of Criminals.

25. The initial charge of child neglect was filed on August 5, 2008, three weeks after Casey's arrest. The grand jury indictment on October 14, 2008, was for three felony charges, including aggravated child abuse, and four misdemeanor obstruction and lying charges. The initial child neglect charge was dismissed a week later by the prosecutor on October 21, 2008.

26. Florida statute Title XLVI, Chapter 827.03, op. cit.

Chapter 10

1. Marcia Clark with Teresa Carpenter, *Without a Doubt* (New York: Viking Penguin, 1997), 130.

2. See https://espn.go.com/sportscentury/features/00016472.html, http://www .profootballhof.com/hof/member.aspx?PLAYER_ID=195.

3. "The O. J. Simpson Case," Appendix 2, http://www.crimelibrary.com/notorious _murders/famous/simpson/brentwood_2.html.

4. The case initially was assigned to homicide detectives (Mark Fuhrman, Brad Phillips, and others) but was turned over to robbery/homicide because it had a lighter caseload. While Fuhrman was kept on the case as an advisor, he admitted that he was unable to influence the direction of the investigation that the robbery/ homicide detectives were pursuing.

5. One eyewitness who knew Simpson placed him near Nicole's house at the time of the murder when she saw him run a red light and nearly collide with another vehicle. (She was not called to testify later because after she gave her testimony to the grand jury, she admitted she lied to sell her story to a magazine.)

6. Clark and Carpenter, *Without a Doubt*, 64–65.

7. For a timeline of these and subsequent events see Doug Linder, "The Trial of Orenthal James Simpson" (2000), http://law2.umkc.edu/faculty/projects/ftrials /Simpson/Simpsonaccount.htm; and "Chronology of the O.J. Simpson Trials," http://law2.umkc.edu/faculty/projects/ftrials/Simpson/Simpsonchron.html.

8. Alan M. Dershowitz, *Reasonable Doubt: The O. J. Simpson Case and the Criminal Justice System* (New York: Simon & Schuster, 1997), 106.

9. See "Closing Arguments of Johnnie Cochran (excerpts)," http://law2.umkc .edu/faculty/projects/ftrials/Simpson/cochranclose.html.

10. Vincent Bugliosi, *Outrage: The Five Reasons Why O. J. Simpson Got Away with Murder* (New York: W. W. Norton, 1996), 61. Bugliosi informed Garcetti that this opinion was incorrect. According to the DA's own grand jury legal adviser, it was common for cases to go back to the judicial district where the crime was committed after indictment.

11. Bugliosi, *Outrage*, 60–61. Los Angeles County uses the "bull's-eye system" to assign jurors in all cases. Jurors eligible for assignment cannot live more than 20 miles from the courthouse.

12. See Samuel Gross, "The Risks of Death: Why Erroneous Convictions Are Common in Capital Cases," *Buffalo Law Review* 44 (1996): 469, 494; and American Psychological Association, "Brief Filed in *Lockhart v. McCree*, 476 U.S. 651, Index Topics: Death Penalty (Death Qualified Juries)" (2007), www.apa.org /psychlaw/lockhart.html.

13. Bugliosi, *Outrage*, 96.

14. Mark Fuhrman, *Murder in Brentwood* (Washington, D.C.: Regnery, 1997).

15. Ibid., 173.

16. Ibid., 94.

17. Jeffrey R. Toobin, "An Incendiary Defense," *New Yorker*, July 25, 1994, 56.

18. Clark and Carpenter, *Without a Doubt*, 122.

19. Bugliosi, *Outrage*, 66.

20. Ibid., 68.

21. Fuhrman, *Murder in Brentwood*, 126.

22. See "Forensics at the OJ Simpson Trial, So . . . What Went Wrong?" (Washington, D.C.: National Museum of Crime and Punishment, 2015).

23. Bugliosi, *Outrage*, 116.

24. Clark and Carpenter, *Without a Doubt*, 124.

25. See http://www.ocregister.com/articles/stuart-529204-simpson-heard.html.

26. Bugliosi, *Outrage*, 107, 97.

27. Ibid., 50–55.

28. Ibid., 35.

29. Dershowitz, *Reasonable Doubt*, 96.

30. In 2010, the office had 30 branch area offices in the county and more than 1,000 attorneys and 300 investigators. It prosecuted about 60,000 felonies and 130,000 misdemeanors.

Chapter 11

1. See: "Ex-GI at Fort Bragg Is Convicted in Killing of 2 Blacks," *New York Times,* February 28, 1997, www.nytimes.com/1997/02/28/us/ex-gi-at-fort-bragg -is-convicted-in-killing-of-2-blacks.html; "Three White Soldiers Charged in Killings of 2 Blacks," *CNN U.S. News,* December 9, 1995, http://edition.cnn.com /US/9512/ft_bragg; "Another Soldier Convicted in Race-based Killings," *New York Times,* May 3, 1997, http://www.nytimes.com/1997/05/03/us/another-soldier -convicted-in-race-based-killings.html; Emery P. Dalesio, "Skinhead Paratrooper Convicted of Murdering Black Couple," *Lubbock Avalanche-Journal* and *Associated Press,* 1997, http://lubbockonline.com/news/022897/skinhead.htm; "Burmeister's Cold Exterior Cracks at Sentencing," WRAL.com, 2011, http://www.wral.com /news/local/story/161276.

2. David T. Morgan, *Murder along the Cape Fear* (Macon, GA: Mercer University Press, 2005), 222.

3. See chapter 6 of this book.

4. Chip Brown, "Cyrus Vance Jr.'s 'Moneyball' Approach to Crime," *New York Times Magazine,* December 7, 2014, www.nytimes.com/2014/12/07/magazine /cyrus-vance-jrs-moneyball-approach-to-crime. A version of this article appeared in print: Chip Brown, "The Data D.A.," *New York Times Sunday Magazine,* December 7, 2014, MM22.

5. Joan E. Jacoby, "Pushing the Envelope—Leadership in Prosecution," *Justice System Journal* 17, no. 3 (1995): 291–303.

6. Some criticized his decision as a form of private prosecution, but the county government supported him and public furor never developed.

7. For a description of the Red Hook Community Court and a comparison with Kings County District Court criminal activity see C. G. Lee, F. Cheesman,

D. Rottman, R. Swaner, S. Lambson, M. Rempel, and R. Curtis, *A Community Court Grows in Brooklyn: A Comprehensive Evaluation of the Red Hook Community Justice Center* (Williamsburg, VA: National Center for State Courts, 2013), http://www .ncsc.org/~/media/Files/PDF/Services%20and%20Experts/Areas%20of%20expertise /Problem%20solving%20courts/11012013-Red-Hook-Exeuctive-Summary.ashx#pa ge=2&zoom=auto,-150,670.

Selected Bibliography

Abramovsky, A. "Victim Impact Statements: Adversely Impacting upon Judicial Fairness." *St. John's Journal of Legal Commentary* (1992): 21–33. http://www.johnhoward.ab.ca/pub/C53.htm.

American Bar Association. *ABA Standards for Criminal Justice: Prosecution Function and Defense Function.* 3rd ed. Washington, D.C.: American Bar Association, 1993.

Anderson, Nick. Review of *The Price of Silence: The Duke Lacrosse Scandal* by William D. Cohan. *Washington Post*, April 18, 2014.

Ashton, Jeff, with Lisa Pulitzer. *Imperfect Justice: Prosecuting Casey Anthony.* New York: HarperCollins, 2011.

Barber, B. R. "Neither Leaders nor Followers: Citizenship under Strong Democracy." In *Essays in Honor of James MacGregor Burns*, edited by M. R. Benchloss and T. E. Cronin. New York: Prentice Hall, 1989.

Bellassi, John P. "A Short History of the Pretrial Diversion of Adult Defendants from Traditional Criminal Justice Processing. Part One: The Early Years." National Association of Pretrial Service Agencies. https://www.rinabook.com/new-read/161096/a-short-history-of-the-pretrial-diversion.html.

Bennis, W., and B. Nanus. *Leaders: The Strategies for Taking Charge.* New York: Harper & Row, 1985.

Blythe, Anne. "Nifong Has No Recall of Session." *News&Observer,* March 3, 2007. http://www.newsobserver.com/141/v-print/story/548876.html.

Blythe, Anne. "With Criminal Case Over, Watch for Civil Action." *News&Observer*, April 12, 2007. http://www.newsobserver.com/141/v-print/story/563042.html.

Boedeker, Hal. "Casey Anthony: Lawson Lamar Defends Seeking Death Penalty." *Orlando Sentinel*, June 24, 2012. http://articles.orlandosentinel.com/2012-06-24/entertainment/os-casey-anthony-lawson-lamar-20120624_1_legal-analyst-bill-sheaffer-casey-anthony-anthony-prosecution.

Brown, Chip. "Cyrus Vance Jr.'s 'Moneyball' Approach to Crime." *New York Times Magazine*, December 7, 2014. www.nytimes.com/2014/12/07/magazine/cyrus-vance-jrs-moneyball-approach-to-crime.

Bryson, J. M., and B. C. Crosby. *Leadership for the Common Good: Tackling Public Problems in a Shared-Power World*. San Francisco: Jossey-Bass, 1992.

Bugliosi, Vincent. *Outrage: The Five Reasons Why O. J. Simpson Got Away with Murder*. New York: W. W. Norton, 1996.

Cairns, Theresa White, and John A. Kruse. "Alaska's Ban on Plea Bargaining Reevaluated." *Judicature* (1991): 1–38. http://www.ajc.state.ak.us/reports/plea 91Exec.pdf.

Church, Thomas W., Jr., Alan Carlons, Jo-Lynne Q. Lee, and Teresa Tan. *Justice Delayed: The Pace of Litigation in Urban Trial Courts*. Williamsburg, VA: National Center for State Courts, 1978.

Clark, Marcia, and Teresa Carpenter. *Without a Doubt*. New York: Viking Penguin, 1997.

Cohan, William D. *The Price of Silence: The Duke Lacrosse Scandal, The Power of the Elite and the Corruption of Our Great Universities*. New York: Scribner, 2014.

Dershowitz, Alan M. *Reasonable Doubt: The O. J. Simpson Case and the Criminal Justice System*. New York: Simon & Schuster, 1997.

"Dominique Strauss-Kahn," Times Topics, *New York Times*, August 4, 2011. http://www.NewYorkTimes.com/timestopics/people/dominiquestrausskahn.

Feuer, Alan, John Eligon, and William K. Rashbaum. "Strauss-Kahn Case Adds to Doubts on Prosecutor," *New York Times*, July 2, 2011. http:www.nytimes.com/2011/07/03/nyregion/collapsing-strauss-kahn-case-adds-to-doubts-on-manhattan-prosecutor.

Finn-DeLuca, Valerie. "Victim Impact Statements." *Criminal Law Bulletin* 30, no. 5 (1994): 403–428.

Flango, C., and B. Ostrum. *Examining the Work of State Courts, 2003, Criminal*. Williamsburg, VA: National Center for State Courts, 2003.

Fuhrman, Mark. *Murder in Brentwood*. Washington, D.C.: Regnery, 1997.

Gershman, Bennett L., and Joel Cohen. "DSK and Bail: But Aren't the French Right?" *HuffPost Politics*, May 24, 2011. www.huffingtonpost.com/bennett-l-gersham/dsk-and-bail-but-arent-the-french-right.

Grisham, John. *The Innocent Man: Murder and Injustice in a Small Town*. New York: Bennington Press, Doubleday, 2006.

Gross, Samuel. "The Risks of Death: Why Erroneous Convictions Are Common in Capital Cases." *Buffalo Law Review* 44 (1996): 469–494.

Hightower, Kyle, Associated Press. "Prosecutors Focus on Duct Tape in Casey Anthony Trial." *Daytona Beach News-Journal*, June 11, 2011. http://www.news-journalonline.com/news/florida/2011/06/11/prosecutors-focus-on-duct-tape-in-casey-anthony-trial.html.

Jacoby, Joan E. *The American Prosecutor: A Search for Identity*. Lexington, MA: Lexington Books, 1980.

Jacoby, Joan E. "Expedited Drug Case Management Programs: Some Lessons in Case Management Reform." *Justice System Journal* 17, no. 1 (1994): 19–40.

Jacoby, Joan E. "Pushing the Envelope—Leadership in Prosecution." *Justice System Journal* 17 (1995): 291–307.

Jacoby, Joan E., P. S. Gilchrist III, and E. C. Ratledge. *Prosecutor's Guide to Police-Prosecutor Relations.* Washington, D.C.: Jefferson Institute for Justice Studies, 1999.

Jacoby, Joan E., H. P. Gramckow, and E. C. Ratledge. *Asset Forfeiture Programs: Impact, Issues, and Implications.* Washington, D.C.: Jefferson Institute for Justice Studies, 1992.

Jacoby, Joan E., H. P. Gramckow, and E. C. Ratledge. *The Impact of Community Policing on the Criminal Justice System.* Washington, D.C.: Jefferson Institute for Justice Studies, 1995.

Jacoby, Joan E., Carl B. Hammond, Edward C. Ratledge, and Stephen Ward. *Evaluation of Illinois' Multi-Jurisdictional Drug Prosecution Programs and Local Drug Prosecutor Support Programs.* Chicago: Illinois Criminal Justice Information Authority, 1999.

Jacoby, Joan E., Charles R. Link, and Edward C. Ratledge. *Some Costs of Continuances: A Multi-Jurisdictional Study.* Washington, D.C.: Jefferson Institute for Justice Studies, 1986.

Jacoby, Joan E., Leonard R. Mellon, Edward C. Ratledge, and Stanley Turner. *Prosecutorial Decisionmaking: A National Study.* Washington, D.C.: U.S. Department of Justice, National Institute of Justice, 1982.

Jacoby, Joan E., L. R. Mellon, and W. F. Smith. *Policy and Prosecution.* Washington, D.C.: U.S. Department of Justice, National Institute of Justice, 1982.

Jacoby, Joan E., and Edward C. Ratledge. *Cold Case Assessment Program: Findings and Recommendations.* Raleigh, NC: North Carolina Conference of District Attorneys, 2005.

Kennedy, Randall. *Nigger: The Strange Career of Jim Crow.* New York: Vintage Books, 2002.

Lee, C. G., F. Cheesman, D. Rottman, R. Swaner, S. Lambson, M. Rempel, and R. Curtis. *A Community Court Grows in Brooklyn: A Comprehensive Evaluation of the Red Hook Community Justice Center.* Williamsburg, VA: National Center for State Courts, 2013. http://www.ncsc.org/~/media/Files/PDF/Services%20and%20Experts/Areas%20of%20expertise/Problem%20solving%20courts/11012013-Red-Hook-Exeuctive-Summary.ashx#page=2&zoom=auto,-150,670.

Lemley, Ellen C., and Gregory D. Russell. "Implementing Restorative Justice by Groping Along: A Case Study in Program Evolutionary Implementation." *Justice System Journal* 23, National Center for State Courts (2002): 157–190.

Lewis, Julia, and Associated Press. "Nifong Guilty of Criminal Contempt; Sentenced to 1 Day in Jail." WRAL.com, 2011. http://www.wral.com%2Fnews%2Flocal%2Fstory%2F1763323.

Lubitz, Robin L., and Thomas W. Ross. "Sentencing Guidelines: Reflections on the Future." In *Sentencing & Corrections, Issues for the 21st Century.* Washington, D.C.: U.S. Department of Justice, National Institute of Justice, Research in Brief 10, 2001. https://www.ncjrs.gov/pdffiles1/nij/186480.pdf.

Mellon, Leonard R. "A Concept for Measuring the Legal Evidentiary Strength of Criminal Cases." Paper presented at the Annual Meeting of the American Society of Criminology, Philadelphia, PA, November 7–10, 1979.

Miller, Frank W. *Prosecution: The Decision to Charge a Suspect with a Crime.* Boston: Little, Brown, 1969.

Mintz, Robert. "Did US Justice Fail in the DSK Case?" *Guardian.co.uk.* July 6, 2011. www.guardian.co.uk/commentisfree/cifamerica/2011/jul/06.

Morgan, David T. *Murder along the Cape Fear.* Macon, GA: Mercer University Press, 2005.

Moses, Ray. *Jury Argument in Criminal Cases.* Houston: Center for Criminal Justice Advocacy, 2001, 5.

Neff, Joseph. "Nifong Ignores Clues from DNA Tests." *News & Observer*, April 16, 2007. http://www.newsobserver.com/100/v-print/story/564692.html.

Neff, Joseph. "Quest to Convict Hid a Lack of Evidence." *News & Observer*, April 14, 2007. http://www.newsobservor.com/1537/v-print/story/564100.htm.

Neff, Joseph, B. Niolet, and A. Blythe. "Lab Chief: Nifong Said Don't Report All DNA Data." *News & Observer*, December 16, 2006. www.newsobserver.com /politics/misconduct/v-print/story/.

Niolet, Benjamin. "DA's Footing in Lacrosse Case Unclear." *News & Observer*, December 22, 2006. www.newsobserver.com/1185/story/539319.html.

Niolet, Benjamin, and Michael Biesecker. "DA: I Haven't Heard Accuser's Account." *News & Observer*, October 28, 2006.

Niolet, Benjamin, and Joseph Neff. "Easley: Nifong Broke His Word." *News & Observer.* February 3, 2007. http://www.newsobserver.com/1185/story/539319.html.

Niolet, Benjamin, Jim Nesbitt, and Joseph Neff. "Two Indicted in Duke Lacrosse Case." *News & Observer*, April 18, 2006. http://www.newsobserver.com/news /crime_safety/duke_lacrosse/v-print/story/429.html.

Nocera, Joe. "The D.A. Did the Right Thing." *New York Times*, May 7, 2011. www .nytimes.com/2011/0705/opinion/05nocera.html.

Rawlings, Nate. "Latest Twist in the DSK Case: A Civil Suit, and Sordid New Details." *Time*, August 9, 2011. www.http://content.time.com/time/nation /article/0,8599,2087648,00.html.

Reeves, Brian A. "Felony Defendants in Large Urban Counties, 2009—Statistical Tables." Washington, D.C.: U.S. Department of Justice, Bureau of Justice Statistics, State Court Processing Statistics, NCJ243777, 2013.

Reiss, Albert J., Jr. "Discretionary Justice." In *Handbook of Criminology*, edited by Daniel Glaser, 679–699. Chicago: Rand McNally College, 1974.

Rozenberg, Joshua. *The Case for the Crown. The Inside Story of the Director of Public Prosecutions.* Wellingborough, Northamptonshire, England: Equation, 1987.

Sellin, Thorsten, and Marvin E. Wolfgang. *The Measurement of Delinquency.* New York: John Wiley & Sons, 1964.

Taylor, Stuart, Jr., and K. C. Johnson. *Until Proven Innocent: Political Correctness and the Shameful Injustices of the Duke Lacrosse Rape Case.* New York: St. Martin's Press, 2007.

Toobin, Jeffrey R. "An Incendiary Defense." *New Yorker*, July 25, 1994.

Turow. Scott. "Reasonable Doubt and the Strauss-Kahn Case." *New York Times*, August 27, 2011. www.nytimes.com/2011/08/28/opinion/sunday/cyrus-vance -jrs-high-marks in-the-strauss-kahn-case.html.

Turrentine, Jeff. "The N-word." *Indyweek*, March 6, 2002. http://www.indyweek .com/indyweek/the-n-word/Content?oid=1185947.

Weinberg, Steve. "Breaking the Rules." Washington, D.C.: Center for Public Integrity, 2003.

Whoriskey, Peter, and Sylvia Adcock. "Prosecutors Drop Duke Rape Counts." *Washington Post*, December 23, 2006, A1.

Wilkins, Leslie T. *Consumerist Criminology*. London: Heinemann Educational Books, and Totowa, New Jersey: Barnes & Noble Books, 1984.

Zacharias, Fred C. "Justice in Plea Bargaining." *William and Mary Law Review* 39 (1998): 1122–1189.

Index

About the Authors

Joan E. Jacoby, BA, sociology, Boston University; MA, statistics, American University, Washington, D.C., is the executive director of the Jefferson Institute for Justice Studies. She is the author of *The American Prosecutor: A Search for Identity*.

Edward C. Ratledge, BS, MA, economics, University of Delaware, is the director of the Center for Applied Demography & Survey Research and associate professor in the School of Public Policy and Administration, University of Delaware, Newark, Delaware. He is a coauthor (with Joan E. Jacoby) of *Handbook on Artificial Intelligence and Expert Systems in Law Enforcement*.